THE BELLUM CIVILE
OF PETRONIUS

EDITED

WITH INTRODUCTION, COMMENTARY, AND
TRANSLATION

BY

FLORENCE THEODORA BALDWIN, Ph.D.

New York
THE COLUMBIA UNIVERSITY PRESS
1911

Norwood Press
J. S. Cushing Co. — Berwick & Smith Co.
Norwood, Mass., U.S.A.

TO

MY SISTER

CONTENTS

THE BELLUM CIVILE OF
PETRONIUS

INTRODUCTION

IN discussing any part of the work of Petronius, we are hampered at the outset by uncertainty as regards the identity of the author. His *Satirae* [1] are not mentioned by any writer prior to the second century A.D.,[2] and even then, although repeatedly cited by grammarians, as Petronius, Petronius Arbiter, or Arbiter alone,[3]

---

[1] For the title, see p. 3, n. 2.

[2] The first reference known is that of Terentianus Maurus, *De Metris*, l. 2489, *Arbiter disertus*, and 2852, *Petronius*. For further references, see Buecheler's editions (Berlin, *Ed. Maior*, 1862, *Ed. Minor*, 1892, 1886, 1895), Collignon, *Pétrone en France* (Paris, 1905), Introd., and Burmann, Ed. (Utrecht, 1709, 1743), Part II, pp. 254, 257, 271.

[3] *E.g.* Serv. *ad Verg. Aen.*, III, 57 ; Fulgent. *Mytholog.*, III, 8, p. 124 (in *Mythographi Latini*, Amsterdam, 1681), and the references in (2) above. In Scaliger's Ms. (see p. 246) he is called C. Petronius Arbiter Afranius.

he is never spoken of as a contemporary or assigned to any period. As a result of this uncertainty, many theories have been advanced and
vigorously contested, placing him anywhere from
the reign of Augustus [1] to the fourth century A.D.[2]
The internal evidence, however, and especially the
two epic fragments, the *Troiae Halosis* [3] and the
Bellum Civile, point decidedly to the reign of
Nero.[4] Beyond this there is a considerable
amount of evidence, not conclusive indeed, but
collectively of no little weight, which leads us to
identify him with the Gaius Petronius of Nero's
court,[5] the *elegantiae arbiter* of whom Tacitus has
left us so striking a portrait.[6] This evidence is:
first the name or designation *Arbiter;* second,
the indications in the fragments that their author
was not only familiar with the writings of members of the imperial court, but took a lively and

---

[1] C. Beck, *The Age of Petronius Arbiter* (Cambridge, Mass.,
1856). He admits that the work may date as late as 34 A.D.

[2] Statilius, *Apologia.*

[3] See p. 5.

[4] This view is held by Teuffel, Buecheler, Ritter, Fried-
länder, Boissier, Studer, Merivale, Mackail, Heitland, Mommsen, and others. All but the first four of those mentioned
accept him also as the Petronius of Tacitus.

[5] Called Titus Petronius by Pliny, *H. N.*, XXXVII, 7, 3,
and Plutarch, *Quomodo Adulator ab amico internoscatur,* 19
(60 E.).

[6] *Ann.*, XVI, 18 ff.

controversial interest in them ; third, the striking
resemblance between the genius of the work and
the character of the brilliant and cynical courtier
who could flay his master's vices with his satire
when the hand of death was already on him ;
fourth, the absence of any record of another
Petronius of literary pretensions or qualifica-
tions.[1] In the following discussion of the relation of the *Bellum Civile* to the *Pharsalia* of
Lucan, therefore, this identity has been assumed, but all conclusions as to the purpose of
the poem have been based upon internal evidence alone.

The *Satirae*[2] of Petronius Arbiter, now lost
except for fragments of the fifteenth and sixteenth

The book books, partakes of the character of a
Menippean satire in its mixture of prose

---

[1] For a list of the other known *Petronii*, see Burmann,
Part II, p. 278.

[2] In the Tragurian Ms. the title is : *Petronii Arbitri Satyri
Fragmenta ex libro* XV *et* XVI ; in Sc., *C. Petronii Arbitri
Afranii Satyrici Liber;* in B, VI, Br., F2, Mess., *Petronii
Arbitri Satyricon* (Br. *Satiricon*); in V2, *Petronii Arbitri Satyricon Liber*. The other Mss. give the author's name only. The
older editors generally accepted the title *Satyricon* (genitive
plural), but Buecheler adopted the Latin *Saturae*. The more
high-sounding Greek title would naturally belong to a later
date than the rest of the work (see Casaubon, *De Satyrica
Poesi*, Paris, 1605, II, p. 326).

and verse, but with important differences. In the *Apocolocyntosis* of Seneca, the only complete specimen of this kind of work extant, the mingling of prose and verse is much like that in the text of an old-fashioned opera. The prose tells the story and furnishes the themes, the verse embroiders them and marks the climaxes. As in the opera it furnished the material for the florid passages, so in the satire it supplied the author with the vehicle for his wildest burlesque. In these *Satirae*, on the other hand, some of the passages in verse are quotations from other authors,[1] others are poems and epigrams introduced as the compositions of some of the characters.[2] Eumolpus, especially,[3] is continually breaking into verse, extemporaneous or premeditated.[4] And of the remaining fragments, which now appear scattered through the work without anything to connect them with the prose, it is probable that many were originally an organic part of the whole.[5] In content the book is a romance, composed by a master hand, of low life and strange adventure

---

[1] 55, 6 ; 68, 4 ; 112, 2.
[2] 5 ; 23, 3 ; 34, 10 ; 133, 3 ; 134, 12.
[3] See p. 7 f.
[4] 89 ; 93, 2 ; 109, 9 ; 119–124.
[5] *E.g.* 83, 10 ; 139, 2.

in southern Italy. Mingled with its fantastic
episodes are more serious passages, in which the
author makes his personages the mouthpiece of
his own views. Such especially are chapters 1–4
on the rhetorical training of the day, 88 on the
decay of arts and sciences,[1] and 118 on poetry.
All of these end with verses. The last two are
assigned to the poet Eumolpus, and the poems
which they introduce are the longest in the book :
the *Troiae Halosis* [2] of 65 iambric senarii, and the
Bellum Civile [3] of 295 hexameters. It may be
noted in passing that Eumolpus recites the Trojan
piece merely *à propos* of a picture at which his
companion is gazing intently, but offers the other
as a practical illustration of his theory of epic
poetry.

As the entire work, or rather all that remains

---

[1] See p. 92.

[2] Teuffel-Schwabe, *History of Roman Literature* (tr. by G.
C. W. Warr, London, 1891–1892), 305, 4, thinks that it alludes
to a poem of Nero's on the same subject. E. Thomas, *L'En-
vers de la société Romaine* (Paris, 1902), p. 93, describes it as a
parody on a juvenile *Iliacon* of Lucan. Its obvious relation is
to the Second Book of the *Aeneid*, which it constantly recalls.

[3] Or *Carmen de Bello Civili*. The Dresden Ms. (see p. 247)
calls it *Satira Petroni poete satyrici contra vicia Romanorum*.
It has also been called *Carmen de luxu Romanorum, Satira de
pessimis Romae moribus, Satira in qua vitia Romanorum
reprehenduntur, De mutatione rei publicae Romanae.*

to us, has been a fruitful source of differences of opinion, so this fragment, dealing with the struggle between Caesar and the Roman Senate, the most ambitious poetic effort contained in it, has become a sort of secondary storm-center. The questions which have been asked about it, and variously answered, may be summarized as follows : Was it intended to give a complete picture in little of the war, or an outline to be filled in, or an introduction to be continued ? What was the author's object in writing it ? Did he intend it to be taken seriously? The first question, while the least important of the three, is also the most difficult to answer with any degree of certainty. The concluding line of the poem :

The poem

factum est in terris quicquid Discordia iussit

might serve equally well to introduce a continuation of it. The fragment might also, though with less probability, be an outline, fairly complete through 244, but from there on to be expanded should the poet decide on an exhaustive treatment of the subject ; as exhaustive, that is, as his theory would allow. Or, finally, it might be already complete,[1] describing the opening scenes

---

[1] Complete, that is, in scope, not finish.

of the struggle and foreshadowing the rest. Perhaps Petronius never took the trouble to make up his mind on this point, but, if any, the last-named choice seems the most likely. The words of the introduction : *tamquam si placet hic impetus, etiamsi nondum recepit ultimam manum,* indicate that it is merely intended for a spirited attack on the subject which, though forever imperfect, would show what the author meant and what he might have done. Nor should it be forgotten that, whatever Eumolpus, as a character in the story, may be supposed to contemplate, it is not likely that Petronius, the satirist, would ever have thought seriously of attempting to expand his verses into a full-fledged epic, independent of his romance.[1] He had made his point, and that would be sufficient.

The second question is complicated at the outset by the manner in which both the *Bellum Civile* and the *Troiae Halosis* are introduced. Eumolpus, into whose mouth they are put, is a wretch whom his creator holds up alternately to ridicule and loathing. His public recitations are greeted with showers of stones, which, from long habit, he receives

The author's purpose

---

[1] Of course such a poem could not have been included in the *Satirae* without destroying its proportions entirely.

calmly enough. On this occasion his companions,
with whom he has just planned a particularly
daring swindle, allow him to hold forth in peace
to beguile a tedious journey on foot. When poem
and journey are ended, literature is dropped without further comment, and the intrigue goes on as
before. All this, on the face of it, might be considered sufficient proof that nothing assigned to
the old poet was to be taken seriously. But it is
Petronius's way to throw a dash of satire even
over what he seriously means. The remarks on
the decay of the fine arts and of science are in-
trusted to this same Eumolpus, and the criticism
of the *declamatores*, the justice of which is proved
by abundant evidence,[1] is divided between the
sponging and shifty Agamemnon and the cowardly
profligate Encolpius. It is in the same spirit that
Apuleius allows the exquisite story of Cupid and
Psyche [2] to be told by the repulsive old hag in the
robbers' den. Either Petronius did not consider
that the incongruity involved made much differ-

---

[1] *E.g.* Pers., III, 44 ff.; Juv., VII., 150 ff.; Quintil., II, 20,
4 ff.; V, 12, 17 ff.; VIII, 3, 76. For examples of the *declamationes*
themselves, see those ascribed to Quintilian, and Seneca's
Controversiae. It should be noted that part of Petronius's
discussion of this subject and the whole chapter on poetry (118)
are included in Saintsbury's *Loci Critici* (Boston, 1903).

[2] *Met.*, IV, 28 . . . VI, 24.

ence, or else he realized that just such inconsistencies of intellect and character are common enough in real life. Looking without prejudice at Eumolpus's discussion, we may disagree with some of his conclusions, but we shall not find anything to ridicule. Beginning with poetry in general, he gives us an appreciation of Horace which has become justly celebrated,[1] and then goes on to the epic and his own ideal of a work freed from the restraint of troublesome facts and elevated above the commonplace by an indirect method of treatment and the introduction of mythological elements : *ut potius furentis animi vaticinatio appareat quam religiosae orationis sub testibus fides.* He then, by way of illustration, offers the much-disputed epic fragment which one party has hailed as superior to Lucan [2] and almost equal to Vergil,[3] and the other has decried as tasteless and stupid bombast.

That Petronius, a mocker and a realist, should engage in the battles of artificial literature, and even essay to contribute to it himself, seems so strange, that the question at once suggests itself : Had he, in composing this poem, any special motive

---

[1] *Horatii curiosa felicitas.*
[2] Dousa, *Praecidanea*, II, 12.
[3] Anton, Ed., note to l. 295.

which can still be discovered? The almost
unanimous answer has been that it was an undis-
Theories as to the au- thor's pur- pose (Petro- nius and Lucan) guised satire upon Lucan.[1]   Westerburg[2] and E. Thomas[3] add that it is
double-edged, ridiculing the conserva-
tives in the person of Eumolpus, even
while attacking the newer school.
The *Troiae Halosis*, whether considered as directed
against Lucan or Nero,[4] is included in all this. More
moderate views are those of Margaritori[5] and
Heitland.[6] Margaritori considers the lines a mere
reproduction of the epic convention of the day,
to which Petronius could not have attached much
importance, since he assigned them to Eumolpus,[7]
while Heitland finds that they were "thrown off
half in rivalry, half in imitation of Lucan." To
Collignon also the poem is "*tout au plus une
refonte partielle du poème d'après une point de vue*

---

[1] *E.g.* Dousa, *l.c.*, Teuffel in *Rhein. Mus.*, Vol. IV (1846),
p. 511 ff. E. ; Thomas, *op. cit.*, p. 93 f. Boissier, *L'Opposition
sous les Césars* (Paris, 1892), V, III, adds that, in attacking
Lucan, Petronius may have intended to please Nero.

[2] *Petron und Lucan, Rhein. Mus.*, Vol. XXXVIII (1883),
p. 92 ff.

[3] *Op. cit.*, Ch. IV, § 1.

[4] See p. 5, n. 2.

[5] *Petronio Arbitro* (Vercelli, 1897), pp. 49 and 54.

[6] Introduction to Haskin's *Lucan* (London, 1887), (31).

[7] But see p. 7 f.

spécielle. Les deux poètes diffèrent sur la façon de comprendre le rôle et le caractère du merveilleux dans l'épopée." [1] Tailhade,[2] in his translation, omits as interpolations *"d'un scholiaste bête"* all verses in the work that are not closely joined to the story (*Avis Prémonitoire*, p. xxvi). This does not seem to include the *Bellum Civile*, but he omits it also, although he translates chapter 118, even to *tamquam si placet hic impetus*, etc., and then, having merely inserted the name of the poem, continues: *"Eumolpus, ayant avec sa rhapsodie*, etc." De Boisjoslin, in his Preface to the book, calls the *Bellum Civile* an *"épisode de hasard, que la déraison du copiste a inseré dans cette aventure."*

The view that Petronius was criticizing or parodying Lucan rests, first upon the language of chapter 118, second upon the internal evidence of the poem itself. The criticism is plain. The words of Eumolpus: *non enim res gestae versibus comprehendendae sunt, quod longe melius historici faciunt,* point directly to the school of which Lucan was the most distinguished member, while the fact that he takes as his example *belli civilis ingens opus,* and that

Examination of the theories

---

[1] Collignon, *Étude sur Pétrone* (Paris, 1892), Ch. V.
[2] *Pétrone, le Satire* (Paris, 1902).

his own lines are so full of reminiscences of the
Pharsalia, shows that he must have had Lucan
himself particularly in mind.[1] But it does not
follow that his purpose was parody or travesty.[2]
Criticism and parody do not go well together,
and it seems utterly unnatural that, having stated
his objections to Lucan's method in a sober and
reasonable manner, he should immediately nullify
them all by offering in support of his own theory
a mere burlesque, or a poem so absurd and
tasteless as to discredit all that he had taken
the trouble to say. Nor, indeed, is it easy to
see how he could have aimed at both schools at
once without inevitably missing both. The fact
that his taste may have been at fault or his proposed plan for the *ingens opus* a bad one, proves
nothing, if it appears that he presented it in
good faith.[3]

---

[1] As Teuffel says (*l.c.*), Petronius probably omits Lucan's
name because he was still alive. His meaning was clear enough
without it.

[2] Westerburg, *op. cit.*, distinguishes the two forms in this
poem, parody in its details, and travesty in the form and spirit
of the whole.

[3] In the argument which follows I shall, of course, be compelled to rely largely upon my own feeling with regard to the
poem. Humor is not to be discovered by analysis, and those
who seek it so are apt to miss it where it is and find it where it
is not.

Let us turn now to the evidence afforded by the parallel passages.[1] The first point that The parallel must strike any one is their number. passages In the historical parts of the poem (including the portents, 122–140, which are treated as history by both authors) they are practically continuous. Those portions devoted to the supernatural element, as is natural, show only incidental reminiscences. The opening passage on Roman decadence is also full of parallels, but Caesar's descent from the Alps, 177–208, appears to be quite independent.[2] Returning for further light to the critics, we are told, first of all, that Petronius "follows Lucan step by step,"[3] and this is taken as evidence of a satirical purpose. It should be remembered, however, that, as both authors are drawing from the same historical sources, this resemblance of outline is only natural. The tragic poets of Athens all used the same cycle of myths and legends, yet, with one exception,[4] they seem to have been content to pursue each his own

---

[1] See p. 71 ff.

[2] For further discussion of this passage, see p. 38.

[3] *Moessler Quaestionum Petronianarum Specimen Alterum et Tertium* (Hirschberg, 1865), p. 9. Boissier, *op. cit.*, V, II, p. 244.

[4] Eurip. *El.*, 520–544. But the intention of criticism here is denied by Murray, in his Translation (London, 1908). Note to ll. 510–545.

course without assailing that of any one else. Going farther, Westerburg [1] finds the whole poem a travesty of the *Pharsalia* both in manner and in spirit ; 1–60 is a "*Kapuzinerpredicht.*" As specific cases of parody he cites *fames premit advena classes*, 16, where Petronius applies to tigers for the arena the words which Lucan had used of Actium : *et quas premit aspera classes Leucas* (I, 42 f). Julia's prophetic words :

> praeparat innumeras puppes Acherontis adusti
> portitor   III, 16 f.

are "very well parodied" by Fortuna :

>   vix navita Porthmeus
> sufficiet simulacra virum traducere cumba ;
> classe opus est.   117–119.

Petronius's

> sentit terra deos mutataque sidera pondus
> quaesivere suum   264 f.

ridicules Lucan's address to Nero :

> aetheris immensi partem si presseris unam,
> sentiet axis onus.   librati pondera caeli
> orbe tene medio.   I, 56–58.[2]

and the *Sullanus ensis* personified, l. 98, and represented as drinking blood, parodies :

---

[1] *Op. cit.*   [2] See p. 19.

sic et Sullanum solito tibi lambere ferrum
durat, Magne, sitis.   I, 330 f.

It will be admitted, I think, that a parody should,
above all things, be amusing. But compare these,
or any of the parallels, with Aristophanes's parodies of Euripides,[1] and it will at once appear how
far from genuine parody they are. Nor is the
poem a burlesque in tone, like the *Apocolocyntosis*
of Seneca. Yet, as Petronius's prose narrative
shows, he had a rare talent for that artistic exaggeration and use of the unexpected and incon-
gruous, which is the very soul of this kind of fun.
Moessler,[2] going more into details, finds in 116–121
a triple reflection on Lucan, III, 14–19. *Fortuna*
is substituted for Julia as the speaker. Tisiphone
is painted more luridly than Lucan's Eumenides,
and *laceratus ducitur orbis* is meant to be at once
simpler and more elegant than *lassant rumpentis
stamina Parcas*. Again, in describing the panic
at Rome, 209–244, answering to Lucan, I, 466–522,
Petronius first exaggerates by giving Caesar a

---

[1] *E.g.* in *Alcestis*, 181–182, the heroine, dying to save her
husband, bids farewell to her marriage-bed : . . . σὲ δ'ἄλλη τις
γυνὴ κεκτήσεται | σώφρων μὲν οὐκ ἂν μᾶλλον, εὐτυχὴς δ'ἴσως.
In *Equites*, 1251–1252, Cleon reluctantly surrenders his wreath
to the man who has proved a greater scoundrel than he : . . .
σὲ δ'ἄλλος τις λαβὼν κεκτήσεται | κλέπτης μὲν οὐκ ἂν μᾶλλον,
εὐτυχὴς δ'ἴσως.

[2] *Quaestionum Specimen Alterum*, p. 18.

fleet, then softens the picture of the flight from
the city by substituting tearful farewells for head-
long desertion, and finally sets 238–244 against
the brevity of Lucan's *Pompeio fugiente timent*, 522.
In weighing the force of these assertions, it will
readily be conceded that Petronius's terms, in the
first passage, *are* stronger than Lucan's, but they
are far from startling for that extravagant age.
And the fleets, although unhistorical, are a smaller
addition to Caesar's forces than :

> inter Rhenum populos Alpesque iacentis
> finibus Arctois patriaque a sede revolsos.   I, 481 f.

Again, in the second passage, the seven lines
about Pompey are not to be set against Lucan's
three words, but against the many long passages
devoted to him throughout the *Pharsalia*.[1] Ob-
serve also that in repeating the storm simile, 233–
237, Petronius ignores Lucan's absurd description of captain and crew jumping overboard
through fear of shipwreck (I, 498–503). As to
the general line of reasoning adopted by these
critics, it will be seen that imitation and varia-
tion, strengthening or softening of terms, are all

---

[1] For a full list, see Heitland, *op. cit.* (38). This is the only
place where Petronius gives Pompey more than a passing
mention.

put into the same category, and interpreted in accordance with the same theory.

In order to appreciate how far from exaggeration Petronius is in his imitations of Lucan, let us take another and more striking case. Caesar's address to his soldiers, 156–176, corresponds, in whole or in part, to two long orations in the *Pharsalia*,[1] and recalls at least three shorter passages.[2] The difference in length is not the point; that follows naturally from the difference in scale between the two poems, but the tone of Petronius is as much quieter as his words are fewer. The lines of thought, argument, and appeal are identical, but in the Pharsalus speech Lucan permits his villain-hero to display a ferocity quite lacking in Petronius's characterization.[3] Compare also 171 f. :

---

[1] I, 299–351, at Ariminum ; VII, 250–329, before Pharsalus.
[2] I, 195–203, 225–227, 288 f.
[3] 292–294. See p. 84.

    sed dum tela micant, non vos pietatis imago
    ulla nec adversa conspecti fronte parentes
    commoveant : vultus gladio turbate verendos.

                            320–322.

Petronius's: victores ite furentes,
    ite mei comites et causam dicite ferro   168 f.
merely answers to VII, 261 f.:

    si pro me patriam ferro flammisque petistis,
    nunc pugnate truces, gladiosque exsolvite culpa.

C

reddenda est gratia vobis,

non solus vici

with Lucan, I, 340–345 ; VII, 257 f., and 264–269.
Petronius's *mei comites* crystallizes feelings upon
which Lucan enlarges again and again. Then
there is the quiet :

quia poena tropaeis

imminet et sordes meruit victoria nostra

172 f.

against the hysterical appeal :

Caesareas spectate cruces, spectate catenas,
et caput hoc positum Rostris effusaque membra

VII, 304 f.

which is immediately weakened by what follows :

vestri cura movet : nam me secura manebit
sors quaesita manu : fodientem viscera cernet
me mea qui nondum victo respexerit hoste.

308–310.

Lastly, there is nothing in the Petronian passage
to recall the absurd :

cuius non militis ensem

agnoscam ? caelumque tremens cum lancea transit
dicere non fallar quo sit vibrata lacerto.

VII, 287–289.

Had ridicule been Petronius's object, he would

scarcely have let pass so tempting an opportunity as that.

In the remaining passages it will be found
that Petronius, while frequently the more obscure of the two, is also as a rule the more re-
strained.   Take, for example, the passage already
quoted :

> sentit terra deos mutataque sidera pondus
> quaesivere suum.   264 f.

This ascription of weight to the gods, also found
repeatedly in Seneca's tragedies,[1] is utterly un-
poetical, and, like the operation of the law of
gravity in general, brings us down to earth with
a thud.   But how does Petronius's use of it
compare with Lucan's ?   That consistent patriot
applies it, not to the old *noblesse* of Olympus,
but to the divine Nero, urging him, when the
day of his apotheosis shall come, to " keep the
heavens trimmed,"[2] by sitting carefully in the
middle![3]   Certainly, Petronius's simple use of
the idea is no match for this high development
of it.   Finally, to understand what would be
necessary in order really to outdo Lucan in his
most reckless mood, the account of the storm in

---

[1] See on 264.
[2] The expression is Heitland's, *op. cit.* (46), d.
[3] For the lines, see p. 14.

which Caesar crossed from Dyrrachium to Brun-
disium [1] should be considered, where the waves
are held down by the clouds, and the sea would
leave its bed to overwhelm the land, did not the
winds, all blowing at once, protect each his own
coast.[2]   And to appreciate what Petronius could
have done, had he chosen to amuse himself with
Lucan and his heroes, we need only turn back to
some of the excursions into mythology and history
made by his wonderful Trimalchio.   "*Rogo, inquit,
Agamemnon mihi carissime, numquid duodecim
aerumnas Herculis tenes, aut de Ulixe fabulam,
quemadmodum illi Cyclops pollicem porcino ex-
torsit? solebam haec ego puer apud Homerum
legere*" (48).   "*Scitis, inquit, quam fabulam agant?*[3]
*Diomedes et Ganymedes duo fratres fuerunt. ho-
rum soror erat Helena. Agamemnon illam rapuit
et Dianae cervam subiecit. ita nunc Homeros dicit,
quemadmodum inter se pugnent Troiani et Paren-
tini. vicit scilicet et Iphigeniam, filiam suam,*

---

[1] V, 560–677. This will also throw some light on the statement of E. Thomas, *op. cit.*, p. 91, that Petronius, in imitating
portions of the *Pharsalia*, had chosen those that we would
condemn *sans réserve*.

[2] It must not be forgotten that this is not represented as a
miracle, wrought by the personal intervention of a god, as in
Verg., Aen., I, 81–123, but a storm weathered — in an open
boat — by a historical personage in a rationalistic epic.

[3] 59. A Homeric scene is about to be acted.

Achilli dedit uxorem. ob eam rem Aiax insanit et statim argumentum explicabit."

One passage remains to be considered, the opening denunciation of luxury and avarice and their attendant evils, which occupies over one fifth of the whole poem, and in fullness of detail far exceeds anything similar in Lucan. It has been remarked [1] that many of these details belong rather to the Empire than to the Republic, and it has accordingly been marked as a special piece of satire, aimed, not at Lucan only, but also at Seneca and other moral writers.[2] It is true that most of the crying evils which it assails had been and continued to be made the object of attacks which were powerless to reform them, but it does not follow that Petronius, in adding his voice, was insincere.[3] Indeed, the length and vehemence of the passage, even its overloaded obscurity, may have been due to a warmth of indignation that marred, instead of making, verses. There is nothing in the words which shows a desire to ridicule those who professed to say such things in earnest. At worst they are simply the stereotyped sermon without

The prologue

---

[1] Moessler, *De Petronii Poemate de Bello Civili* (Breslau, 1842), § 15.

[2] Westerburg, *op. cit.*, p. 93.

[3] Cf. the position of Juvenal.

which no serious poem of that time was complete.[1] And there is quite as much probability that Petronius, with his broad if perverse outlook,[2] would sometimes be stirred by such abuses, as that they would move Lucan, absorbed in his epic and its wonderful author. As to the disproportionate length of the passage, which occupies more space than any other single division of the poem, it may be due merely to the lack of *ultima manus* which would have removed superfluities and adjusted the parts to the whole.

Why, then, if satire or positive criticism was not his purpose, did Petronius, after declaring Imitations against the historically conducted epic, of other follow its prophet so closely? In seeking poets ing to answer this we must bear in mind that Lucan is not the only poet from whom Petronius has borrowed, but merely the chief of

---

[1] See the notes on this passage.

[2] For a touch of human sympathy, cf. Trimalchio's words (71) : "*amici, inquit, et servi homines sunt et aeque unum lactem biberunt etiam si illos malus fatus oppressit.*" The man into whose mouth these words are put treats his slaves as a spoiled child his toys, but still, what he says here, ungrammatically and in a moment of drunken sentimentality, reads like the honest conviction of his creator. Cf. also the frequently repeated phrase, *homo inter homines*, applied to the freed slave, and at the same time illuminating the other side of the great gulf.

many. A large number of parallel passages, from various authors, will be found scattered through the notes.[1] Those from the tragedies of Seneca are the most numerous, outside of Lucan, and most noteworthy. A comparison of the quotations from the works of the uncle and nephew will show, incidentally, some of the many resemblances between them, and show also that if, in his borrowings, Petronius generally went to Lucan for his language, the line of thought is apt to be closer to that of Seneca. This is especially true of the figures with which he embroiders his web. The points of the compass,[2] the laws of physics,[3] have a potent attraction for these men, to whom really poetical ideas so seldom come.[4] There are also the same set descriptions of nature in her angry moods, of yawning chasms and unfruitful fields. Tombs "ope their ponderous and marble jaws," and the light of day is suddenly flashed

---

[1] Those from later writers will serve to illustrate the general prevalence of the custom.

[2] See on l. 2.

[3] *E.g.* the center of gravity, 264 f.; the conflict between weight and supporting power, 85.

[4] Contrast such a fancy as that of Vergil, where Aeneas in the Underworld sees Dido:

obscuram, qualem primo qui surgere mense
aut videt aut vidisse putat per nubila lunam. VI, 453 f.

upon the realms of everlasting night.　A conceit
of which Seneca is particularly fond, introducing
it, *commutatis verbis atque sententiis*, no less than
four times,[1] is the enumeration of the grim phantoms at the gates of Hades.　In this he is following Vergil,[2] and is followed in turn by Petronius,[3]
but Lucan, although his witch Erichtho[4] has
much to say about the Lower World, never mentions them.　Comparisons drawn from storms at
sea are found almost everywhere in Latin poetry,
but there is a link between the similes of this
trio made by their fondness for the word *regimen*.
The Furies, too, are the common property of
the poets of the Empire, who overwork them
mercilessly.　For the *locus communis* of reflections on the fates of the members of the First
Triumvirate, or of Pompey and his two sons, see
the notes to ll. 61–66.

　To sum up, Petronius has drawn, first and
chiefly, from Lucan ; secondly, but still
Conclusion
for a great amount, considering the
difference in subjects, from Seneca ;[5] thirdly, from

---

　　[1] *H. F.*, 92–103, 690–696 ; *Oed.*, 588–592, 650 f.
　　[2] *Aen.*, VI., 273 ff.
　　[3] Letumque Insidiaeque et lurida Mortis imago, 257.
　　[4] VI, 507 ff.
　　[5] Or perhaps from the same traditional literary stock from
which Seneca drew.

Vergil,[1] Horace, Catullus, rarely from Lucretius,[2] perhaps never directly from Ennius. In like manner, later poets borrow from him as well as from more voluminous writers.[3] His epic fragment, while not original enough to lend much weight to the theory which it illustrates, is, when judged by contemporary standards, the reverse of absurd. For its object, it appears, as Heitland [4] says, "to have been thrown off half in rivalry, half in imitation of Lucan." Probably the versatile author wished to add to his *satira* of moods and manners a specimen of legitimate epic poetry, as then understood. Perhaps, too, piqued by Lucan's air of possessing the entire field, he wished to show how easily such conventional work might be done. It does not follow that he thought the result great poetry, or expected any one else to think so. It is also probable that he really did

---

[1] One sometimes finds in Vergil a phrase which has roused several echoes in Petronius, none of them complete. *E.g. Ge.*, II, 510: *gaudent perfusi sanguine fratrum.* Cf. 75, 214.

[2] But in chapter 134, 12, 4 f. there is a distinct Lucretian reminiscence: *mihi pontus inertes | summittit fluctus.* There are other echoes of Lucretius in the same poem. The resemblance here is not in sense but in sound.

[3] Cf. Stat. *Theb.*, III, 661 : *primus in orbe deos fecit timor*, and Petr., *Frag.* 27 (Buecheler), *Poetae Latini Minores*, XLIII, 76 (Teub.)

[4] *Op. cit.* (31).

believe in keeping epic poetry within the realm of imagination — as he understood it — and distinct from history.   What he failed to see was the futility of attempting such treatment with a subject which was, and must remain, historical, whose persons could not be demigods and did not deserve to be puppets.   By his manner of introducing the poem he contrived, first, to disarm criticism to a certain extent, and, second, as Tacitus says of his indomitable Petronius,[1] to show that his *ignavia* had achieved as much as the *industria* of others. Finally, in so far as it is critical, its criticism is of a negative kind, incompatible with parody or travesty, which consists in writing sensibly where Lucan allowed himself to drift into folly.[2]   The many close resemblances to the *Pharsalia* would serve precisely to bring out the differences and make his readers reflect on them.[3]   Besides this, in handling Lucan's subject, he probably felt that, until superseded, Lucan had said the last word on it, and therefore he borrowed from him whenever convenient as frankly as Lucan himself

---

[1] *L.c.*

[2] " It reads like a fair copy written to show Lucan how to do it."   Heitland, *op. cit.* (6).

[3] Collignon, *Etude sur Pétrone*, Ch. V, gives as a reason for not considering the poem a parody of the *Pharsalia:* " *Elle lui fait trop d'emprunts non déguisés.*"

from Vergil [1] and Vergil from Ennius; nay, even more, for Petronius was not, either by nature or training, a poet, and needed outside assistance to make up the deficiency.

At this point the question presents itself: How much of the *Pharsalia* did Petronius know? [2]

Petronius's knowledge of the *Pharsalia* Following the words of the Life of Lucan attributed to the sixth-century grammarian Vacca,[3] it has been generally believed that only the first three books of his epic were published during this author's lifetime. His suicide, commanded by Nero for his participation in Piso's conspiracy, took place in 65 A.D., Petronius's in 66, Nero's own in 68. It would stand to reason that, under

---

[1] See Heitland, *op. cit.* (51), for a list of Vergilian reminiscences covering 16 pages, and Nisard, *Les Poètes latins de la décadence* (3d ed., Paris, 1867), vol. 2, p. 333 ff., for a discussion of Lucan's debt to Vergil, *Ge.*, I, 466–488.

[2] Assuming him to have been C. Petronius.

[3] *Quippe et certamine pentaeterico acto in Pompeii theatro laureis recitante Nerone fuerat coronatus; et ex tempore Orphea scriptum in experimentum ingenii ediderat et III libros quales videmus . . . (ad fin.) sua sponte coactus vita excedere venas sibi praecidit . . ., non sine iactura utilitatis cum patriae quae tantam immature amisit indolem tum studiorum quoque. reliqui enim VII belli civilis libri locum calumniantibus tamquam mendosi non darent. qui tametsi sub vero crimine non egent patrocinio, de iisdem dici quod in Ovidii libris praescribitur potest: 'emendaturus si licuisset erat.'* (A list of his other writings follows.)

the circumstances, Lucan's friends would not
have dared to publish the remaining books until
after the Emperor's death, so that Petronius
could not have read them. Westerburg,[1] however, noticing Petronius's unmistakable imitations of the Seventh Book, admitted this also,
attributing his knowledge of it to recitations.
Outside of these four books he found but one
parallel, that between VI, 817 f. :

> Europam, miseri, Libyamque Asiamque timete;
> distribuit tumulos vestris Fortuna triumphis.

and Petronius's epitaph on the First Triumvirate,
61–66. This he considered accidental, as indeed,
if it stood alone, it might well be.[2] Heitland,
however, though he does not mention this case,
finds six others, making no distinction between
Book VII and the rest of the group, and inclines
to the belief that Petronius knew them all.[3]
In addition to these the following striking instances may be noted :

> maerentia tecta
> Caesar habet vacuasque domos.   *Phar.* V, 30 f.

cf. 225 :

---

[1] *Op. cit.*, p. 95.
[2] See p. 24 and notes to 61–66.
[3] He cites IX, 706 f. (14–16); X, 133 f. (21 f.); IX, 426–
430 (27–29); X, 338 f. (64); VI, 718 (95–97); VII, 125–127,
(235–237).

rumoris sonitu maerentia tecta relinquunt.
auribus incertum feralis strideat umbra.

VI, 623.

cf. 138 :

umbrarum facies diro stridore minantur.

haud multum terrae spatium restabat Eoae
ut tibi nox tibi tota dies tibi curreret aether,
omniaque errantes stellae Romana viderent.

VII, 423–425.

and X, 155–158 :

quod terra quod aer [1]
quod pelagus Nilusque dedit, quod luxus inani
ambitione furens toto quaesivit in orbe,
non mandante fame.

cf. 1–2 :

orbem iam totum victor Romanus habebat
qua mare qua terrae qua sidus currit utrumque.

primaque Thessaliam Romano sanguine tinxit.

VII, 473.

cf. 294 :

Thessalicosque sinus Romano sanguine tingue.[2]

spumantis caede catervas VII, 699.[3]

cf. 214 :

perfusas sanguine turmas

---

[1] For parallels from other authors, see notes on 1–2.
[2] For the reading, see Notes.
[3] For the Vergilian parallel, see p. 25, n. 1.

and 281 :
> toto fluitantes orbe catervas.

> quae seges infecta surget non decolor herba?
>
> VII, 851.

cf. 99 :
> extulit in lucem nutritas sanguine fruges.

Taking the *Pharsalia* as a whole, and arranging
the books according to the number of times that
Petronius appears to have drawn upon them,[1]
. we have the following series : I, VII, X, VI, II,
III, IV, IX, VIII, V.   The number of parallels
from I–III and from IV–X are almost equal.
The reason for the preponderant influence of
Books I and VII is not far to seek.   Petronius,
even if he had known all ten books equally well,
could hardly have found space for borrowings
from every part of them unless he had made his
295 lines a mere cento of Lucan.   The books
which naturally fixed his attention were the
First, containing the opening scenes of the war,
to which he has devoted most of his own poem, and
the Seventh, treating of Pharsalus, the climax of
both the struggle and the epic.   But admitting

---

[1] For a full list of parallel passages, see p. 71 ff.   The reck-
oning is, of course, only approximate, as there would inevitably
be a difference of opinion as to how many passages were
certainly, and how many only probably, conscious imitations.

all these evidences that Petronius was acquainted
with the last seven books of the *Pharsalia*, how,
if he died before their publication, could he have
gained his knowledge? The question is easily
answered. First, there were the "author's readings," so much in vogue at that time, where not
only short poems, but passages from longer ones,
not yet published, were declaimed. Heitland [1]
has remarked on the disastrous effects of this
custom upon Lucan's work. Even when there
were books still to write, and improvements to
make in those already written, Lucan's favorite
passages, those which had stirred his imagination
most, would probably have been perfected and
read to the court circle before the ban of the imperial displeasure silenced him. [2] Another — or
an additional — explanation is offered by Heitland : "My own view of the probabilities of the
case is that the words of the earlier (or Suetonian)
Life, relating to Lucan's emendation of some verses
just before his death, [3] are the foundation of the
notion that the later books are uncorrected.
There was some record of the publication of three
books, none of the rest. Out of these materials

---

[1] *Op. cit.* (27).

[2] Tac., *Ann.*, XV, 49. Dio, LXII, 29. Vacca.

[3] *Impetrato autem mortis arbitrio libero codicillos ad patrem
corrigendis quibusdam versibus suis exaravit.*

the story of the later Life [1] was made up, and
has no authority : though it may for all that be
true." [2]

Such, then, is the *Bellum Civile* of Petronius,
and as such, although an unfinished fragment, it
General   claims a place in the poetic literature
estimate of of its period. This period, known as
the poem   the Silver Age of Latin Literature, is
one of decadence. In poetry it includes Lucan,
Seneca, Persius, Silius Italicus, Statius, Juvenal,
Martial, and some lesser names.   Its characteristics are those which belong naturally to a genera-
tion devoid of original inspiration : rhetoric at all
times, overdevelopment of trivial themes, ceaseless
rehandling of a small and rather cheap set of ideas,
worn thin in the continual effort to polish them
to new lustre, endless straining after sensational
effects, *sententiae*, antitheses, paradoxes, a general
lack of subtlety, of the ability to produce great
effects by suggestion and restraint, of beauty,
delicacy, and real passion ; a ceaseless shouting,
quibbling, and reveling in bloodshed and physical
horrors.[3]   This does not mean that the poetry of

---

[1] See p. 27, n. 3.

[2] *Op. cit.* (32).

[3] *E.g.* Lucan, II, 173–190 (the murder of the brother of Marius) ; VI, 507–830 (episode of Erichtho) ; Seneca, *Oed.*, 960–

the Silver Age is devoid of dignity, force, and brilliant workmanship, but its finer growths are always in danger of being choked by the weeds that spring up with them. To take oneself very seriously was perhaps the first requisite of success in this school ; to be of fastidious taste would have been a fatal handicap. In view of all this, even were there nothing else to commend his work, Petronius would deserve praise for self-restraint, for moderation in the use of meaningless details and the invention of absurdities, and for sparing us any nauseating tale of horrors. But this is not all. Into his fragment of less than 300 lines he has worked a remarkably full and suggestive narrative. Such little vignettes as 61-66, 87-88, and the prophecy of the great series of battles, 111-115, open up deep vistas to any one familiar — as was Petronius's original public — with the history of those times. There is power — the power of a keen mind to summarize, and the power of a strong imagination to visualize — in such bits as :

ut bibat humanum populo plaudente cruorem.

18.

978 ; and the entire *finale* of *H. O.* (1132-) and *Med.* (868-). Contrast Vergil's treatment of the Deiphobus episode *Aen.*, VI, 494 ff.

D

non homo pulsus erat, sed in uno victa potestas
Romanumque decus, quare tam perdita Roma
ipsa sui merces erat et sine vindice praeda. 48–50.

luxuriam spoliorum et censum in damna furentem.
86.

the grim summing up :

iam pridem nullo perfundimus ora cruore
nec mea Tisiphone sitientis perluit artus
ex quo Sullanus bibit ensis et horrida tellus
extulit in lucem nutritas sanguine fruges. 96–99.

and the fine picture of the unconquerable Caesar
defying the elements, and lifted by sheer strength
of will and purpose to a level with the gods (201–
208). In these passages, as in the bulk of the poem,
the style is terse and vigorous, with the suggestion of some strong motive power behind it.
But there are also bits of great beauty, refreshing
spots beside the road over which the poet is driv-
ing his muse so relentlessly. For instance :

iam Phasidos unda
orbata est avibus, mutoque in litore tantum
solae desertis adspirant frondibus aurae. 36–38.

and :

(non) verno persona cantu
mollia discordi strepitu virgulta loquuntur. 72 f.

With a considerable variety of subject and treatment, and with remarkable freedom from the ver-

bosity and exaggeration of its time, the poem
ranks high when compared with its more preten-
tious fellows. If it falls short of the brilliance
of Lucan's best work, it escapes his worst bathos.
If it lacks the grace and charm of Statius, it is
free from the mere prettiness into which these
so often degenerate. It is in every way superior
to the *Bellum Punicum* of Silius. And all this,
it must not be forgotten, is achieved by a writer
whose regular *métier* — whoever he may have
been — was as far as possible from epic poetry.

As to the soundness of our author's theory, it
merely represents one horn of a dilemma. *Per*
ambages deorumque ministeria seems a
strange course for a narrative of well-
known public events to pursue. But
the severely historical treatment, on the other
hand, makes poetry well-nigh impossible. Nisard [1]
finds two ways in which the *Pharsalia* might
have been composed : *"C'était ou de receuillir à*
Rome et par toute l'Italie les souvenirs nationaux
sur ces dernières guerres de la liberté, de courir en
Grèce, en Egypte, sur les traces de Pompée et de
César, d'interroger les pâtres de la Thessalie, et de
composer une épopée de tous ces bruits populaires;
ou bien de peindre à grands traits la corruption d'où

*Petronius's
epic
theory*

---

[1] *Op. cit.*, II, p. 123 f.

*sortirent les guerres civiles, et d'expliquer le grand
changement qui rendit César maître du monde."*
Lucan chose neither of these ways, but it will be
observed that the second is not unlike what
Petronius attempted. And before one utterly
condemns the plan of compelling the weary gods
once more to put their shoulders to the wheel, it
should be noted that what Petronius meant, as
indicated by what he did, was not, like Silius, to
reduce his characters to mere pawns pushed about
by divine players, but simply to have the gods
set the terrific engine grinding — as who would
venture to say that Caesar and the Senate of the
moment could alone have wrought such a thing?
— to oversee, to prophesy, and to furnish an im-
posing background for human activities, but without putting any constraint upon human will and
reason. The gain by such a method would have
been mainly negative, in the escape from the mass
of details, military and political, which give the
impression of *religiosae orationis sub testibus fides,*
and the effect of the work as a whole would inevitably have been one of incongruity. But so is
that of the *Pharsalia.*[1] At best, had the author

---

[1] It must not be forgotten that Lucan does not dispense
with the supernatural entirely. *Fortuna* flits through his epic,
except where forced to yield to the sterner abstraction, *Fatum,*
Fama helps to carry the tidings of war to Rome (I, 469–472).

of such an epic possessed sufficient ability, he might, like Lucan, have made it memorable for fine passages which would compel the reader to forget for a moment the faulty design of the whole.

The worst positive defect of the *Bellum Civile*, its frequent obscurity, is a fault shared with The poem in detail. Obscurity other poets of the age — Lucan, Persius, Juvenal — who wrote under high pressure of one sort or another. It doubtless arose, in the first instance, from a striving after the unusual and epigrammatic, the constant effort to catch and hold the attention. Petronius is by no means a prime offender; but the contrast with his smooth-flowing prose makes the contortions of some of his metrical passages all the more noticeable, and perhaps these contortions, with the violent and jerky effect of the struggling lines, have helped the idea that the author meant to make what he imitated ridiculous. But besides the general tendency to obscurity at that time there is, in this case, the additional excuse of lack of experience in poetical composition, lack of *ultima manus*, and the problem of crowd-

---

Patria appears to Caesar at the Rubicon (I, 185 ff.), the shade of Julia terrifies the sleeping Pompey (III, 9 ff.), a woman prophesies the course of the war (I, 673 ff.), and the witch Erichtho exercises the blackest of black arts for the benefit of Pompey's son (VI, 507 ff.).

ing much material into a small compass. It is also more than likely that some of the most desperate difficulties are due to the corruption of the text, and would disappear if we could recover what Petronius really wrote.

The most independent passage in the poem, 177–208, is at the same time one of the least suc-
177–208   cessful.   The   author's   indebtedness here   is   not   to   other   poets,   but   to Livy,[1] and in his effort to adapt to his purpose and at the same time magnify to epic proportions the historian's account of Hannibal's crossing of the Alps and the Apennines — which, by the way, had lost their terrors by Caesar's time — he has shown pretty clearly that clouds and mountain-peaks were not favorable to the flowering of his imagination.   Were it not for the poetical inde-pendence of the whole paragraph, the crabbed Latin and tangled meteorological phenomena might well have lent color to the burlesque theory.   The parallel description by Silius Itali-cus [2] forms an interesting comparison.   The work of a poet as much more tasteless as he was more ambitious, it not only equals Petronius in

---

[1] XXI, 35–36 and 58.   See the Notes.
[2] III, 500 ff. and 547 ff.; IV, 749 ff.   See notes on 187 ff. and 203.

exaggeration, but leaves him far behind, telling, for instance, how the broken ice amputated the limbs of those who fell, and then was melted by their blood.

In striking contrast to this florid descriptive passage is that immediately preceding,[1] contain-

Caesar's speech

ing Caesar's speech to his army. Its twenty lines are perhaps the finest in the poem, and in simplicity, clearness, and dignity of thought and expression are not unworthy of the man to whom they are assigned. It is marked by soldierly brevity and a strong man's moderation of speech. Caesar's affection for his soldiers and his absolute confidence in them are revealed without undue protestation. The rewards of victory and the penalty of inaction — the possibility of failure is not considered — are brought out by single firm touches. The only thing which is not in keeping is the scornful reference to the Roman *plebs* (164–166). This is doubly inappropriate, first, as it makes of Caesar a reactionary of the school of the Scipios; and second, as it throws the responsibility for the war on the people instead of on the Senatorial oligarchy, where it belonged. Petronius's object, of course, was merely to make use of the younger Scipio's sting-

---

[1] 156–176.

ing retort to his political enemies,[1] and after more
than a century, during which Caesar had been
canonized, anathematized, and generally misun-
derstood, the inaccuracy is pardonable.   The
metrical form of this admirable bit of rhetoric
is appropriately measured and dignified, lending
special effectiveness to the two lines which are
allowed four dactyls each

dum Gallos iterum Capitolia nostra petentes.
                                                161.

representing the terrific downward sweep of the
Gallic invasion ; and

at reor, haud impune, nec hanc sine vindice dextram
vinciet ignavus.   167 f.

where Caesar's calmness is broken for a moment
by the thought of the vindictive injustice of his
enemies.   The whole ends with a line finely expressive of his unshaken confidence in the out-
come :

inter tot fortes armatus nescio vinci.[2]   176.

Points of   Examining our author's style more
style   minutely, we notice the following characteristics :
   Fondness for paradox or contrast :

---

[1] See note on l. 166.   [2] See p. 58.

detritaque commoda luxu
vulneribus reparantur. inops audacia tuta est.

	56 f.
muneribusque meis irascor.	108.
vincendo certior exul.	162.
sanguine Germano sexagintaque triumphis esse nocens coepi.	163 f.
causam dicite ferro.	169.
quia poena tropaeis imminet et sordes meruit victoria nostra.	172 f.
gaudet Roma fuga.	224.
praedamque in proelia ducit.[1]	232.

This device was, of course, especially popular with the Stoic Seneca. Used in moderation, it is a highly effective means of setting the irony of things clearly before the reader, but overdone it soon becomes tiresome, the word-play giving an exaggerated and artificial importance to the thought, instead of the thought ennobling the words. Petronius, however, has used it with discretion, and in Caesar's speech it becomes a powerful means of bringing out the injustice of the position into which he has been forced.

Fondness for startling and novel expressions:

---

[1] Cf. Lucan, I, 504: *in bellum fugitur.* Examples from the *Troiae Halosis* (89) : *ibat iuventas capta dum Troiam capit,* 27. *iacet sacerdos inter aras victima,* 51. *contraque Troas invocat Troiae sacra,* 65.

belua dente	
ad mortes pretiosa.	15 f.
fames premit advena classes.	16.
(mensa) maculis mutatur vilius aurum.	29.
ingeniosa gula est.	33.
sitientis . . . artus.	97.
nimbos . . . ligatos. (*i.e. ice*)	187.
vincta fluctus stupuere ruina.[1]	191

This tiresome trick arose from the decay of true imagination and originality and the pernicious training of the schools of oratory, with their impossible *controversiae* and *suasoriae*.[2] Petronius the novelist laughed at them,[3] but Petronius the poet laid aside for the moment his splendid sense of humor and copied — though not in their most desperate forms — the foibles of his serious-minded contemporaries.[4]

Sententiae are few, and the author has kept his own rule [5] against introducing them in digressions. One is woven into the address to *Fortuna:*

---

[1] Examples from the *Troiae Halosis;*

in suo voto latent.	10.
peritura Troia perdidit primum deos.	53.

[2] See p. 8, n. 1.
[3] Chs. 1–4. See p. 89 ff.
[4] His own words (88, 6) : *vitia tantum docemus et discimus,* are not without application to some of his poetry.
[5] 118, 5. See p. 1.

Fors cui nulla placet nimium secura potestas,
quae nova semper amas et mox possessa relinquis. 80 f.

Others are appended as tags to the lines which
suggest them :

inops audacia tuta est.	57.
hos gloria reddit honores.	66.

Colloquial expressions have sometimes been
admitted in spite of the poet's ban.[1] *E.g.* the use
of *accersere*,[2] 117, 158.

esse nocens coepi.[3]	164.

Legal or quasi-legal expressions are :

sine vindice praeda.	50.
nullum sine pignore corpus.	53.
causam dicite. (*ironical*)	169.
causa peracta est.	175.

On the other hand, the language has many of the
characteristics which distinguish poetry from
prose. *E.g.*:

The free use of verbs and adjectives which
practically personify the noun to which they
belong :

---

[1] 118, 4. See p. 1.

[2] Lucan is also fond of this word. See notes to 158.

[3] Cf. Ov., *Met.*, X, 132 : *velle mori statuit*. Such circumlocu-
tions are plebeian. Cf. the redundant *tun* in vulgar German.

(tellus) *hostis* erat.	6.
ingeniosa gula est.	33.
maiestas *auro corrupta iacebat.*	44.
hoc *mersam* caeno Roman *somnoque iacentem.*	58.
ira *rebellat.*	105.
laceratus ducitur orbis.	121.
(tellus) armis *laeta* meis.	157.
non *pugnavit* humus.	186.
consensit . . . timor.	246.
terras . . . *furentes.*	247.
lacerataque tecta *rebellent.*	287.

Transferred epithet :

corruptis miles vagus exstruit armis.   32.

Effect for cause :

rigido . . . flamine.   196.

Zeugma :

qua mare qua terrae qua sidus currit utrumque. 2.
bustorum flammis et cana sparsa favilla.   77.

Middle passive :

tu . . . satiare ruina.[1]   119.

Frequent use of possessive pronouns : *e.g.* *sua* . . . *arva*, 12 ; *mea Tisiphone*, 97 ; *mei comites*, 169 ; *Caesaris sui*, 267. These, how-ever, are never superfluous, but always have some special emotional fitness. See the Notes.

---

[1] See note on *mutatur*, 29.

Difficulties. — In addition to the obscurities already mentioned, the poem contains some lines which, in spite of the Latin words, hardly read or construe as Latin. Such are:

hinc Numidae accusant, illinc nova vellera Seres
atque Arabum populus sua despoliaverat arva.   11 f.
         hunc nive dura
claudit hiems canoque ad sidera vertice tollit.[1]   146 f.
       pepulitque meatibus auras.   178.
atque hoc Romano tonitru ferit omnia signa.   212.
atque inter torto laceratam pectore vestem.   276.

The difficulties in 24–27 and 229–231 are probably due to the corruption of the text.

In sharp contrast with the *ingenti volubilitate verborum* of his prose, Petronius has employed but a small vocabulary for his poem.

Language

He was, of course, obliged to dispense with many of the picturesque expressions which lend color to the narrative, and does not seem to have had a sufficiently large store of *voces a plebe semotae* to replace them. Thus there is much repetition. *Vincere* appears a dozen times, reinforced by *victor* and *victoria, quaerere* in various senses eight times, *rumpere* (usually the past participle) and its compounds ten times, *tellus* ten times, *pulsus* and *pulsatus* nine times together,

---

[1] See Notes.

orbis six times. The following words are used from three to five times each : [1]

arx, bella (the plural by preference), *clades, concretus, corrumpere, damnum, efferre, frangere, furere* and *furor, horridus, iacere, incendia, ingens, laetus, late, maerere, mergere* and compounds, *orbis, perdere,* and *perire,*[2] *perfundere* and other compounds of *fundere, personare,* and *persona, petere, placere, pondus, potestas, rebellare, regnum, ruina, sanguineus, sanguis, sidus, solvere, strepitus, sumere, tritus,* and *detritus, turma, vertex, vincire, vulnera, vultus.* Besides these repetitions, *submissa* is applied to the waters of the Bosporus in 242 and to *Fides* in 252. *Fortuna* and *Fama* are both *volucer.*[3] The world distracted by civil strife, the garments of *Discordia,* and the war-swept *tecta* are all *lacerata.*[4] *Gradiens* is used first of the caged tiger and second of *Discordia.*[5] The language of 50 :

> ipsa sui merces erat et sine vindice praeda.

---

[1] This list is not meant to be exhaustive, and includes only the more important words so repeated. Others are mentioned in the Notes.

[2] Especially *periturus.* See note to 19.

[3] 78 and 210.

[4] 121, 276, 287. Cf. *anserem laceratum verubus confixit,* 137, 12.

[5] 17 and 279.

is recalled in another connection by *mercedibus emptae*, 165, followed two lines below (167) by *sine vindice*. A particular weakness is the repetition of a word within a few lines but in a different connection, and where there is nothing to gain by it, as where *quaerere* occurs five times in twenty-one lines.[1] Thus we find *eruta* (*mensa*), 27; *eruta . . . conchylia*, 35. *Moles*, which stands for the unwieldy bulk of Rome in 83 and 109, is used between them, in 91, of the masses of rock excavated from the earth. *Insolitae voces*, 180, is followed by *insolitos . . . ausus*, 184.[2] In the description of the panic at Rome we have *maerentia tecta*, 225, and *maerentia pectora*, 229. The repetition of *cerno*, 111 and 114, has a purpose. That of *potestas*, 79–80, may be intended for an antithesis: "Power that hatest power," but the effect is not pleasing.[3]

A comparison of the *Bellum Civile* with the rest of the *Satirae* will show that, as far as possible, Petronius has simply transferred to the poem his prose vocabulary, shorn of its exuberances, and augmented by a few new terms. Words for which he shows a marked fondness in one part

---

[1] 7, 10, 14, 24, 27.

[2] Cf. *ignibus insolitis*, 136; Ch. 136, 6: *planctibus insolitis*.

[3] For a similar habit of Lucan's, cf. Heitland, *op. cit.* (47) E.

of the work reappear frequently in the other.
Thus *perfundere,* a special favorite, occurs in the
prose no less than twelve times, together with
other compounds of *fundere.* *Accersere* [1] appears
five times ; *periturus* three times in the *Bellum
Civile* and six times outside of it.[2] *Eruta,*[3] 33, 4,
and *vindicta,*[4] 95, 7 and 136, 7, may also be noted.[5]
There is, besides, the author's characteristic use
of *male* to indicate that an act or condition is
unreal, ineffectual, incomplete, or unfortunate.[6]
In the prose :

> 12, 1: fidem male ambulantem.
> 86, 4: male dormientis.
> 87, 3: male repugnanti.
> 103, 6: male soporati.
> 132, 8, v. 3: male dabat usum.

Bellum Civile :

> 20: male pubescentibus annis.
> 30: male nobile lignum.

---

[1] See p. 43.

[2] Cf. p. 46, n. 2. Cf. also *Fr.,* XXX, 13 (Buecheler) : *aut
premit eversam periturus navita puppem,* a characteristically
Petronian line.

[3] Cf. 27 and 35. See preceding paragraph.

[4] Cf. 142.

[5] For *turbare,* see on 30.

[6] Cf. Verg., *Aen.,* II, 735 ; IV, 8 ; Propert., IV, 6, 63 ; Sen.,
Tro., 548 ; Stat., *Theb.,* I, 314 f. ; *Anth. Lat.,* I, 402.

85: male sustinet.
193: male fida.

This double use of his vocabulary is made possible, not only by the comparatively prosaic tone of the verse, but also by the tendency of the characters in his romance to indulge in melodramatic rant and describe their sordid doings in language filched from epic, tragedy, and oratory.[1] The resemblance sometimes passes beyond single words to whole expressions. Cf. 26, 7: *tot vulneribus confossis fuga . . . placebat*[2] with:

oraque mille
vulneribus confossa.   259 f.

---

[1] *E.g. Macte virtute esto*, 94, 1. In 101, 1, Encolpius, describing his emotions on finding that he had unwittingly set sail in his enemy's ship, says: "*intremui post hoc fulmen attonitus, iuguloque detecto, 'aliquando, inquam, totum me, Fortuna, vicisti.'* " Cf. also Eumolpus's high-sounding plea for peace, 108, 14. The address of Encolpius to the dead Lichas, 115, 12 ff., beginning: "*ubi nunc est iracundia tua?* " is surprisingly like much that Hamlet says in the Graveyard (V, 1). Of course all this does not make the *Bellum Civile* burlesque, any more than the lyric outbursts of Pyramus and Thisbe, or the fustian of Ancient Pistol destroy the sincerity of Elizabethan tragedy. On this comic abuse of lofty and serious language in the *Satirae*, see the article by E. Klebs, *Philologus*, n. f. 1 (vol. 47, 1889), p. 623 ff. He points out especially a vein of burlesque analogies to the *Odyssey* running through the story.

[2] Also one of the author's favorite words. Cf. 7, 25, 56, 80, and the list, p. 46.

E

and 108, 7 : *turbam diducit in partes*, with :

omnis regia caeli
in partes diducta ruit.   265 f.

111, 10 : *porrexit . . . victam manum* is recalled
by :

abscondit . . . victum caput.   250.

Parallels from the other poems in the book are :

Troiae Halosis	*Bellum Civile*
14: mens . . . in damna potens.	censum in damna furentem. 86.
33: premunt classes mare.	fames premit . . . classes. 16.
34: pulsumque marmor . . . gemit.	freta pulsa carinis. 3.
56: sepultos Priamidas nocte et mero.[1]	turba sepulta mero. 31.
62: Bellumque sumunt.	sumite bellum. 174.

Ch. 128, 6, v. 4 :

thesaurosque rapit.	thesaurosque rapis? 292.

Ch. 136, 6, vv. 4–5 :

---

[1] An echo of Verg., *Aen.*, II, 265 :

invadunt urbem somno vinoque sepultam.

tremuit perterritus aether
planctibus insolitis, confusaque regia caeli.

ignibus insolitis	136.
omnis regia caeli	265.

Use of words. — The following points may be noted :

triumphis, 157, 163; *acies*, 156; *tropaeis*, 172; *ovantem*, 240; are all used by metonymy for "battles," "triumphs," "victories," "glory," with a vagueness and a free interchange of meanings which is quite modern.

Other words used in a figurative or unusual sense are :

acta, 267, "deeds" (not yet done), "enterprises."
averti, 248, "shun," "leave." [1]
concutere, 288, "rouse," "excite."
deploratus, 195, 227, "abandoned," "lost."
desolatus, 286, "enfeebled," "deprived of strength."
deprimere, 209, "descend." [2]
fervere, 214, "swarm." [3]

---

[1] Cf. Verg., *Ge.*, III, 498 f. :

immemor herbae
victor ecus fontisque avertitur.

and Stat., *Theb.*, VI, 192. This use of the word (as also of *aversari*. Cf. ἀποστρέφεσθαι) becomes more and more frequent as time goes on. For examples, see *Thesaurus Linguae Latinae* (Leipzig, 1900–).

[2] The only use of the word in this sense that I have been able to find.

[3] Common in poetry. Cf. Verg., *Aen.*, I, 436 ; IV, 407, 409, 567.

gaudere, 75, "abound in,"; 224, "give oneself up to."
geminus, 51, 111, 238 = *duo*. Common in poetry.
laetior, 181, "more brilliant." [1]
mitis, 186, "slight," "soft." In its regular sense, 247.
obsessa, 275, "covered with," "surrounded by" (of personal appearance). [2]
peragere, 4, "traverse." [3]
personare, 177. An exaggerated word to apply to Caesar's delivery of his speech. In 113:

iam fragor armorum trepidantes personat aures.

it is more appropriate. This straining of language was a plebeian trait which worked its way up into literary Latin. [4]
premere, 16, "weigh heavy on."
sepulta, 31, "dead drunk." [5]
stare, 274, "be thick with." [6]
strues, 62, denotes the process of destruction. In 195 it refers to the result, as regularly.
tumidus, 209, "lofty," "huge." [7] 198, *tumida grandine*, comes nearer the literal meaning, "swollen."

---

[1] In 72 it is used in its ordinary tropical sense, as in *laeta seges*. This is simply a further extension to the light of the sun.

[2] *Obsitus* is more common in this sense.

[3] See Notes.

[4] See note on *calcavit*, 152.

[5] See p. 50, n. 1.

[6] Frequently used thus in poetry of something conspicuous or startling. See note to 274.

[7] Cf. Ov., *Am.*, II, 16, 5, 51 f.:

at vos, qua veniet, tumidi subsidite montes
et faciles curvis vallibus este, viae.

A rare word used by Petronius is *persona*,[1] "ringing with," 72.

Unusual expressions are :

incendia ducit	139.
omina . . . dedit[2]	178.
incendia portat	263.
acta . . . ducit.	267.

Syntax The following constructions belong to poetical, colloquial, or late Latin.

Use of cases :

Genitive: hoc dedecoris (sc. est), 47.

Dative: rapuisse Catoni, 46. Instead of the more usual *eripuisse*.

>*certaverat ostro*,[3] 10.
>*dextrae coniungere dextram*,[4] 100.

Ablative. — As is common in poetry, this case appears in many constructions so loose as to defy the ordinary grammatical classifications. The Ablative of Place without a preposition[5] is

---

[1] Used also by Val. Flac., IV, 418 : *ovanti persona sistro* (active) ; and Mamert. *Gratiarum Actio*, x : *lata camporum balatu, hinnitu, mugitibus persona.*

[2] See Notes.

[3] Cf. Verg., *Aen.*, I, 107 : *furit aestus harenis.*

[4] See Notes.

[5] *E.g. quaesitus tellure nitor*, 10.

so frequent in the poets that I have not collected the instances of its use here. The following extensions of (a) the Instrumental, and (b) the Ablative of Attendant Circumstances, are worth noting :

> (a) quaeritur . . . auro fera, 14.
> auspiciis patuere deum, 127.
> fax stellis comitata,[1] 139.
> (b)[2] ferali circum tumulata cupressu, 75.
> canoque . . . vertice tollit,[3] 147.
> vincta . . . stupuere ruina, 191.
> inter torto laceratam pectore vestem
> sanguineam tremula quatiebat lampada dextra.
>
> > 276 f.

Prepositional phrases:

> ad mortes pretiosa, 16.
> de parte sinistra, 179.
> in . . . bella paratis, 6.
> in damna furentem, 86.
> nixus in hastam, 203.
> per damna renovare, 36.
> super arma cadebant,[4] 199.

---

[1] Cf. Verg., *Aen.*, I, 312 : *uno . . . comitatus Achate.*

[2] The first three phrases might really belong to either division.

[3] See Notes.

[4] So constantly in his prose. *E.g. consedit . . . super ectum,* 9, 2 ; *candelabrum . . . super mensam eversum,* 64, 10 ;

Infinitive:

sufficiet . . . traducere, 118.

Subjunctive. — There is nothing unusual in Petronius's use of this mood, but his fondness for the Ideal Second Person is noticeable. In the poem we find *putares*, 129 and 190 *putes*, 148. In the prose he is constantly appealing to his audience with *putares, putes, scires,* and *crederes.*

Trampe, in his dissertation [1] on the versification of Lucan, claims that Petronius has made his Prosody, hexameters *Vergiliani, non Lucaniani,* etc. with the intention of criticizing Lucan's manner as well as his matter. He supports this by an analysis of the poet's usage in the matter of verse-endings, elisions, pauses, etc. To the reader, however, these verses are utterly un-Vergilian in their effect, and resemble those of Lucan in many points, especially defects. Nor does this seem unnatural when one reflects that Petronius, evidently not a poet either by instinct or by long practice, wrote his poem with the *Pharsalia* vividly before his mind.[2] It is but another case

---

me . . . *praecipitat super lectum,* 94, 9 ; *anumque . . . deiectam super foculum mittit,* 136, 1.

[1] *De Lucani Arte Metrica* (Berlin 1884), p. 78.

[2] See p. 27 ff.

of *vitia tantum ... discimus.*[1]   Like Lucan, Petronius has wrought his verses with a heavy hand.
They are correct and vigorous, but monotonous
and often unmusical, and create an impression of
having been hammered out with careful regard to
the fundamental rules, but without much feeling
for subtler effects or perception of the variety of
treatment which might be achieved within them.
In the following notes I have endeavored to point
out their most striking characteristics and also
the chief points of resemblance to Lucan.[2]

Pauses. — Like Lucan, Petronius is fond of
pauses after the strong penthemimeral and hep-
themimeral caesuras, repeating them until the
cadence becomes insistent and tiresome, *e.g.*:

3: nec satiatus erat.

4: iam peragebantur.

7: quaerebantur opes.

11: hinc Numidae accu-
sant.

27: quaeque virum quae-
runt.

36: ut renovent per
damna famem.

90: en etiam mea regna
petunt.

117: atque animas ac-
cerse novas.

127: auspiciis patuere
deum.

135: sideribus tremefacta
ciet.

---

[1] See p. 42, n. 4.

[2] For the salient points of Lucan's versification, see Heitland,
op. cit. (49).

More Vergilian is his fondness for the pause after
the bucolic diaeresis, which we find in nearly seven
per cent of the lines, *e.g.* :

31: turba sepulta mero circum venit, omniaque orbis.
34: ad mensam vivus perducitur, atque Lucrinis.
131: et lucem sceleri subduxit. rupta tonabant.
132: verticibus lapsis montis iuga, nec vaga passim.
272: extulit ad superos Stygium caput. huius in ore.
289: Curio. tu fortem ne supprime, Lentule, Martem.
292: thesaurosque rapis? nescis tu, Magne, tueri.[1]

Rhythm. — The great defect here, as in Lucan,
is want of variety. Take, for example, the speech
of *Fortuna*, 103–121. The same metrical combinations are repeated over and over again.
There are also a few lines which are positively
unpleasant :

50: ipsa sui merces erat et sine vindice praeda.
195: armaque congesta strue deplorata iacebant.
258: quas inter Furor, abruptis ceu liber habenis.

In the proportion of dactyls to spondees, Petronius keeps carefully to a middle course, with an
evident preference for slowness of movement.
There are in the whole poem only eight lines of
five dactyls each [2] which serve to accelerate the

---

[1] In 131 and 292 this pause is preceded by a spondee.
[2] 3, 12, 33, 42, 115, 136, 178, 272.

ordinarily staid progress of the verse, *e.g.*:

Actiacosque sinus et Apollinis arma timentes.   115.

depicts the tumult and mêlée of the battle.

iamque Aetna voratur
ignibus insolitis et in aethera fulmina mittit.   136.

omina laeta dedit pepulitque meatibus auras.   178.

and :

extulit ad superos Stygium caput: huius in ore. 272.

produce the same impression of swift motion. Contrasting with these eight lines there are sixteen which contain but one dactyl apiece.[1] Their slow and stately movement is effective at the opening of the poem :

orbem iam totum victor Romanus habebat.   1.

and of the solemn remonstrance addressed by *Dis* to *Fortuna*:

rerum humanarum divinarumque potestas.   79.

It also closes Caesar's speech :

inter tot fortes armatus nescio vinci.   176.

---

[1] 1, 38, 58, 77, 79, 82, 93, 101, 128, 171, 176, 187, 261, 274, 291, 295.

and the entire poem :

> factum est in terris quicquid Discordia iussit. 295.

Outside of these the most notable cases are :

> solae desertis adspirant frondibus aurae. 38.

expressing the loneliness of the bird-deserted Phasis ;

> hoc mersam caeno Romam somnoque iacentem. 58.

of the helplessly mired and wallowing city ;

> ecquid Romano sentis te pondere victam ? 82.

of the crushing weight with which she bore upon others ;

> deformis Titan vultum caligine texit. 128.

of the eclipse of the sun, and :

> stabant aerati scabra rubigine dentes. 274.

enforcing the repulsive picture of *Discordia*.

Sameness in the endings of lines is also noticeable. There are no monosyllabic endings,[1] and the only ones which are at all abnormal are *pro-*

---

[1] This does not take into account endings like *ille est*, 45, where there is an elision.

spexit et ambas, 154, and *quem ter ovantem,* 240.
To these may be added a single spondaic line:

> alta petit gradiens iuga nobilis Appennini.[1]   279.

which is also the only one in the poem ending
with a word of more than three syllables. This
extreme uniformity is made all the more evident by Petronius's fondness for repeating some
of his verse-endings. *Potestas* occurs four times
in this position,[2] *Martem* three times,[3] *dehiscit,*
putares, *triumphis,* and *furentes* twice each;[4]
160 closes with *sanguine tinguo;* and 294 with
sanguine tingue.

Hiatus does not occur.

Final assonance is found only once: *potestas*
. . . *potestas,* 79–80.[5]

Metrical licenses. — The only ones which Petronius allows himself are *belua* as a trisyllable,

---

[1] *Appenninus* as a verse-ending is used repeatedly by the
poets. Cf. Ov., *Met.,* II, 226; Lucan, II, 396; Pers., I, 95;
Sil. Ital., II, 314; IV, 744. Of Ovid's line Haupt says:
"*Der spondeische Versausgang beschliesst die lange Aufzählung
mit aushallendem Klange.*" Cf. also Lucan, I, 689:

> nubiferae colles atque aeriam Pyrenen.

[2] 43, 48, 79, 80.

[3] 134, 158, 289.

[4] 90, 254; 129, 190; 157, 163; 168, 247, respectively.
86 ends with *furentem.*

[5] See p. 47.

15; *Catŏ*, 45; and *Curiŏ*,[1] 289; *mihĭ*, 104; and *tibĭ*, 105; *fervĕre*,[2] 214.

Elision is rather sparingly used, though more frequently than in the *Pharsalia*,[3] about one case to every four lines. Of these nearly one third are elisions of *-que*, and so of little importance. There are no hypermetric syllables. The lines in which Petronius has made the freest and most effective use of elision are:

nec posse ulterius perituram extollere molem. 83.
luxuriam spoliorum et censum in damna furentem. 86.
classe opus est. tuque ingenti satiare ruina. 119.

in all of which there are double elisions, an uncommon thing in the poem. The best instance of all is the description of the fiends crowding up from Hades:

emergit late Ditis chorus, horrida Erinys,
et Bellona minax, facibusque armata Megaera,
Letumque insidiaeque et lurida Mortis imago.
255–257.

---

[1] So also Lucan. With Curio's name it is a metrical necessity.

[2] Cf. Verg., *Ge.*, I, 456; *Aen.*, IV, 409, 567. Varro, *Sat. Menipp.*, *Desultorius*: fervere piratis vastarique omnia circum.

[3] Winbolt, *Latin Hexameter Verse* (London, 1903), p. 182, estimates one elision to 6½ lines for Lucan.

Alliteration is used continually, but rather weakly. The best instances are :

tres tulerat Fortuna duces, quos obruit omnes.   61.
qui furit effusus, funesto spargitur aestu.   70.
aedificant auro sedesque ad sidera mittunt.   87.
Actiacosque sinus et Apollinis arma timentes.   115.
qualis Caucasea decurrens arduus arce
Amphitryoniades.   205 f.
hic vehit imprudens, praedamque in proelia ducit.   232.
Pax prima ante alias niveos pulsata lacertos.   249.
vulneribus confossa cruenta casside velat.   260.

Metrical treatment of repeated words. — Another characteristic of the author's hammering method is the intentional repetition of words in the same line or in succeeding lines, a device effective in moderation, but wearisome when often employed. When the emphasis is strongest, the metrical treatment is identical. Thus Caesar says to his men :

                    victores ite furentes,
ite mei comites.   168 f.

and *Discordia* shrieks :

sumite nunc gentes accensis mentibus arma,
sumite [1] et in, etc.   283 f.

---

[1] There is here the slight difference caused by elision in one place.

201 f. :

victa [1] erat ingenti tellus nive *victa*que cæli
sidera, *victa* suis haerentia flumina ripis.

lead up to the climax, *nondum Caesar erat*, 203.
Again, similar and different treatment are combined :

tu legem, Marcelle, tene. *tu* concute plebem
Curio. *tu* fortem ne supprime, Lentule, Martem.
quid porro *tu*, Dive, *tuis* cunctaris in armis? 288–290.

In 45 f. two pairs of words and two kinds of treatment are combined :

pellitur a populo *victus Cato;* tristior ille est
qui *vicit*, fascesque pudet rapuisse *Catoni*.

So also in 170 :

namque *omnes unum* crimen vocat, *omnibus una*.

Finally, a single important word is repeated, with
similar position in each clause, but with different
metrical treatment :

venalis populus, *venalis* Curia patrum. 41.
testor, ad has acies *invitum* accersere Martem,
invitas me ferre manus. 158 f.

---

[1] There is here the slight difference caused by elision in one
place.

Moessler,[1] with the German passion for law and order, has raised a question as to the relations of *Dis, Fortuna,* and *Discordia* to each other and to the opening of the poem. He finds an inconsistency between the account given in 1–60 of the tendencies which were making for civil war and the later appearance of *Fortuna.* "*Quum Fortuna caussa alicuius rei declaratur, nullus locus est aliis caussis.*" He concludes that Petronius has constructed a double narrative, part mythological, part historical, with two independent chains of causation. But he still seems troubled by the question of precedence between *Dis* and *Fortuna,* and by the fact, as he says, that *Discordia* merely repeats what has already been told in the historical portion of the poem. The true explanation of Petronius's system — if, indeed, he had one — seems to be about as follows : The civil war which we see preparing in 1–60 is the design of Fate, whose power has degraded the Romans past all hope of mild remedy.[2] But Fate often leaves the execution of even the highest decrees to lesser powers, and grants them considerable liberty in the matter of details. So in 61 we find *Fortuna* sending Pompey, Caesar, and

Dis, Fortuna, and Discordia

---

[1] *De Petronii Poemate de Bello Civili,* p. 61 ff.
[2] See note on l. 6. Cf. also 58–60.

Crassus upon the earth, and then abandoning
them to the Erinys. In the next passage *Dis*
rises and summons her. He speaks, not in
command, but in remonstrance, pleading for
a renewal of bloodshed to refresh himself and
his agent Tisiphone. When he speaks of the
insane extravagance and luxury of the Romans,
he does not, as Moessler says, mean that they
are the cause of his action, but merely that
they furnish a justification of his demands.
Fortuna, in a tone of authority, grants his
prayer.[1]

Si modo vera mihi fas est impune profari. 104.

is an admission of the supreme dominion of Fate,
but within that limit she is herself supreme. Even
Jupiter merely falls in with her plans. His lightnings, which terrify his brother, make no impression on her except as aids. The other gods
now second Jupiter with portents which announce
clades hominum venturaque damna (126), and
Caesar, with characteristic energy, forms his
resolution and acts on it at once. Portents con-
tinue to encourage him amid the difficulties of
his march. Meanwhile *Fama* fills Rome with

---

[1] vota tibi cedent, 105. destruet istas . . . et mihi cordi,
108 f.

F

an exaggerated account of what is happening, and
Consuls, Senate, and people promptly lose their
heads, even Pompey fleeing before the fickle goddess who had so long been his "dear lady." [1]
The gods themselves are next swept into the vor-
tex.   The spirits of goodness and peace flee·from
the earth, while the powers of darkness rise to
bear their part in the coming destruction.   The
greater gods divide to the opposing camps according to their sympathies.   It is now Discordia's
turn to appear.   She does not really, as Moessler thinks, repeat what has already been said.
The   incidental   information   supplied   by   her
words brings out details which had not yet been
made clear.   But her chief duty is to give the
signal for the struggle, to hark on Roman against
Roman, and divide the world against itself.   She,
too, speaks in a tone of authority, but as we know
her to be one of the servants of *Dis*, who had
not been able to precipitate the war himself,
it is plain that she is merely acting under
orders.   *Fortuna*, like the mightier Fate, has
announced her will and then left its execution to
subordinates.

The best account of the traces of Petronius to

---

[1] Cf. 243 f.

be found in later writers is contained in Collignon's *Pétrone en France*, running through
the entire book. Comparatively few of
them relate to the *Bellum Civile*. Heiric,
however, of the monastery at Auxerre,
from which came the present *Codex
Bernensis*,[1] has introduced some striking imitations
into his *Vita Sancti Germani* (about 876):

(margin note: Reminis-cences of the Bellum Civile in Medieval Latin)

I, 20:[2]   perparva et vilia scitu

       si qua patent usquam: cara et praegrandia
       censet
       si qua latent.

  24:     orbem iam totum victor Romanus habebat,

       qua mare, qua tellus, qua cardo invergit
       uterque.
       si quod in orbe fretum, si quis sinus abditus
       usquam,
       si quod clima fores Phoebeae lampadis expers,
       si qua fuit regio, fulvum quae gigneret aurum,
       nil nisi Romani vivebat nominis umbra.

V, 131:   hinc subit aerias meritis sublimior Alpes.

Other less striking resemblances will be found
in Buecheler, *Ed. Maior, Praefatio*, p. xi, and
Collignon, *Pétrone en France*, Introd., p. 7 f.

---

[1] See p. 247.

[2] The references are to book and paragraph, according to
J. P. Migne, *Patrologiae Cursus Completus* (Paris, 1879), Vol. 124.

Vincent de Beauvais,[1] in his *Speculum His-toriale*, XX, 25, attributes to Petronius, Bishop of Bologna,[2] a number of fragments, both prose and verse, culled from our author, beginning with :

quid faciant leges ubi sola pecunia regnat? (Ch. 14, 2.)

Towards the end we read :

ingeniose gula est.   (33.)
ad praedam strepitumque lucri suffragia vertunt. (40.)
venalis populus, venalis curia patrum   (41.)
ipsaque maiestas auro corrupta iacebit.   (44.)
quaerit se natura nec invenit.   omnibus ergo
scorta placent fractique nervi serpere gressus
et laxi crines et tot nova nomina vestis.   (24–26.)

Guillaume le Breton,[3] *Philippis*, II, 44, has the line :

iudice Fortuna bellum committere vellet.   Cf. 174.

Jean de Montreuil,[4] *Epp.*, 14 : *ut inquiit Aufranius :*[5] *scorta placent fractique enervi corpore*

---

[2] *De quodam libro Petronii partim metrico, partim prosaico, pauca haec moralia, quae sequuntur, excerpta notavi.*
[3] Thirteenth century.
[4] 1354–1418.
[5] Afranius, the author of *togatae*.   So Scaliger's Ms. (see. p. 246) calls our author C. Petronius Arbiter Afranius.

gressus, et laxi crines et tot nova nomina vestis quaeque virum quaerunt turba sepulta mero circumvenit. est favor in precio senibusque libera virtus excidit omnibus una impendet clades arma cruor caedes incendia totaque bella ante oculos volitant.[1]

Sarrasin's *Guerre Espagnole* (Paris, 1675) is imitated from the *Bellum Civile.*

The *Editio Princeps* of Petronius was published at Milan, by Franciscus Puteolanus, 1482. The Editions and translations sixteenth and seventeenth centuries saw many more editions, the eighteenth and nineteenth a rapidly decreasing number of them. Full lists may be found in the prefaces to the editions of Burmann, Anton, the Bipontine Society, and Collignon, *Pétrone en France.* Only the oldest and most recent editions and some of the most important which intervene are given here:

Vitales, Venice, 1499.

H. Busch, Leipzig, 1500 and 1508. *Bellum Civile* alone, 1500.

Régnault-Chaudière, Paris, 1520.

J. Wouweren (Wouwerius), Amsterdam, 1524; Leyden, 1596, 1604, 1624.

---

[1] Cf. ll., 25–27, 31, 42 f., 170 f., 215 f.

Sambucus, Vienna, 1564; Antwerp, 1565.

Tornaesius (Jean de Tournes), Lyons, 1575.

Pithoeus (P. Pithou), Paris, 1577, 1589.   Published by
   Mamert Patisson.

Ed. Lugd. Batavorum, Ioannis Paetsii, Leydèn, 1583.

J. Dousa, Leyden, 1585.

Frellon, Lyons, 1608, 1615.

G. Erhard (M. Goldast), Frankfort, 1610.

Bourdelot, Paris, 1618, 1645.

Gabbema, Utrecht, 1654.

Hadrianides, Amsterdam, 1669.

Burmann, Utrecht, 1709, 1743.   Part II contains the
   prefaces and commentaries of many of the earlier
   scholars, some of whom did not publish editions.

Reiske, Leipzig, 1748.

C. G. Anton, Leipzig, 1781.

Ed. Societatis Bipontinae, Zweibrücken, 1790.

De Guerle, Paris, 1834.

Buecheler, Ed. Maior, Berlin, 1862; Ed. Minor, 1882,
   1886, 1895.

Many translations of the *Satirae*, in whole and in
   part, have been made, but the versions of the
   Bellum Civile are generally very free.   Three of
   the most available are : De Guerle, Paris, 1798,
   1816, 1834 (*Collection Pankoucke*), 1861 ; Bail-
   lard (in Nisard, *Collection des auteurs latins*
   (Paris, 1856), v. 14) ; H. Wagner (English), London, 1873.

PARALLEL PASSAGES

PETRONIUS AND LUCAN

Petronius, 1–60, 82–89.
Lucan, I, 158 ff.:
hae ducibus causae suberant: sed publica belli
semina, quae populos semper mersere potentis.
namque, ut opes mundo nimias fortuna subacto
intulit et rebus mores cessere secundis
praedaque et hostiles luxum suasere rapinae :
non auro tectisque modus : mensasque priores
aspernata fames : cultus gestare decoros
vix nuribus rapuere mares : fecunda virorum
paupertas fugitur ; totoque accersitur orbe
quo gens quaeque perit.   167

*   *   *   *   *   *

inde irae faciles ; et quod suasisset egestas   173
vile nefas ; magnumque decus ferroque petendum
plus patria potuisse sua ; mensuraque iuris
vis erat : hinc leges et plebescita coactae,
et cum consulibus turbantes iura tribuni :
hinc rapti fasces pretio sectorque favoris
ipse sui populus, letalisque ambitus urbi,
annua venali referens certamina Campo :
hinc usura vorax avidumque in tempora faenus
et concussa fides et multis utile bellum.

Petronius, 1–2.
Lucan, I, 110.   (populi potentis fortuna):
quae mare quae terras quae totum continet orbem.

VII, 423–425:
haud multum terrae spatium restabat Eoae
ut tibi nox tibi tota dies tibi curreret aether
omniaque errantes stellae Romana viderent.

Cf. also the movement of X, 155 f.   (See under
31 ff.)

Petronius, 14–16.
Lucan, I, 41–43:
his, Caesar, Perusina fames Mutinaeque labores
accedant fatis; et quas premit aspera classes
Leucas.

IX, 706 f.:
sed quis erit nobis lucri pudor?   inde petuntur
huc Libycae mortes et fecimus aspida mercem.

Petronius, 21.
Lucan, X, 133 f.   (Cleopatra's slaves):
nec non infelix ferro mollita iuventus
atque exsecta virum.

Petronius, 27–29.

Lucan, IX, 426–430:

tantum Maurusia genti
robora divitiae quarum non noverat usum,
sed citri contenta comis vivebat et umbris.
in nemus ignotum nostrae venere secures,
extremoque epulas mensasque petivimus orbe.

X, 144 f.:
dentibus hic niveis sectos Atlantide silva
imposuere orbes.

Petronius, 31 ff.
Lucan, IV, 373–376:

o prodiga rerum
luxuries numquam parvo contenta paratu,
et quaesitorum terra pelagoque ciborum
ambitiosa fames et lautae gloria mensae.

X, 155 ff. (wealth of Egypt):
infudere epulas auro, quod terra quod aer
quod pelagus Nilusque dedit, quod luxus inani
ambitione furens toto quaesivit in orbe
non mandante fame.

Petronius, 41.
Lucan, IV, 816–818:
perdita tunc urbi nocuerunt saecula, postquam
ambitus et luxus et opum metuenda facultas
transverso mentem dubiam torrente tulerunt.

Petronius, 50.
Lucan, II, 655 f.:
ipsa caput mundi bellorum maxima merces,
Roma capi facilis.

Petronius, 51.
Lucan, I, 181:
hinc usura vorax avidumque in tempora faenus.

Petronius, 63.
Lucan, VIII, 698 ff.:
litora Pompeium feriunt truncusque vadosis
huc illuc iactatur aquis?   adeone molesta
totum cura fuit socero servare cadaver?   700
hac Fortuna fide Magni tam prospera fata
pertulit : hac illum summo de culmine rerum
morte petit, cladesque omnes exegit in uno
saeva die quibus immunes tot praestitit annos :
Pompeiusque fuit qui numquam mixta videret 705
laeta malis : felix nullo turbante deorum,
et nullo parcente miser.   semel impulit illum
dilata Fortuna manu.   pulsatur harenis,
carpitur in scopulis, hausto per vulnera fluctu,
ludibrium pelagi : nullaque manente figura   710
una nota est Magno capitis iactura revolsi.
ante tamen Pharias victor quam tangat harenas
Pompeio raptim tumulum Fortuna paravit,
ne iaceat nullo, vel ne meliore sepulcro.

Also I, 685 f.   (See on 111–115 below.)

Petronius, 64.
Lucan, X, 338 f.
dignatur Pharias isto quoque sanguine dextras
quo Fortuna parat victos perfundere patres.

Also I, 691.   (See on 111–115 below.)

Petronius, 65 f.
Lucan, VI, 817 f. (Erichtho to Sextus Pompeius):
Europam, miseri, Libyamque Asiamque timete :
distribuit tumulos vestris Fortuna triumphis.

Petronius, 75.
Lucan, III, 442:
et non plebeios luctus testata cupressus.

Petronius, 79–81.
Lucan, I, 510 f.:
o faciles dare summa deos eademque tueri
difficiles.

II, 12 f.:
sive nihil positum est sed Fors incerta vagatur
fertque refertque vices et habet mortalia casus.

Petronius, 82–86.
Lucan, I, 3.   (populum):
in sua victrici conversum viscera dextra.

I, 70–72:
invida fatorum series, summisque negatum
stare diu ; nimioque graves sub pondere lapsus
nec se Roma ferens.

I, 81:
in se magna ruunt.

Petronius, 95–99.
Lucan, VI, 718 (Erichtho to the powers of the Un-
    derworld):
si bene de vobis civilia bella merentur.

Petronius, 98 f.
Lucan, I, 330 f.:
sic et Sullanum solito tibi lambere ferrum,
durat, Magne, sitis.

VII, 317:
                 quanto satiavit sanguine ferrum !

VII, 851 f. (Pharsalus):
quae seges infecta surget non decolor herba?
quo non Romanos violabis vomere manes?

865:
          surgentem de nostris ossibus herbam.

Petronius, 111–115.
Lucan, I, 679–694 (the frenzied matron):
                 video Pangaea nivosis
cana iugis latosque Haemi sub rupe Philippos. 680

quis furor hic, o Phoebe, doce : quo tela manusque
Romanae miscent acies bellumque sine hoste est ?
quo diversa feror ? primos me ducis in ortus
qua mare Lagei mutatur gurgite Nili.
hunc ego fluminea deformis truncus harena   685
qui iacet agnosco : dubiam super aequora Syrtin
arentemque feror Libyen quo tristis Erinys
transtulit Emathias acies. nunc desuper Alpis
nubiferae colles atque aeriam Pyrenen
abripimur. patriae sedes remeamus in urbis   690
impiaque in medio peraguntur bella senatu.
consurgunt partes iterum totumque per orbem
rursus eo. nova da mihi cernere litora Ponti
telluremque novam. vidi iam, Phoebe, Philippos.

Petronius, 116–121.
Lucan, III, 14 ff. (the vision of Julia):
                    vidi ipsa tenentis
Eumenidas quaterent quas vestris lampadas armis :
praeparat innumeras puppes Acheruntis adusti
portitor : in multas laxantur Tartara poenas.
vix operi cunctae dextra properante sorores
sufficiunt : lassant rumpentis stamina Parcas.

Petronius, 126–140.
Lucan, I, 522–583:
                    tum ne qua futuri
spes saltem trepidas mentes levet addita fati

peioris manifesta fides superique minaces
prodigiis terras implerunt aethera pontum.   525
ignota obscurae viderunt sidera noctes,
ardentemque polum flammis, caeloque volantis
obliquas per inane faces, crinemque timendi
sideris et terris mutantem regna cometen.
fulgura fallaci micuerunt crebra sereno.   530
et varias ignis denso dedit aere formas :
nunc iaculum longo nunc sparso lumine lampas
emicuit caelo.   tacitum sine nubibus ullis
fulmen et Arctois rapiens e partibus ignem
percussit Latiale caput : stellaeque minores   535
per vacuum solitae noctis decurrere tempus
in medium venere diem : cornuque coacto
iam Phoebe toto fratrem cum redderet orbe
terrarum subita percussa expalluit umbra.
ipse caput medio Titan cum ferret Olympo   540
condidit ardentis atra caligine currus
involvitque orbem tenebris, gentesque coegit
desperare diem : qualem fugiente per ortus
sole Thyesteae noctem duxere Mycenae.
ora ferox Siculae laxavit Mulciber Aetnae ;   545
nec tulit in caelum flammas sed vertice prono
ignis in Hesperium cecidit latus.   atra Charybdis
sanguineum fundo torsit mare, flebile saevi
latravere canes.   Vestali raptus ab ara
ignis ; et ostendens confectas flamma Latinas   550

scinditur in partes geminoque cacumine surgit
Thebanos imitata rogos. tum cardine tellus
subsedit, veteremque iugis nutantibus Alpes
discussere nivem. Tethys maioribus undis
Hesperiam Calpen summumque implevit
    Atlanta. 555

*   *   *   *   *   *

compositis plenae gemuerunt ossibus urnae. 568
tum fragor armorum magnaeque per avia voces
auditae nemorum, et venientes comminus umbrae.
quique colunt iunctos extremis moenibus agros
diffugiunt : ingens urbem cingebat Erinys
excutiens pronam flagranti vertice pinum
stridentisque comas. 574

*   *   *   *   *   *

insonuere tubae et quanto clamore cohortes 578
miscentur tantum nox atra silentibus umbris
edidit : et medio visi consurgere Campo
tristia Sullani cecinere oracula manes :
tollentemque caput gelidas Anienis ad undas
agricolae fracto Marium fugere sepulcro. 583

    II, 1–4:
iamque irae patuere deum manifestaque belli
signa dedit mundus : legesque et foedera rerum
praescia monstrifero vertit natura tumultu
indixitque nefas.

Petronius, 137 f.
Lucan, VI, 623:
auribus incertum feralis strideat umbra.

VII, 179 f.:
defunctosque patres et cunctas sanguinis umbras
ante oculos volitare suos.

Petronius, 152–154.
Lucan, I, 183–185:
iam gelidas Caesar cursu superaverat Alpes,
ingentesque animo motus bellumque futurum
ceperat.

Petronius, 156–176.
Lucan, I, 195–203 (Caesar to the vision at the Ru-
      bicon):
mox ait : o magnae qui moenia prospicis urbis
Tarpeia de rupe Tonans Phrygiique penates
gentis Iuleae et rapti secreta Quirini
et residens celsa Latialis Iuppiter Alba
Vestalesque foci summique o numinis instar
Roma fave coeptis : non te furialibus armis
persequor : en adsum victor terraque marique
Caesar ubique tuus, liceat modo, nunc quoque,
      miles.
ille erit ille nocens qui me tibi fecerit hostem.

299–351 (speech at Ariminum):
bellorum, o socii, qui mille pericula Martis
mecum, ait, experti decimo iam vincitis anno, 300
hoc cruor Arctois meruit diffusus in arvis,
vulneraque et mortes hiemesque sub Alpibus
    actae?
non secus ingenti bellorum Roma tumultu
concutitur quam si Poenus transcenderet Alpes
Hannibal. implentur valido tirone cohortes. 305
in classem cadit omne nemus : terraque marique
iussus Caesar agi. quid? si mihi signa iacerent
Marte sub adverso ruerentque in terga feroces
Gallorum populi? nunc, cum Fortuna secundis
mecum rebus agat, superique ad summa vocantes
temptamur. veniet dux longa pace solutus 311
milite cum subito partesque in bella togatae
Marcellusque loquax et nomina vana Catones.
scilicet extremi Pompeium emptique clientes
continuo per tot sociabunt tempora regno? 315

   *   *   *   *   *   *

post Cilicasne vagos et lassi Pontici regis 336
proelia barbarico vix consummata veneno
ultima Pompeio dabitur provincia Caesar?
quod non victrices aquilas deponere iussus
paruerim? mihi si merces erepta laborum est 340
his saltem longi non cum duce praemia belli
reddantur : miles sub quolibet iste triumphet.
   G

conferet exsanguis quo se post bella senectus?
quae sedes erit emeritis? quae rura dabuntur
quae noster veteranus aret? quae moenia fessis?
an melius fient piratae, Magne, coloni?   346
tollite iampridem, victricia tollite signa:
viribus utendum est quas fecimus: arma tenenti
omnia dat qui iusta negat: nec numina deerunt.
nam nec praeda meis neque regnum quaeritur
          armis,   350
detrahimus dominos urbi servire paratae.

VII, 250–329 (before Pharsalus):
o domitor mundi, rerum fortuna mearum,
miles, adest totiens optata copia pugnae.
nihil opus est votis; iam fatum accersite ferro.
in manibus vestris, quantus sit Caesar, habetis.
haec est illa dies mihi quam Rubiconis ad undas
promissam memini, cuius spe movimus arma,   255
in quam distulimus vetitos remeare triumphos.
haec eadem est hodie quae pignora quaeque pe-
          nates
reddat, et emerito faciat vos Marte colonos.
haec fato quae teste probet, quis iustius arma
sumpserit: haec acies victum factura nocentem
          est.   260
si pro me patriam ferro flammisque petistis
nunc pugnate truces gladiosque exsolvite culpa.
nulla manus belli mutato iudice pura est.

non mihi res agitur, sed vos ut libera sitis
turba precor, gentes ut ius habeatis in omnes. 265
ipse ego privatae cupidus me reddere vitae,
plebeiaque toga modicum componere civem.
omnia dum vobis liceant nihil esse recuso.
invidia regnate mea. nec sanguine multo
spem mundi petitis : Graiis delecta iuventus 270
gymnasiis aderit studioque ignava palaestrae,
et vix arma ferens, et mixtae dissona turbae
barbaries ; non illa tubas non agmine moto
clamoren latura suum. civilia paucae 274
bella manus facient : pugnae pars magna levabit
his orbem populis Romanumque obteret hostem.
ite per ignavas gentes famosaque regna
et primo ferri motu prosternite mundum :
sitque palam quas tot duxit Pompeius in urbem
curribus unius gentes non esse triumphi. 280
Armeniosne movet Romana potentia cuius
sit ducis ? aut emptum minimo vult sanguine
    quisquam
barbarus Hesperiis Magnum praeponere rebus ?
Romanos odere omnes dominosque gravantur;
quos novere, magis. sed me Fortuna meorum
commisit manibus, quorum me Gallia testem
tot fecit bellis. cuius non militis ensem 287
agnoscam ? caelumque tremens cum lancea tran-
    sit,

dicere non fallar quo sit vibrata lacerto.
quod si signa ducem numquam fallentia vestrum
conspicio faciesque truces oculosque minaces,   291
vicistis.   videor fluvios spectare cruoris
calcatosque simul reges, sparsumque senatus
corpus, et immensa populos in caede natantis. 294

*   *   *   *   *   *

aut merces hodie bellorum aut poena paratur : 303
Caesareas spectate cruces spectate catenas,
et caput hoc positum rostris effusaque membra,
Septorumque nefas, et clausi proelia Campi.
cum duce Sullano gerimus civilia bella.
vestri cura movet : nam me secura manebit
sors quaesita manu : fodientem viscera cernet
me mea qui nondum victo respexerit hoste.   310
        (The speech continues to 329.)

   I, 225–227 (after crossing the Rubicon):
hic, ait, hic pacem temerataque iura relinquo,
te, Fortuna, sequor. procul hinc iam foedera
        sunto.
credidimus fatis.   utendum est iudice bello.

Petronius, 160.
Lucan, VII, 473:
primaque Thessaliam Romano sanguine tinxit.

Petronius, 164 f.

Lucan, I, 288 f. (Curio to Caesar):
livor edax tibi cuncta negat : gentesque subactas
vix impune feres.

Petronius, 209–244.
Lucan, I, 466–522:
Caesar ut immensae collecto robore vires
audendi maiora fidem fecere, per omnem
spargitur Italiam vicinaque moenia complet.
vana quoque ad veros accessit fama timores
irrupitque animos populi clademque futuram 470
intulit et velox properantis nuntia belli
innumeras solvit falsa in praeconia linguas.
est qui tauriferis ubi se Mevania campis
explicet audaces ruere in certamina turmas
adferat, et qua Nar Tiberino illabitur amni 475
barbaricas saevi discurrere Caesaris alas :
ipsum omnes aquilas collataque signa ferentem
agmine non uno densisque incedere castris.
nec qualem meminere vident : maiorque ferusque
mentibus occurrit victoque immanior hoste. 480
hunc inter Rhenum populos Alpesque iacentis
finibus Arctois patriaque a sede revolsos
pone sequi, iussamque feris a gentibus urbem
Romano spectante rapi. sic quisque pavendo
dat vires famae : nulloque auctore malorum 485
quae finxere timent. nec solum volgus inani
perculsum terrore pavet : sed curia et ipsi

sedibus exsiluere Patres invisaque belli
consulibus fugiens mandat decreta Senatus.   489
tum quae tuta petant et quae metuenda relinquant
incerti, quo quemque fugae tulit impetus urgent
praecipitem populum, serieque haerentia longa
agmina prorumpunt.   credas aut tecta nefandas
corripuisse faces aut iam quatiente ruina
nutantis pendere domos : sic turba per urbem   495
praecipiti lymphata gradu, velut unica rebus
spes foret adflictis patrios excedere muros,
inconsulta ruit.   qualis, cum turbidus Auster
reppulit a Libycis immensum Syrtibus aequor
fractaque veliferi sonuerunt pondera mali,   500
desilit in fluctus deserta puppe magister
navitaque et nondum sparsa compage carinae
naufragium sibi quisque facit : sic urbe relicta
in bellum fugitur.   nullum iam languidus aevo
evaluit revocare parens coniunxve maritum   505
fletibus aut patrii dubiae dum vota salutis
conciperent tenuere Lares : nec limine quisquam
haesit et extremo tum forsitan urbis amatae
plenus abit visu : ruit irrevocabile vulgus.
o faciles dare summa deos eademque tueri   510
difficiles ! urbem populis victisque frequentem
gentibus et generis coeat si turba capacem
humani facilem venturo Caesare praedam
ignavae liquere manus.   514

*   *   *   *   *   *

tu tantum audito bellorum nomine, Roma 519
desereris ; nox una tuis non credita muris.
danda tamen venia est tantorum danda pavorum,
Pompeio. fugiente timent. 522

(Here follows the catalogue of portents quoted
on 126–140 above.)

Petronius, 214.
Lucan, VII, 699:

spumantis caede catervas.[1]

Petronius, 216.
Lucan, VII, 180:
ante oculos volitare suos.

Petronius, 225.
Lucan, V, 30 f.:

maerentia tecta
Caesar habet vacuasque domos.

Petronius, 235–237.
Lucan, VII, 125–127:

ut victus violento navita Cauro
dat regimen ventis, ignavumque arte relicta
puppis onus trahitur.

Petronius, 264.
Lucan, I, 56–58:
aetheris immensi partem si presseris unam

---

[1] See p. 29.

sentiet axis onus.   librati pondera caeli
orbe tene medio.

Petronius, 276.
Lucan, VII, 568:
sanguineum veluti quatiens Bellona flagellum.[1]

Petronius, 280 f.[2]
Lucan, VII, 649–651:
                    stetit aggere campi
eminus, unde omnes sparsas per Thessala rura
adspiceret clades quae bello obstante latebant.

Petronius, 291.
Lucan, II, 443 f.:
            non tam portas intrare patentis
quam fregisse iuvat.

Petronius, 294.   (See on 160.)

With *Troiae Halosis* (Ch. 89), 4–6 :
                    caesi vertices
Idae trahuntur scissaque in molem cadunt
robora.

    Cf. Lucan, I, 306:
in classem cadit omne nemus.

---

[1] Cf. Verg., *Aen.*, VIII, 703 :
        quam cum sanguineo sequitur Bellona flagello.
[2] See 214 above and note.

PETRONII SATIRAE

1. 'num alio genere furiarum declamatores
inquietantur, qui clamant : "haec vulnera pro
libertate publica excepi ; hunc oculum pro vobis
impendi : date mihi ducem, qui me ducat ad liberos
meos, nam succisi poplites membra non susti-
nent ?" haec ipsa tolerabilia essent, si ad eloquentiam ituris viam facerent.   nunc et rerum tumore
et sententiarum vanissimo strepitu hoc tantum
proficiunt, ut cum in forum venerint, putent se in
alium orbem terrarum delatos.   et ideo ego adu-
lescentulos existimo in scholis stultissimos fieri, quia
nihil ex his, quae in usu habemus, aut audiunt aut
vident, sed piratas cum catenis in litore stantes, sed
tyrannos edicta scribentes, quibus imperent filiis
ut patrum suorum capita praecidant, sed responsa
in pestilentiam data, ut virgines tres aut plures
immolentur, sed mellitos verborum globulos et omnia dicta factaque quasi papavere et sesamo sparsa.
2. qui inter haec nutriuntur, non magis sapere
possunt, quam bene olere, qui in culina habitant.
pace vestra liceat dixisse, primi omnium eloquentiam perdidistis. levibus enim atque inanibus
sonis ludibria quaedam excitando effecistis, ut
corpus orationis enervaretur et caderet.   nondum iuvenes declamationes continebantur, cum
Sophocles aut Euripides invenerunt verba quibus

deberent loqui. nondum umbraticus doctor in-
genia deleverat, cum Pindarus novemque lyrici
Homericis versibus canere timuerunt. et ne
poetas [quidem] ad testimonium citem, certe
neque Platona neque Demosthenen ad hoc genus
exercitationis accessisse video. grandis et ut ita
dicam pudica oratio non est maculosa nec tur-
gida, sed naturali pulchritudine exsurgit. nuper
ventosa istaec et enormis loquacitas Athenas ex
Asia commigravit animosque iuvenum ad magna
surgentes veluti pestilenti quodam sidere afflavit,
semelque corrupta regula eloquentia stetit et ob-
mutuit. ad summam, quis postea Thucididis,
quis Hyperidis ad famam processit? ac ne carmen
quidem sani coloris enituit, sed omnia quasi eodem
cibo pasta non potuerunt usque ad senectutem
canescere. pictura quoque non alium exitum
fecit, postquam Aegyptiorum audacia tam magnae
artis compendiariam invenit.'

3. non est passus Agamemnon me diutius
declamare in porticu quam ipse in schola suda-
verat, sed 'adulescens' inquit 'quoniam sermonem
habes non publici saporis et, quod rarissimum est,
amas bonam mentem, non fraudabo te arte secreta. *nihil* nimirum in his exercitationibus
doctores peccant, qui necesse habent cum in-
sanientibus furere. nam nisi dixerint quae adu-

lescentuli probent, ut ait Cicero, "soli in scholis
relinquentur." sicut [ficti] adulatores cum cenas
divitum captant, nihil prius meditantur quam id
quod putant gratissimum auditoribus fore : nec
enim aliter impetrabunt quod petunt, nisi quasdam
insidias auribus fecerint : sic eloquentiae magister, nisi tamquam piscator eam imposuerit hamis
escam, quam scierit appetituros esse pisciculos,
sine spe praedae morabitur in scopulo.

4. quid ergo est? parentes obiurgatione digni
sunt, qui nolunt liberos suos severa lege proficere.
primum enim sic ut omnia, spes quoque suas
ambitioni donant. deinde cum ad vota prope-
rant, cruda adhuc studia in forum pellunt et
eloquentiam, qua nihil esse maius confitentur,
pueris induunt adhuc nascentibus. quod si pa-
terentur laborum gradus fieri, ut studiosi iuvenes
lectione severa irrigarentur, ut sapientiae prae-
ceptis animos componerent, ut verba atroci stilo
effoderent, ut quod vellent imitari diu audirent,
ut persuaderent sibi nihil esse magnificum, quod
pueris placeret : iam illa grandis oratio haberet
maiestatis suae pondus. Nunc pueri in scholis lu-
dunt, iuvenes ridentur in foro, et quod utroque
turpius est, quod quisque perperam didicit, in
senectute confiteri non vult.'

* * * * * * *

88. erectus his sermonibus consulere pruden-
tiorem coepi . . . aetates tabularum et quaedam
argumenta mihi obscura simulque causam desidiae
praesentis excutere, cum pulcherrimae artes peris-
sent, inter quas pictura ne minimum quidem
sui vestigium reliquisset.   tum ille 'pecuniae' inquit 'cupiditas haec tropica instituit.   priscis enim
temporibus, cum adhuc nuda virtus placeret, vigebant artes ingenuae summumque certamen inter
homines erat, ne quid profuturum saeculis diu
lateret.   itaque herbarum omnium sucos Democ-
ritus expressit, et ne lapidum virgultorumque vis
lateret, aetatem inter experimenta consumpsit.
Eudoxos [quidem] in cacumine excelsissimi montis consenuit, ut astrorum caelique motus depre-
henderet, et Chrysippus, ut ad inventionem suffi-
ceret, ter elleboro animum detersit.   verum ut
ad plastas convertar, Lysippum statuae unius
lineamentis inhaerentem inopia extinxit, et My-
ron, qui paene animas hominum ferarumque aere
comprehenderat, non invenit heredem.   at nos
vino scortisque demersi ne paratas quidem artes
audemus cognoscere, sed accusatores antiquitatis
vitia tantum docemus et discimus.   ubi est dia-
lectica?   ubi astronomia?   ubi sapientiae cultis-
sima via?   quis umquam venit in templum et
votum fecit, si ad eloquentiam pervenisset?   quis,

si philosophiae fontem attigisset? ac ne bonam
quidem mentem aut bonam valetudinem petunt,
sed statim antequam limen Capitolii tangant,
alius donum promittit, si propinquum divitem
extulerit, alius, si thesaurum effoderit, alius, si ad
trecenties sestertium salvus pervenerit. ipse senatus, recti bonique praeceptor, mille pondo auri
Capitolio promittere solet, et ne quis dubitet
pecuniam concupiscere, Iovem quoque peculio
exornat. noli ergo mirari, si pictura defecit, cum
omnibus diis hominibusque formosior videatur
massa auri, quam quicquid Apelles Phidiasque,
Graeculi delirantes, fecerunt. 89. Sed video te
totum in illa haerere tabula, quae Troiae halosin
ostendit. Itaque conabor opus versibus pandere :

iam decima maestos inter ancipites metus
Phrygas obsidebat messis et vatis fides
Calchantis atro dubia pendebat metu,
cum Delio profante caesi vertices
Idae trahuntur scissaque in molem cadunt   5
robora, minacem quae figurarent equum.
aperitur ingens antrum et obducti specus,
qui castra caperent. huc decenni proelio
irata virtus abditur, stipant graves
Danai recessus, in suo voto latent.   10
o patria, pulsas mille credidimus rates

solumque bello liberum : hoc titulus fero
incisus, hoc ad furta compositus Sinon
firmabat et mens semper in damnum potens.
 iam turbà portis libera ac bello carens 15
in vota properat. fletibus manant genae
mentisque pavidae gaudium lacrimas habet,
quas metus abegit. Namque Neptuno sacer
crinem solutus omne Laocoon replet
clamore vulgus. mox reducta cuspide 20
uterum notavit, fata sed tardant manus,
ictusque resilit et dolis addit fidem.
iterum tamen confirmat invalidam manum
altaque bipenni latera pertemptat. fremit
captiva pubes intus, et dum murmurat, 25
roborea moles spirat alieno metu.
ibat iuventus capta, dum Troiam capit,
bellumque totum fraude ducebat nova.
 ecce alia monstra : celsa qua Tenedos mare
dorso replevit, tumida consurgunt freta 30
undaque resultat scissa tranquillo minor,
qualis silenti nocte remorum sonus
longe refertur, cum premunt classes mare
pulsumque marmor abiete imposita gemit.
respicimus : angues orbibus geminis ferunt 35
ad saxa fluctus, tumida quorum pectora
rates ut altae lateribus spumas agunt.
dat cauda sonitum, liberae ponto iubae

consentiunt luminibus, fulmineum iubar
incendit aequor sibilisque undae fremunt.   40
stupuere mentes.   infulis stabant sacri
Phrygioque cultu gemina nati pignora
Lauconte.   quos repente tergoribus ligant
angues corusci.   parvulas illi manus
ad ora referunt, neuter auxilio sibi,   45
uterque fratri :   transtulit pietas vices
morsque ipsa miseros mutuo perdit metu.
accumulat ecce liberum funus parens,
infirmus auxiliator.   invadunt virum
iam morte pasti membraque ad terram trahunt. 50
iacet sacerdos inter aras victima
terramque plangit.   sic profanatis sacris
peritura Troia perdidit primum deos.

   iam plena Phoebe candidum extulerat iubar
minora ducens astra radianti face,   55
cum inter sepultos Priamidas nocte et mero
Danai relaxant claustra et effundunt viros.
temptant in armis se duces, ceu ubi solet
nodo remissus Thessali quadrupes iugi
cervicem et altas quatere ad excursum iubas.   60
gladios retractant, commovent orbes manu
bellumque sumunt.   Hic graves alius mero
obtruncat et continuat in mortem ultimam
somnos, ab aris alius accendit faces
contraque Troas invocat Troiae sacra.'   65

PETRONII SATIRAE

118. 'multos,' inquit Eumolpus ' o iuvenes carmen decepit. nam ut quisque versum pedibus
instruxit sensumque teneriorem verborum ambitu
intexuit, putavit se continuo in Heliconem venisse.
sic forensibus ministeriis exercitati frequenter ad 2
carminis tranquillitatem tamquam ad portum
feliciorem refugerunt, credentes facilius poema
exstrui posse, quam controversiam sententiolis
vibrantibus pictam. ceterum neque generosior 3
spiritus vanitatem amat, neque concipere aut
edere partum mens potest nisi ingenti flumine
litterarum inundata. refugiendum est ab omni 4
verborum, ut ita dicam, vilitate et sumendae voces
a plebe semotae, ut fiat "odi profanum vulgus et
arceo." praeterea curandum est, ne sententiae 5
emineant extra corpus orationis expressae, sed
intexto versibus colore niteant. Homerus testis
et lyrici Romanusque Vergilius et Horatii curiosa
felicitas. ceteri enim aut non viderunt viam, qua
iretur ad carmen, aut visam timuerunt calcare.
ecce belli civilis ingens opus quisquis attigerit, 6
nisi plenus litteris, sub onere labetur. non enim
res gestae versibus comprehendendae sunt, quod

longe melius historici faciunt, sed per ambages
deorumque ministeria et fabulosum sententiarum tormentum praecipitandus est liber spiritus,
ut potius furentis animi vaticinatio appareat
quam religiosae orationis sub testibus fides :
tamquam si placet hic impetus, etiam si nondum
recepit ultimam manum.'

119. 'orbem iam totum victor Romanus ha-
    bebat,
qua mare, qua terrae, qua sidus currit utrumque.
nec satiatus erat. gravidis freta pulsa carinis
iam peragebantur ; si quis sinus abditus ultra,
si qua foret tellus, quae fulvum mitteret aurum, 5
hostis erat, fatisque in tristia bella paratis
quaerebantur opes. non vulgo nota placebant
gaudia, non usu plebeio trita voluptas.
aes Ephyreiacum laudabat miles in unda ;
quaesitus tellure nitor certaverat ostro ;   10
hinc Numidae accusant, illinc nova vellera Seres,
atque Arabum populus sua despoliaverat arva.
ecce aliae clades et laesae vulnera pacis :
quaeritur in silvis auro fera, et ultimus Hammon
Afrorum excutitur, ne desit belua dente   15
ad mortes pretiosa ; fames premit advena classes,
tigris et aurata gradiens vectatur in aula,
ut bibat humanum populo plaudente cruorem.

H

heu, pudet effari perituraque prodere fata,
Persarum ritu male pubescentibus annis   20
surripuere viros exsectaque viscera ferro
in venerem fregere, atque ut fuga mobilis aevi
circumscripta mora properantes differat annos,
quaerit se natura nec invenit.   omnibus ergo
scorta placent fractique enervi corpore gressus 25
et laxi crines et tot nova nomina vestis,
quaeque virum quaerunt.   ecce Afris eruta terris
ponitur ac maculis mutatur vilius aurum   29
citrea mensa greges servorum ostrumque reni-
        dens,   28
quae censum turbat.   hoc sterile ac male nobile
        lignum   30
turba sepulta mero circum venit, omniaque orbis
praemia corruptis miles vagus exstruit armis.
ingeniosa gula est.   Siculo scarus aequore mersus
ad mensam vivus perducitur, atque Lucrinis
eruta litoribus vendunt conchylia cenas,   35
ut renovent per damna famem.   iam Phasidos unda
orbata est avibus, mutoque in litore tantum
solae desertis adspirant frondibus aurae.
nec minor in campo furor est, emptique Quirites
ad praedam strepitumque lucri suffragia vertunt 40
venalis populus, venalis curia patrum,
est favor in pretio.   senibus quoque libera virtus
exciderat, sparsisque opibus conversa potestas

ipsaque maiestas auro corrupta iacebat.
pellitur a populo victus Cato ; tristior ille est,   45
qui vicit, fascesque pudet rapuisse Catoni.
namque — hoc   dedecoris   populo   morumque
      ruina —
non homo pulsus erat, sed in uno victa potestas
Romanumque decus.   quare tam perdita Roma
ipsa sui merces erat et sine vindice praeda.   50
praeterea gemino deprensam gurgite plebem
faenoris illuvies ususque exederat aeris.
nulla est certa domus, nullum sine pignore corpus,
sed veluti tabes tacitis concepta medullis
intra membra furens curis latrantibus errat.   55
arma placent miseris, detritaque commoda luxu
vulneribus reparantur.   inops audacia tuta est.
hoc mersam caeno Romam somnoque iacentem
quae poterant artes sana ratione movere,
ni furor et bellum ferroque excita libido ?   60
    120. tres tulerat Fortuna duces, quos obruit
      omnes
armorum strue diversa feralis Erinys.
Crassum Parthus habet, Libyco iacet aequore
      Magnus,
Iulius ingratam perfudit sanguine Romam.
et quasi non posset tot tellus ferre sepulcra   65
divisit cineres.   hos gloria reddit honores.
    est locus exciso penitus demersus hiatu

Parthenopen inter magnaeque Dicarchidos arva,
Cocyti perfusus aqua ; nam spiritus, extra
qui furit effusus, funesto spargitur aestu.   70
non haec autumno tellus viret aut alit herbas
caespite laetus ager, non verno persona cantu
mollia discordi strepitu virgulta locuntur,
sed chaos et nigro squalentia pumice saxa
gaudent ferali circum tumulata cupressu.   75
has inter sedes Ditis pater extulit ora
bustorum flammis et cana sparsa favilla,
ac tali volucrem Fortunam voce lacessit :
"rerum humanarum divinarumque potestas,
Fors; cui nulla placet nimium secura potestas,   80
quae nova semper amas et mox possessa relinquis,
ecquid Romano sentis te pondere victam,
nec posse ulterius perituram extollere molem ?
ipsa suas vires odit Romana iuventus
et quas struxit opes male sustinet.   aspice late 85
luxuriam spoliorum et censum in damna furentem.
aedficant auro sedesque ad sidera mittunt,
expelluntur aquae saxis, mare nascitur arvis,
et permutata rerum statione rebellant.
en etiam mea regna petunt.   perfossa dehiscit 90
molibus insanis tellus, iam montibus haustis
antra gemunt, et dum vanos lapis invenit usus,
inferni manes caelum sperare fatentur.
quare age, Fors, muta pacatum in proelia vultum

Romanosque cie ac nostris da funera regnis.   95
iam pridem nullo perfundimus ora cruore,
nec mea Tisiphone sitientis perluit artus,
ex quo Sullanus bibit ensis et horrida tellus
extulit in lucem nutritos sanguine fruges."
   121. haec ubi dicta dedit, dextrae coniungere
       dextram   100
conatus rupto tellurem solvit hiatu.
tunc Fortuna levi defudit pectore voces :
"o genitor, cui Cocyti penetralia parent,
si modo vera mihi fas est impune profari,
vota tibi cedent ; nec enim minor ira rebellat 105
pectore in hoc leviorque exurit flamma medullas.
omnia, quae tribui Romanis arcibus, odi
muneribusque meis irascor. destruet istas
idem, qui posuit, moles deus. et mihi cordi   109
quippe cremare viros et ·sanguine pascere luxum.
cerno equidem gemina iam stratos morte Philippos
Thessaliaeque rogos et funera gentis Hiberae.
iam fragor armorum trepidantes personat aures,
et Libyae cerno tua, Nile, gementia castra,
Actiacosque sinus et Apollinis arma timentes. 115
pande, age, terrarum sitientia regna tuarum
atque animas accerse novas. vix navita Porth-
       meus
sufficiet simulacra virum traducere cumba ;
classe opus est. tuque ingenti satiare ruina,

pallida Tisiphone, concisaque vulnera mande : 120
ad Stygios manes laceratus ducitur orbis."
122. vixdum finierat, cum fulgure rupta corusco
intremuit nubes elisosque abscidit ignes.
subsedit pater umbrarum, gremioque reducto
telluris pavitans fraternos palluit ictus.   125
continuo clades hominum venturaque damna
auspiciis patuere deum.   namque ore cruento
deformis Titan vultum caligine texit :
civiles acies iam tum spectare putares.
parte alia plenos extinxit Cynthia vultus   130
et lucem sceleri subduxit.   rupta tonabant
verticibus lapsis montis iuga, nec vaga passim
flumina per notas ibant morientia ripas.
armorum strepitu caelum furit et tuba Martem
sideribus tremefacta ciet, iamque Aetna voratur 135
ignibus insolitis et in aethera fulmina mittit.
ecce inter tumulos atque ossa carentia bustis
umbrarum facies diro stridore minantur.
fax stellis comitata novis incendia ducit,   139
sanguineoque rubens descendit Iuppiter imbre.
haec ostenta brevi solvit deus.   exuit omnes
quippe moras Caesar, vindictaeque actus amore
Gallica proiecit, civilia sustulit arma.
    Alpibus aeriis, ubi Graio numine pulsae
descendunt rupes et se patiuntur adiri,   145
est locus Herculeis aris sacer : hunc nive dura

claudit hiems canoque ad sidera vertice tollit.
caelum illinc cecidisse putes : non solis adulti
mansuescit radiis, non verni temporis aura,
sed glacie concreta rigent hiemisque pruinis :   150
totum ferre potest umeris minitantibus orbem.
haec ubi calcavit Caesar iuga milite laeto
optavitque locum, summo de vertice montis
Hesperiae campos late prospexit et ambas
intentans cum voce manus ad sidera dixit :   155
"Iuppiter omnipotens, et tu, Saturnia tellus,
armis laeta meis olimque onerata triumphis,
testor, ad has acies invitum accersere Martem,
invitas me ferre manus, sed vulnere cogor,
pulsus ab urbe mea, dum Rhenum sanguine tin-
        guo   160
dum Gallos iterum Capitolia nostra petentes
Alpibus excludo, vincendo certior exul.
sanguine Germano sexagintaque triumphis
esse nocens coepi.   quamquam quos gloria terret,
aut qui sunt qui bella vident ?   mercedibus emp-
        tae   165
ac viles operae, quorum est mea Roma noverca.
at reor, haud impune, nec hanc sine vindice dex-
        tram
vinciet ignavus.   victores ite furentes,
ite mei comites, et causam dicite ferro.   169
namque omnes unum crimen vocat, omnibus una

impendet clades. reddenda est gratia vobis,
non solus vici. quare, quia poena tropaeis
imminet et sordes meruit victoria nostra,
iudice Fortuna cadat alea. sumite bellum
et temptate manus. certe mea causa peracta
    est :   175
inter tot fortes armatus nescio vinci."
   haec ubi personuit, de caelo Delphicus ales
omina laeta dedit pepulitque meatibus auras.
nec non horrendi nemoris de parte sinistra
insolitae voces flamma sonuere sequenti.   · 180
ipse nitor Phoebi vulgato laetior orbe
crevit et aurato praecinxit fulgure vultus.
   123. fortior ominibus movit Mavortia signa
Caesar et insolitos gressu prior occupat ausus.
prima quidem glacies et cana vincta pruina 185
non pugnavit humus mitique horrore quievit.
sed postquam turmae nimbos fregere ligatos
et pavidus quadrupes undarum vincula rupit,
incaluere nives. mox flumina montibus altis
undabant modo nata, sed haec quoque — iussa
    putares —   190
stabant, et vincta fluctus stupuere ruina,
et paulo ante lues iam concidenda iacebat.
tum vero male fida prius vestigia lusit
decepitque pedes ; pariter turmaeque virique
armaque congesta strue deplorata iacebant. 195

ecce etiam rigido concussae flamine nubes
exonerabantur, nec rupti turbine venti
derant aut tumida confractum grandine caelum.
ipsae iam nubes ruptae super arma cadebant,
et concreta gelu ponti velut unda ruebat. 200
victa erat ingenti tellus nive victaque caeli
sidera, victa suis haerentia flumina ripis ;
nondum Caesar erat, sed magnam nixus in hastam
horrida securis frangebat gressibus arva,
qualis Caucasea decurrens arduus arce 205
Amphitryoniades, aut torvo Iuppiter ore,
cum se verticibus magni demisit Olympi
et periturorum disiecit tela Gigantum.
    dum Caesar tumidas iratus deprimit arces,
interea volucer motis conterrita pinnis 210
Fama volat summique petit iuga celsa Palati
atque hoc Romano tonitru ferit omnia signa :
iam classes fluitare mari totasque per Alpes
fervere Germano perfusas sanguine turmas.
arma, cruor, caedes, incendia totaque bella 215
ante oculos volitant. ergo pulsata tumultu
pectora perque duas scinduntur territa causas.
huic fuga per terras, illi magis unda probatur
et patria pontus iam tutior. est magis arma
qui temptare velit fatisque iubentibus uti. 220
quantum quisque timet, tantum fugit. ocior ipse
hos inter motus populus, miserabile visu,

quo mens icta iubet, deserta ducitur urbe.
gaudet Roma fuga, debellatique Quirites
rumoris sonitu maerentia tecta relinquunt.   225
ille manu pavida natos tenet, ille penates
occultat gremio deploratumque relinquit
limen et absentem votis interficit hostem.
sunt qui coniugibus maerentia pectora iungant,
grandaevosque patres onerisque ignara iuven-
        tus   230
† id pro quo metuit, tantum trahit.† omnia secum
hic vehit imprudens praedamque in proelia ducit.
ac velut ex alto cum magnus inhorruit auster
et pulsas evertit aquas, non arma ministris,
non regimen prodest, ligat alter pondera pinus, 235
alter tuta sinus tranquillaque litora quaerit :
hic dat vela fugae Fortunaeque omnia credit.
quid tam parva queror? gemino cum consule
        Magnus
ille tremor Ponti saevique repertor Hydaspis
et piratarum scopulus, modo quem ter ovantem 240
Iuppiter horruerat, quem fracto gurgite pontus
et veneratus erat submissa Bosporos unda,
pro pudor, imperii deserto nomine fugit,
ut Fortuna levis Magni quoque terga videret.
124. ergo tanta lues divum quoque numina
        vicit,   245
consensitque fugae caeli timor. ecce per orbem

mitis turba deum terras exosa furentes
deserit atque hominum damnatum avertitur ag-
    men.
Pax prima ante alias niveos pulsata lacertos
abscondit palla victum caput atque relicto   250
orbe fugax Ditis petit implacabile regnum.
huic comes it submissa Fides et crine soluto
Iustitia ac maerens lacera Concordia palla.
at contra, sedes Erebi qua rupta dehiscit,
emergit late Ditis chorus, horrida Erinys   255
et Bellona minax facibusque armata Megaera
Letumque Insidiaeque et lurida Mortis imago.
quas inter Furor, abruptis ceu liber habenis,
sanguineum late tollit caput oraque mille
vulneribus confossa cruenta casside velat ;   260
haeret detritus laevae Mavortius umbo
innumerabilibus telis gravis, atque flagranti
stipite dextra minax terris incendia portat.
    sentit terra deos mutataque sidera pondus
quaesivere suum ; namque omnis regia caeli   265
in partes diducta ruit.   primumque Dione
Caesaris acta sui ducit, comes additur illi
Pallas et ingentem quatiens Mavortius hastam.
Magnum cum Phoebo soror et Cyllenia proles
excipit ac totis similis Tirynthius actis.   270
    intremuere tubae ac scisso Discordia crine
extulit ad superos Stygium caput.   huius in ore

concretus sanguis, contusaque lumina flebant,
stabant aerati scabra rubigine dentes,
tabo lingua fluens, obsessa draconibus ora,   275
atque inter torto laceratam pectore vestem
sanguineam tremula quatiebat lampada dextra.
haec ut Cocyti tenebras et Tartara liquit,
alta petit gradiens iuga nobilis Appennini,
unde omnes terras atque omnia litora posset   280
aspicere ac toto fluitantes orbe catervas,
atque has erumpit furibundo pectore voces :
"sumite nunc gentes accensis mentibus arma,
sumite et in medias immittite lampadas urbes.
vincetur, quicumque latet ; non femina cesset,   285
non puer aut aevo iam desolata senectus ;
ipsa tremat tellus lacerataque tecta rebellent.
tu legem, Marcelle, tene.   tu concute plebem,
Curio.   tu fortem ne supprime, Lentule, Martem.
quid porro tu, dive, tuis cunctaris in armis,   290
non frangis portas, non muris oppida solvis
thesaurosque rapis ? nescis tu, Magne, tueri
Romanas arces ? Epidamni moenia quaere   293
Thessalicosque sinus Romano sanguine tingue."
   factum est in terris, quicquid Discordia iussit.

COMMENTARY

118. 1. *teneriorem:* "subtler."

verborum ambitu: figurative or allusive language, into which the thought is woven, not lying on the surface, but gleaming out here and there.

Heliconem: a mountain in Boeotia, sacred to Apollo and the Muses. Erhard, cf. Mart., VII, 63, 12 (of Silius Italicus):

> proque suo celebrat nunc Helicona foro.

2. *forensibus ministeriis exercitati:* trained for the bar. Cf. preceding note.

controversiam: cf. Ch. 1-4 (see p. 89 ff.). Pupils in the schools of rhetoric were required to plead on both sides of imaginary cases, often of the most absurd description. See Introd., p. 8 n. 1. An amusing account of these *controversiae* will be found in Boissier, *Tacite* (Paris, 1904), *Les Ecoles de déclamation à Rome.*

sententiolis vibrantibus: the jingling phrase, with its affected diminutive, is a fit echo of the tawdry style in which these "flashing little epigrams" were dressed.

pictam: contrast *exstrui* above. The poem is to be a solid structure; the *controversia*, supposed to belong to the serious business of life, is merely a painted show.

3. *vanitatem:* mere empty words,

> "full of sound and fury,
> Signifying nothing."

109

inundata: "quickened."

4. *vilitate:* "cheapness," "vulgarity." Also "slovenliness." Cf. Quintil., VIII, 3, 49 (*vilis oratio* opposed to *accurata*).

a plebe semotae: not cheapened by indiscriminate and undiscriminating use, as has been the fate of many a fine word in our own tongue.

odi . . . arceo: Hor., *Carm.,* III, 1, 1.

5. *sententiae:* "glittering generalities" and epigrams (in the modern sense).

intexto: cf. *intexuit* above.

lyrici: the Greek melic poets (including Pindar).

curiosa felicitas: the perfection of Horace's lyrics lies in their exquisitely finished workmanship, which yet has the effect of something perfectly fresh, simple, and natural — the result of a happy inspiration. If Petronius's reputation as a critic rested on these two words alone, it would still be very high.

ceteri: how severe is Petronius's standard will at once appear if the roll of those whom he excludes from his canon be recalled.

timuerunt: because they preferred an easier, if less glorious, road to fame. De Salas, cf. Propert., III, 1, 14 f.

plenus litteris: throughout the *Satirae* Petronius uses the ablative after *plenus* instead of the more common genitive.

6. *ecce . . . labetur:* see Introd., p. 11 f.

res . . . gestae: the actual events, just as they occurred, with all their uninspiring details.

quod longe melius historici faciunt: cf. Quintil., X,

1, 90 : *Lucanus ardens, et concitatus, et sententiis claris-
simus, et, ut dicam quod sentio, magis oratoribus quam
poetis adnumerandus.*

ambages: "détours," *i.e.* indirection.

deorum . . . ministeria: the activities of the gods
are to show us those of man by reflection. Cf. 76–122,
283–295.

fabulosum sententiarum tormentum: the projection of
thought through the realms of the imagination.

liber: freed from the trammels of fact.

furentis: of poetic frenzy. Cf. Verg., *Aen.*, VI, 100.

religiosae: scrupulously exact.

fides: conscientious accuracy.

impetus: continuing the figure of *tormentum, praecipitandus.* The poem is compared to the flight of a
missile or the swoop of a bird, brief but forceful. Moessler translates by *Anlauf. Impetus* is often used of a
sudden manifestation of power or passion, as contrasted
with a steady, even effort, or the operation of a force
which can be calculated. Cf. Liv., V, 6, 7; XLII,
29, 11. Quintil., XII, 2, 1. Also Ov., *F.*, VI, 5 f. :

> est deus in nobis, agitante calescimus illo.
> impetus hic sacrae semina mentis habet.

ultimam manum: cf. Ov., *Tr.*, I, 7, 27 f. :

> nec tamen illa legi poterunt patienter ab ullo
> nesciet his summam si quis abesse manum.

30 : *ultima lima.* II, 555; *Met.*, VIII, 200; XIII,
402 : *manus ultima.* Solinus, *Ad Adventum:* *summa
manus.*

ANALYSIS OF THE POEM

1–60. General introduction : ·Rome the mistress of the world. Her abuse of power. Its reaction. Civil war inevitable.

61–66. Subsidiary introduction. The human leaders in the struggle.

67–121. The Powers of Evil make their compact. Preparations to begin the work of destruction.

122–143. Signs and omens. Transition to the war itself and its dominating figure.

144–208. Caesar. (a) His defense (144–176). (b) Descent from the Alps. His will in conflict with the elements (177–208).

209–243. Effect of his approach on the opposite party.

244–270. The gods become involved in the struggle.

271–294. *Signa canunt.*

295. Conclusion.

1–60. An ever popular subject with Roman writers. Cf. Ch. 55, 6 (quoted from Publilius Syrus) ; Verg., *Ge.*, II, 463–465; 503–506 :

sollicitant alii remis freta caeca, ruuntque
in ferrum penetrant aulas et limina regum ;
hic petit excidiis urbem miserosque penatis
ut gemma bibat et Sarrano dormiat ostro.

Sen., *Hipp.*, 205–209 ; *Octavia*, 424–438, 528–530. Sil. Ital., XI, 33–47. Sulpicia, *Satira de Corrupto Statu Rei Publicae Temporibus Domitiani*, 27 ff. :

sic itidem Romana manus, contendere postquam
destitit, et pacem longis frenavit habenis,
ipsa domi leges, et Graia inventa retractans,
omnia bellorum terra quaesita marique
praemia consilio et molli ratione regebat. 31.

* * * * * * *

Romulidarum igitur longa et gravis, exitium, pax. 57.

(For other related passages, see on 87 ff.)

In soberer prose we find contemporary testimony
to some of the conditions at which Petronius claimed
to be looking back. Cic., *Pro Lege Manilia*, 22,
65 ff. Sall., *Cat.*, 10 ff. ; *Jug.* 41. Florus, a rhetorician
rather than a historian, frequently recalls Petronius in
manner as well as matter. Cf. *Ep.*, III, 12, 7 : *quae
enim res alia furores civiles peperit, quam nimia felicitas ?*
IV, 2, 1–2 : *iam paene toto orbe pacato maius erat imperium Romanum quam ut ullis exteris viribus extingui
posset. itaque invidens Fortuna principi gentium populo,
ipsum illum in exitium suum armavit.*

Cf. also Tac., *Agr.*, 30, 6 f. : *raptores orbis postquam
cuncta vastantibus defuere terrae, iam et mare scrutantur
. . . quos non Oriens, non Occidens satiaverit. soli
omnium opes atque inopiam pari affectu concupiscunt
. . . atque ubi solitudinem faciunt, pacem appellant.*
Ann., II, 33, 1 ; III, 52, 1 ; 53, 5 ; 54, 9 ; 55, 1.

Plin., *H. N.*, XII, 1, 2 : *quo magis ac magis admirari
subit . . . caedi montes in marmora, vestes ad Seres peti,
unionem in Rubri maris profundo, smaragdum in ima
tellure quaeri.*

I

Sen., *Controv.*, II, 9, 1: *bella civilia aurato Capitolio gessimus*, etc. Lact., V, 9.

Cf. also Amm. Marc., XIV, 6.

1. *orbem:* cf. Ov., *F.*, I, 717 :

> horreat Aeneadas et primus et ultimus orbis.

Aurel. Vict., *Ep.* 39, 1: *ubi orbis Romani potentiam cepit.* And the formula of the Roman Catholic Church : *Urbi et Orbi.*

victor Romanus: "the victorious Roman," just as we say "the Turk" and the like, usually with an adjective. In the same way Livy uses *victor hostis* (XXII, 49, 10), and frequently writes *Poenus* where it cannot be said to refer to Hannibal alone. Cf. *Parthus*, 63.

With this and the following line cf. Sallust, *Cat.*, 36: *imperium populi Romani . . . cui . . . ad occasum ab ortu solis omnia domita armis parerent.*

And Cic., *Arch*, 10, 23.

2. Hadrianides reads *terra*, against the Mss., and also against Lucr., I, 278 :

quae mare, quae terras, quae denique nubila caeli.

Verg., *Aen.*, I, 236 :

> qui mare qui terras omni dicione tenerent.

and Lucan, I, 110 (see Introd., p. 72), of which this line is an obvious and close imitation.

sidus utrumque: East and West, implying that the sun never set on the Roman Empire. Cf. Cic., *Cat.*, III. 11, 26 ; IV, 10, 21. Tac., *Agr.*, 30 (see note to 1–60). Stat., *Silv.*, I, 1, 94 : *Romana dies.* Claud., IV *Cons.*

Hon., 42 f. Anth. Lat., 424, 4. Also Sen., *H. O.*,
1700, 1840. The exact meaning of *sidus utrumque* has
been variously given as (1) the morning and evening
star, (2) the sun and moon (Burmann), (3) the rising
and setting sun, *i.e.* East and West (Hadrianides,
Anton). For (1) cf. Sen., *Med.*, 71 f. For (2) Plin.,
H. N., II, 12. But by far the greater number of similar
expressions, in both poetry and prose, support (3).
E.g. Verg., *Aen.*, VII, 99–101:

> nepotes
> omnia sub pedibus, qua sol utrumque recurrens
> aspicit Oceanum, vertique regique videbunt.

Ov., *Her.*, IX, 16. Stat., *Theb.*, I, 157 f. Rutil.
Namat., II, 28. Claud., *Bell. Gild.*, 48; *In Eutrop.*,
II, *Prol.*, 35. IV, *Cons. Hon.*, 131.

For *sidus = sol*, cf. Ov., *Met.*, XIV, 172 f. :

> quod loquor et spiro caelumque et sidera solis
> respicio.

Amm Marc., XVIII, 7, 5 : *at ubi solis radiis exarserit
tempus . . . vapore sideris . . . agitantur.*

Hadrianides. Cf. also Pindar, *Olymp.*, I, 5 f., and
the comment of the Scholiast : καὶ δὲ ἥλιος ἀστήρ.

3. *satiatus:* cf. Tac., *Agr.*, 30 (note to 1–60).

gravidis: referring rather to soldiers sent out from
Italy than to cargoes arriving there, as the next few
lines show. The metaphor is a natural one. Cf.
Enn., *Alex.*, *Fr.*, X : *gravidus armatis ecus.*

Verg., *Aen.*, II, 237 f. : *machina . . . feta armis.*

Tennyson, *The Revenge :*

"But anon the great 'San Philip' she bethought herself
and went,
Having that within her womb that had left her ill-
content."

pulsa: Burmann adopted the reading of *Trag.*,
pressa, in support of which he cites Ch. 89, 33 : *classes
premunt mare.* But *pulsa*, found in all the other Mss.,
is undoubtedly the correct reading, as it is certainly
the more vigorous. Cf. Enn., *Ann.*, XIV, 385 : *spumat
. . . sale rate pulsum.* Catull., LXIV, 58 : *pellit vada
remis. Octavia*, 316 f. : *resonant remis pulsata freta,*
more exactly. Moessler thinks that *pulsa* expresses
the eagerness of the Romans for their plunder, but
this is perhaps an over-refinement. Rubenius proposed
the reading *Graiis freta pulsa carinis.* "*Nempe Pontus
et loca, per quae Iason cum suis ad aureum vellus
profectus est.*" This is a typical instance of the mis-
directed energy of the old commentators, who have,
between them, offered almost as many emendations
as there are words in the poem for which others
could be substituted without wrecking the meter or
destroying the sense beyond their own powers of
elucidation.

4. *peragebantur:* cf. Ov., *Her.*, XV, 65 (*Sappho
Phaoni*) : *peragit freta caerula remo.*

ultra: beyond the regular Roman "sphere of influence."

5. *mitteret:* potential ; which might become a source
of revenue.

6. *hostis erat:* was treated as an enemy. Cf. the formula: *in hostium numero* ⎰ *habere.* Cf. Sall., *Jug.,* ⎱ *ducere*

81: *Romanos iniustos, profunda avaritia, communis omnium hostis esse . . . uti quisque opulentissimus videatur, ita Romanis hostem fore.*

Also *Hist.,* IV (Letter of Mithridates). Flo., IV, 12, 1–2. Tac., *Ann.,* III, 54, 9.

tristia bella: the "irrepressible conflict" in which Fate was preparing to involve the Romans. To refer the words, as Moessler does, to the wars for plunder, is to lose sight of the purpose of the passage. Civil war was to be the consequence and the punishment of outrages committed abroad. See Introd., p. 64 ff.

7. *quaerebantur:* the regular word for a laborious and far-reaching search. Cf. 10, 14, ch. 93, 2, 10 (see on 33). Lucan, X, 157: *toto quaesivit in orbe,* and Sulpicia, 26 (see on 1–60).

7–8. *non . . . voluptas:* cf. Ch. 93, 1: *vile est, quod licet, et animus errore lentus iniurias diligit.* (The verses which follow are quoted on 33.) Sen., *Epp.,* XC, 18: *nos omnia nobis difficilia facilium fastidio fecimus.*

9. A most difficult line. The reading of Heinsius, *aes Ephyreiacum,* appears to be the one indicated by the various strange combinations of letters found in most of the Mss. Those which begin with *spolia* apparently represent a very early attempt to restore a line already corrupt and unintelligible. Nor is *aes Ephyreiacum* hard to explain. The famous Corinthian bronze (Ephyra = Corinth), the manufacture of which had

long been one of the lost arts, was highly prized by
Roman collectors, and fabulous prices were .paid for
vessels made of it (see Plin., *H. N.*, XXXIV, 3, and the
comic discussion in Petr., Ch. 50). The literature of
the Empire abounds in references to it. *In unda*, if it
is what Petronius wrote, must then mean " over seas "
(cf. Tac., *Agr.*, 30, quoted on 1–60), but the expression
is a strange and doubtful one. Still, the poet's general
meaning is clear. The soldiers of Rome, no longer strong
in their ignorance of everything but the business of
war, were turned connoisseurs and collectors of *objets
d'art* for themselves and their countrymen. Although in
many respects Petronius has his own times especially
in view, there is probably a reference here to Caesar's
indulgence of his men. Cf. Suet., *Iul.*, 67: *iactare
solitus* (*sc. Caesar*) *milites suos etiam unguentatos bene
pugnare posse . . . habebatque tam cultos ut argento
et auro politis armis ornaret.* (For the other side of the
picture, see Caes., *B. C.*, III, 96.) Of the other readings
proposed, *Assyria concham* (de Tournes) at first recommends itself because it makes *in unda* more intelligible,
but it pointlessly anticipates *ostro*, 10, a waste of words
which Petronius would not have been likely to allow
himself here. *Hesperium coccum* (Saumaise; Moessler,
Hesperiae) departs from the Mss. without elucidating *in
unda.*

Sil. Ital., XIV, 655 f., although very corrupt and
perhaps an interpolation, contain a manifest imitation
of this line, which, incidentally, supports the reading
of Heinsius:

non aera iuvabat
quaesisse ex Epyre : fulvo haud certaverat auro.

10. *nitor:* at first sight this would seem to indicate
some other brilliant pigment which had come to rival
ostrum, the Tyrian purple, made from the secretion of
a shell-fish. But *coccum*, which would best answer
this description, was made from the egg of an insect
(Plin., *H. N.*, IX, 62, 3 ; 65, 3 ; XVI, 12, 1 ; XXI, 22,
1 ; XXII, 3, 1), and minium, cinnabar, and similar
products of the earth appear to have been used not
for dyes, but for paints. It is therefore necessary
either to assume that Petronius is opposing things used
for different purposes, or to seek another explanation
of *nitor*. Probably, as Anton says, it means gems
(cf. Plin., quoted on 1–60). *Certaverat* shows that the
rivalry had already existed for some time. Cf. *despoliaverat*, 12.

11–12. The language of these two lines is highly
elliptical. *Hinc Numidae accusant* — sc. *Romanos
praedandi atque vastandi. Despoliaverat* is a zeugma.
*Seres arboribus vellera despoliaverant et Arabum populus
sua arva ture et odoribus despoliaverat.* For the tense
of *despoliaverat*, see on *certaverat*, above.

Owing to the obscurity of expression here, various
attempts at emendation have been made. One class
substitutes an accusative for *accusant* (*crustas*, Scaliger ;
gallos or *citros*, Reiske ; *silices*, Stephanus ; *lapides*,
Palmer), making *despoliaverat* serve for all three subjects.
The difficulty with these readings is that, with the

possible exception of *crustas*, they are utterly unlike the Mss. The others supply a verb, to be understood with *Seres* also (*accumulant*, early corrupted to *acculant*, Heinsius ; *accurant*, Delbenius ; *adtulerant*, de Guerle). This is better, but it is very harsh to construe the same verb absolutely with *Numidae* and transitively with *vellera Seres*. The Mss. reading, while harsh, too, has authority to support it. The form *accusati*, preserved in one Ms., looks like a weak attempt to improve the more difficult forms.

The Numidians were exposed to Roman rapacity by the fame of their beautiful marble, the Arabians by their incense and perfumes. The Seres (Chinese), too distant for attack, are thought of as exhausting their treasures of silk to meet the demands of trade.

vellera: Roman writers continually speak of silk as "fleece" gotten from trees. *E.g.* Verg., *Ge.*, II, 120 f. :

quid nemora Aethiopum molli canentia lana
velleraque ut foliis depectent tenuia Seres ?

Sen., *Hipp.*, 390 ; *H. O.*, 667 f. Plin., *H. N.*, VI, 20, 2. Sil. Ital., VI, 4. That they confused its production with that of cotton is evident from many passages.

The wearing of silk is one of the luxuries of the Empire which Petronius carries back into the Republic. Its use by men was forbidden by Tiberius (Tac., *Ann.*, II, 33, 1), and was considered extremely effeminate until the Empire had become thoroughly orientalized (Contrast Suet., *Cal.*, 52 ; and Claud., IV *Cons. Hon.*, 601).

Moessler would have 12 also refer to fabrics, but

mention of Arabia as the land of incense and perfumes is so common in Latin literature that when, as here, nothing is specified, the Roman reader would naturally have thought of them. Cf. Verg., *Aen.*, I, 416 f. Tibull., II, 2, 3 f. Ov., *F.*, IV, 569. Sen., *H. F.*, 909 f. *H. O.*, 793 f.; *Hipp.*, 69; *Med.*, 711. Also Shakspere, *Macbeth*, V, 1: "All the perfumes of Arabia," and *Othello*, V, 2:

> "Drop tears as fast as the Arabian trees
> Their medicinal gum."

13–18. Moessler doubts whether these lines are in place, because, in the recapitulation, 24–27, no reference is made to the circus. For this reason he thinks that they may belong after 38, the *furor circensis* immediately preceding the *furor campi*. But 24–27 do not really recapitulate, or they might as well be criticized for omitting to mention the subjects of 9 and 10. They are extremely vague, but so far as they refer to anything outside themselves, it is to what immediately precedes.

With these lines cf. Salv., *De Gubern. Dei*, VI, 2, 10: *primum, quod nihil ferme vel criminum vel flagitiorum est, quod in spectaculis non sit, ubi summum deliciarum genus est mori homines, . . . expleri ferarum alvos humanis carnibus, comedi homines . . . conspicientium voluptate. . . . atque ut hoc fiat, orbis impendium est: magna enim cura id agitur et elaboratur, adeuntur etiam loca abdita, lustrantur invii saltus, peragrantur silvae inexplicabiles, conscenduntur nubiferae Alpes, penetrantur*

*inferae valles et ut devorari possint a feris viscera homi-
num, non licet naturam rerum aliquid habere secretum.*

13. *laesae vulnera pacis:* a curious expression.
Northern Africa was one of the chief sources of the
grain supply of Rome, and it was an abuse of peace as
bad as continual warfare to traffic in ravenous and
destructive beasts to the exclusion of the useful products
of the country. *Laesae* is proleptic.

14. *auro fera:* the emendation *Mauro* (Anton.;
Ed. Lugd. Batavorum, Mauri) at first commends itself.
But *auro*, besides being the reading indicated by the
Mss., is really the best word for the context. Petronius is here complaining of the abuse of commerce
(see on 13) : the gold which should have been given for
things of real value is squandered on creatures which
should have been left in their native wilds, as far from
civilization as possible.

ultimus Hammon Afrorum: the remotest — *i.e.*
westernmost — part of Africa. Cf. Hor., *Carm.*, II,
18, 4 f. : *ultima . . . Africa.*

15. *excutitur:* is ransacked. *Excutere* was the regular Latin word for searching a person by shaking out
his toga.

belua: the African lion. Cf. Hor., *Carm.*, I, 22,15 f.:

> Iubae tellus . . . leonum
> arida nutrix.

Belua cannot mean "elephant" here, as *ad mortes*, 16,
depends on *dente . . . pretiosa*, and indicates some
animal whose value lay in his ferocity. Claud., *de*

Cons. Stil., III, 317 f. ; *quodcumque tremendum dentibus.*
Elephants could not be depended upon to show fight
in the arena. *Belva*, too, although most commonly
applied to them, was also used frequently of other
animals, according to the point of view. *Fera*, above,
refers to wild beasts in general. In this line and 16 f.
Petronius specifies the two most formidable varieties.

dente: de Salas, cf. the expression *ferae dentatae*
(*venatione* . . . *denis bestiis et IV feris dentatis, C. I. L.,*
X, 3704).

16. *ad mortes:* purpose.

fames . . . *advena:* in apposition to *tigris*, 17. The
tiger is called an "immigrant hunger" because of its
voracity, and also because it was allowed to occupy
the ships which should have been employed to bring
foodstuffs to the city. Hadrianides, cf. Suet., *Nero*, 45.

For the form of expression, cf. Ch. 45, 12 (of cowardly
gladiators) : *plane fugae merae.* Lucan, IX, 707 : *Libycae mortes* (serpents). Mart., X, 96, 9: *pretiosa fames*
means that even semi-starvation was expensive.

premit . . . *classes:* cf. the line quoted, p. 48 n. 2;
de Salas, cf. Claud., De III *Cons. Stil.*, 326 f. :

exsanguis dextera torpet
remigis et propriam metuebat navita mercem.

17. *tigris:* Anton explains that Petronius must have
meant the panther, because tigers were not brought
to Rome until the reign of Augustus. But historical
accuracy of this kind was as unknown in Petronius's
day as in Shakspere's, and the magnificent creatures,

once seen, made a profound impression upon the Roman imagination, as is shown by the frequent references to them in Silver Latin. Martial and Seneca (Tragedies) are especially fond of them.

aurata gradiens . . . in aula: pacing his gilded cage.

18. In spite of the almost unparalleled brutality of the Romans, there must have been many who, like Cicero, if not shocked, were at least bored by these exhibitions. *Quae potest homini esse polito delectatio, cum aut homo imbecillus a valentissima bestia laniatur, aut praeclara bestia venabulo transverberatur?* (*Ad Fam.*, VII, 1, 3). Seneca takes a stronger position, and his Letters and Essays contain repeated condemnations of the butcheries of the arena and their reaction on the spectators. *E.g. Epp.*, XC, 45; XCV, 33.

19. *peritura . . . fata:* cf. 83: *perituram . . . molem;* 208. Ch. 89, 53: *peritura Troia;* 115, 17: *periturum corpus.* Sall., *Jug.*, 35, 10: *urbem . . . mature perituram.* Also Verg., *Ge.*, II, 498. Lucan, VII, 329; VIII, 692. Quintil., *Decl.*, VIII, 1: *perituro laborasse fato* (Wernsdorff). See Introd., pp. 46 and 48.

Some editors, finding difficulty in the bold expression here, have read *paritura* (*sc. perniciem,* Meller), or *facta* (Burmann), with reference to the evils mentioned below. But the illogical combination of words really lends force to the thought without obscuring it. *Peritura* is transferred from the doomed Romans to the Fates that have doomed them, and whose purpose might have been read in the ἄτη (a conception for which the Greeks alone have found a name), which compelled them to plunge themselves into ever deepening guilt.

20. *Persarum ritu:* cf. Amm. Marc., XIV, 6, 17.

male = vix: cf. Stat., *Theb.*, I, 21: *vix pubescentibus annis.* For Petronius's use of *male*, see Introd., p. 48 f.

Moessler thinks that Petronius had his own times in mind here : *"puerorum castrationes iam ante bellum civile Romae frequentatas esse non satis constat."* Silver Latin, on the other hand, abounds in references to the practice.

21–22. *surripuere viros:* this is commonly explained : *virilitatem ademerunt* (Forcellini), an interpretation which is supported by Plaut., *Asin.*, I, 3, 84. Catull., LXIII. 6. Lucan, X, 133 f. Arnob., I, 41; V, 13, 39. But this makes *exsecta . . . fregere* a mere repetition. It also seems strange that in the whole sentence, 19–24, there should be no word directly referring to the persons under discussion. It is therefore better to understand *male pubescentibus annis . . . viros* as meaning "boys" (cf. Amm. Marc., *l.c.*: *teneros mares*). *Surripuere* is natural because the worst features of the slave-trade, even though not illegal, would have been kept out of the public ʼye. It may also refer to the kidnapping of children by slave-dealers and their agents.

in venerem: purpose. In Jerome, *Epp.*, 43, 2: *histrio . . . in Venerem frangitur*, it refers to impersonating the character.

fregere: a common word in this connection. Cf. Stat., *Silv.*, III, 4, 74 : *frangere sexum.*

mobilis: this seems to have more point than the other reading, *nobilis*, as it was a frequent epithet of

time, and closely associated with the idea of flight.
Cf. Hor., *Epp.*, II, 2, 172 : *puncto . . . mobilis horae.*
Sen., *Hipp.*, 447, 1141 f.

23. *circumscripta* agrees with *fuga*, above.

properantes differat annos: "puts off the hurrying
years," *i.e.* keeps them from hurrying to their natural
goal. Cf. Sen., *Epp.*, XLVII, 7 : *alius vini minister
in muliebrem modum ornatus cum aetate luctatur. non
potest effugere pueritiam: retrahitur.*

24. *quaerit . . . invenit:* "*natura marium ita cor-
rumpitur ut se mares esse non amplius sentiant.*" (Anton.)
Cf. Mart., II, 83, 2 f.

24–27. *omnibus . . . quaerunt.:* a strange jumble.
Fracti . . . gressus and *laxi crines* are appropriate
to what has preceded, but *tot . . . vestis* is thrown in
irrelevantly; the beginning is flat and the end feeble.
On the whole, it looks as though something had been
lost from the text, and the mutilated remainder patched
up to fit in between *invenit*, 24, and *ecce*, 27.

25. *fracti . . . gressus:* a mincing gait. Cf. Quintil.,
V, 9, 14 : *ut fortasse corpus vulsum, fractum incessum,
vestem muliebrem dixerit mollis et parum viri signa.*
Salv., *De Gubern. Dei*, VII, 19, 83.

enervi corpore: cf. Ch. 2, 2 : *ut corpus orationis enervaretur.*

26. *laxi crines:* flowing locks.

tot . . . vestis: Anton hails this abrupt change —
"*hic demum carpitur luxus mulierum*" — but wrongly,
for Petronius in this poem has nothing to say about
the women, confining his attention to those whom he

holds responsible for the war. Even if something has
been lost here, it is plain that *tot . . . vestis* cannot
belong to any one but the *scorta*. For the capricious
change of names, however, without any implication as to
the sex of the wearers, cf. Plaut., *Epid.*, II, 2, 48 :

quid istae quae vesti quotannis nomina inveniunt nova ?

27. *eruta:* suggests the labor involved in dragging
the "unfruitful lumber" from the remote forests of
Africa to Rome. It is used in its literal sense, 35.

29. The order of lines followed here seems to be
required by the relative clause which begins at 30
(however read), and which otherwise is joined too
loosely to what precedes.

ponitur: is set forth.

maculis: the markings of the citrus wood, which,
together with the size of the *orbis,* determined its value
(see on *citrea mensa* below). (Cf. Plin., *H. N.*, XIII,
29 f., for statistics.) Sen., *de Tranquill.*, I, 4 : *placet
. . . mensa non varietate macularum conspicua* (contrast
Cassius Dio's statement, note on 28). Tertull., *de Pall.*,
5 : *hem quantis facultatibus aestimavere ligneas maculas!*

mutatur (Trag.) : must be the right reading, as
imitatur does not make sense. The words may mean :
"the table is set forth, and gold, as a thing of less value,
is exchanged for its markings," but it is more reasonable
to take the verb as a middle : "the table is set forth and
exchanges the less valued gold (*i.e.* causes it to be exchanged) for its markings." In either case *maculis* is, of
course, ablative, the regular construction with *mutare.*

vilius: better than *vilibus.* Cf. Mart., XIV, 89 ;
Citrea Mensa:

> accipe felices, Atlantica munera, silvas :
> aurea qui dederit dona, minora dabit.

28. *citrea mensa:* cf. Sil. Ital., XIII, 354 : *mensaeque
alia tellure petitae.* Round tables made of cross-sec-
tions of the citrus tree from northern Africa, mounted
on ivory feet, brought fabulous prices at Rome. Pliny
(see on 29) says that Cicero paid 1,000,000 *sestertii*
(about $40,000) for one of them. Some enthusiasts
collected them in large numbers. According to Cassius Dio (LXI, 10, 3), Seneca had 500 ἴσους καὶ ὁμοίους.
Cf. also Mart., IX, 22, 5 :

> ut Mauri Libycis centum stent dentibus orbes.

greges servorum: cf. Sen., *Consol. ad Helv.,* 11 :
turba. Tac., *Ann.,* III, 53 : *familiarum . . . nationes;*
and the humorously exaggerated statements in Petr.,
Ch. 37, 9, and 53, 2. For numbers cf. Tac., *Ann.,*
XIV, 43. Athen., VI, 104.

ostrumque: purple hangings and couch draperies.
Cf. Verg., *Aen.,* I, 700.

renidens: the highly polished surface of the table
reflects the objects about it. Cf. Hor., *Carm.,* II, 18,

2 :   non ebur neque aureum
> mea renidet in domo lacunar.

On the extravagances of the wealthy in the matter
of slaves and banquets, cf. Sen., *Epp.,* XCV, 24 ff.

30. With the exception of the last three or four words,

this line appears very badly confused in the Mss., and even with the best emendation the first part is so flat as to suggest that perhaps a marginal note has displaced the original words, especially as *quae . . . turbat* bears so strong a esemblance to the equally unworthy *quaeque . . . quaerunt*, 30. A similar correspondence between two suspicious bits will be found in 221 and 231 (see note on the latter). *Male nobile lignum*, on the other hand, bears the genuine impress of Petronius's style and connects naturally with what follows.

censum: cf. Cicero (quoted by Nonius, III, p. 202 M, s. *censum*, neutr.) :

quorum luxuries fortunam ac censa peredit.

turbat: a word, with its compounds, frequently used by Petronius and the writers of his period. Cf. Ch. 16, 3 ; 18, 2 ; 74, 8 ; 105, 1, 6 ; 106, 2 ; 108, 1 ; 109, 1 ; 110, 3 ; 111, 7 ; 130, 4 ; 131, 4 ; 136, 3.

male nobile: see Introd., p. 48 f.

31. *turba:* see on 247. •

sepulta mero: cf. Ch. 89, 56 (see Introd. p. 95). Enn., *Ann.*, VIII, 292. Lucr., I, 133 ; V, 475. Verg., *Aen.*, II, 265 ; III, 630. Propert., III, 11, 56.

omniaque orbis praemia: cf. Tac., *Agr.*, 30, and Sulpicia, *Sat.* 30 f. (See note to 1–60.)

32. *corruptis:* differs in but one letter from the Mss. reading, but is infinitely more expressive and imaginative. Of course it is not meant literally, but is a transferred epithet belonging to the soldier's character and the purposes for which his arms are employed.

K

vagus: because of the space over which their operations spread. Cf. 1–6.

exstruit: Moessler is right in contending that this fits the sense better than *esurit.* The latter would refer to the tastes and desires of the degenerate soldiers themselves, as in 9, but the point here is that the whole tremendous power of the armed Empire is made to serve the appetites of the besotted *turba* at Rome. The soldiers are *luxuriae ministri,* and heap up delicacies for them.

33. *ingeniosa gula est:* the same expression is found in Mart., XIII, 62, 2.

For an expansion of the ideas in this and the following lines, cf. Ch. 93, 2 :

> alis Phasiacis petita Colchis
> atque Afrae volucres placent palato
> quod non sunt faciles : at albus anser
> et pictis anas renovata pennis
> plebeium sapit. ultimis ab oris
> attractus scarus atque arata Syrtis
> si quid naufragio dedit, probatur   7.
>
>   *   *   *   *
>
> quicquid quaeritur, optimum videtur.   10.

Sallust, *Cat.,* 13 : *vescendi causa terra marique omnia exquirere,* etc. Sen., *Thy.,* 460–462 ; *Consol. ad Helv.* 9. Juv., V, 92–100. Gell. VII, 16.

scarus: a great dainty with the Romans at all periods. Cf. Enn., *Heduphag.,* 7. Hor., *Epod.,* II, 50 ; *Serm.,* II, 2, 22. Mart., XIII, 84. Plin., *H. N.,* IX, 29, says

that Tiberius transplanted them from the waters east
of Crete to the coast of Campania.

Siculo . . . aequore mersus; "*ex Siculo mare petitum,
in eiusdem maris aqua appositum,*" Moessler. Cf.
Mart., XIII, 79, *Mulli Vivi:*

> spirat in advecto, sed iam piger, aequore mullus :
> languescit. vivum da mare : fortis erit.

34. *vivus* cf. Mart., quoted on 33. Sen., *Nat. Quaest.*,
III, 17 : *quanto incredibiliora sunt opera luxuriae,
quotiens naturam aut mentitur aut vincitur? in cubili
natant pisces, et sub ipsa mensa capitur, qui statim
transferatur in mensam. parum videtur recens mullus,
nisi qui in convivae manu moritur. vitreis ollis inclusi
offeruntur, et observatur morientium color, quem in multas
mutationes mors luctante spiritu vertit . . . et oculos, antequam gulam, pavit (piscis).*

Plin., *H. N.*, IX, 30 *ad fin.* Sen., *Epp.*, XC, 7.

Lucrinis: the Lucrine lake, near Baiae in Campania, was famous for its oysters. Cf. Mart., XIII, 82,
Ostrea:

> ebria Baiano modo veni concha Lucrino :
> nobile nunc sitio luxuriosa garum.

Sen., *Epp.*, LXXVIII; 23.

35. *eruta:* dug from the oyster-beds. Moessler
reads *obruta*, meaning that the oysters were brought
sand and all, and compares 34, but the emendation is
quite uncalled for.

vendunt: some editors have taken exception to this,
the Mss. reading, and have adopted *condunt* from

Heinsius, explaining that the oysters were served last. *Condere cenam*, however, would not mean "end the meal," but rather — if possible at all — would mean that they constituted the whole meal. Cf. Verg., *Ecl.*, IX, 51 f. :

> longos
> cantando . . . condere soles.

Hor., *Carm.*, IV, 5, 29 :

> condit quisque diem collibus in suis.

Stat., *Theb.*, X, 54 : *condiderant iam vota diem* (of a day spent in prayer). The only piece of evidence on the other side is Mart., X, 37, 9, where the question depends on the meaning of *summa mensa*. No instance of *condere* in this sense is quoted. *Vendunt*, on the other hand, is easily explained and much more vigorous. Hor., *Epp.*, II, 1, 74 f. :

> versus paulo concinnior unus et alter
> iniuste totum ducit venditque poema.

and Juv., VII, 135 f. :

> purpura vendit
> causidicum, vendunt amethystina.

mean that the brilliant line and the showy attire lend distinction and bring success. In the same way Petronius evidently means that oysters were considered necessary to make the feast acceptable. Barth's explanation : "*totarum coenarum pretiis conchylia comparantur* " lacks authority to support it.

36. Cf. Manil., V, 370 :

> Numidarum pascimur oris
> Phasidos et damnis.

Hor., *Serm.*, II, 2, 95 f. :

> grandes rhombi patinaeque
> grande ferunt una cum damno dedecus.

ut renovent per damna famem: oysters were served to whet the appetite. Cf. Sen., *Epp.*, CVIII, 15. Petronius scornfully points out that their real power lay in their exorbitant cost. Cf. Hor., *Serm.*, II, 2, 23–26. Sen., *Consol. ad Helv.*, 9. Anton, cf. Claud. *In Eutrop.*, II, 329 : *qui ventrem invitant pretio.* Cf. also Petronius's own lines, quoted on 33.

per damna: cf. 86.

Phasidos unda: from the Phasis, at the eastern end of the Black Sea, now the Rion, came the *aves Phasianae*, pheasants.

Moessler doubts whether Republican Rome really knew pheasants, as the first reference to them is found in Suet., *Cal.*, XXII.

37. Sen., *H. F.*, 536 :

> mutis tacitum
> litoribus mare.

Hipp., 475: solus et aer pervius ventis erit.

39. The subject changes sharply from luxury to political corruption.

Sall., *Cat.*, 3, says of his own youth (about this same time) : *pro pudore, pro abstinentia, pro virtute; audacia, largitio, avaritia vigebant.* Cf. Cic., *Cat.*, IV, 6, 13. (Quoted on 43.) Also Sen., *H. F.*, 169–174.

Campo: The Campus Martius, where elections were held.

furor: cf. Sen., *Hipp.*, 541 : *impius lucri furor.*

40. *praedam:* suggests " spoils " in its modern political sense, but it refers especially to the plunder of conquered provinces, showered on the Roman populace in the form of shows, largesses of grain and money and bribes of all sorts.

strepitumque lucri: the chink of money. *suffragia vertunt* = *suffragia mutant* (Anton). These electors always vote the "straight ticket" of corruption, directing their votes to the source from which the greatest benefits have flowed in the past or promise to flow in the future.

41. *venalis . . . venalis:* cf. Jugurtha's caustic comment on Rome (Sall., *Jug.*, 35, 10) : *urbem venalem . . . si emptorem invenerit.* With the connection of ideas in this and the preceding line, cf. Lucan, I, 180 : *venali campo.*

curia patrum: in Sall., *Jug.*, 52, Cato calls the Senators : *pecuniae . . . servitis.* Anton suggested putting a period after *curia*, making *patrum* depend on *favor* in the next line; a bad arrangement, for, although it makes the two clauses of 41 balance exactly, it limits the meaning of *favor* in 42, which is evidently meant to sum up the thought of the last three lines.

42. *favor* is one of those Janus-words of which Latin possesses a considerable number. On one face it means

the support bestowed on the popular idol; on the other, the influence which he possesses. Cf. the different aspects of *fides, opinio, gratia.* Such combinations are rarer in English, but the adjective "grateful" is a good example.

senibus = patribus, with reference to the origin of the word *senatus*. Cf. Sil. Ital., XI, 47 *senectus* (see on 1–60), and the Spartan Γερουσία, from γέρων.

libera virtus: the free spirit which made them fit to govern. *libera virtus excidit:* recalls Hor., *A. P.*, 282 : *in vitium libertas excidit*, and the line quoted on 43.

43. *exciderat:* cf. Hor., *Carm.*, III, 5, 29 :
> *vera virtus, cum semel excidit.*

sparsisque opibus: cf. Cic., *Cat.*, IV, 6, 13 (of the time of the Gracchi) : *largitionis voluntas tum in re publica versatus est.* Cf. Suet., *Iul.*, 26 ff. and Dio XL, 60, on Caesar's use of his Gallic spoils.

potestas: the civil authority.

44. *maiestas:* the sacred dignity of Rome. This closes the series (*libera virtus, potestas, maiestas*) of attributes of the state embodied in the person of her magistrates and degraded by their corruption. Moessler would refer *maiestas* to foreign dominion in contrast to the civil power, thus making it = *imperium*. But internal corruption, not misrule abroad, is now the topic. *Maiestas*, moreover, does not denote a special kind of power, but the highest aspect of any lawful power whatsoever : *potestas, imperium, regnum*, or omnipotence itself.

45–6. For another reference to Cato, cf. Ch. 137, 9, 6 :

> et peragat causas, sitque Catone prior.

Cato was defeated for praetor (Plut., *Cato Minor*, 42), and for consul (*ibid.*, 49). He was also roughly handled by mobs on several occasions (*ibid.*, 28, 32, 41). Petronius is combining all these rebuffs into one, as the culmination of Roman infamy.

populo : the mob.

tristior: sc. Catone. In this and *pudet* Petronius is projecting into Cato's own times the feelings which his name later inspired. Beginning with Cicero's panegyric, written immediately after Cato's suicide, and which Caesar thought important enough to answer, he was gradually raised to the position of patron saint of republicanism and Stoicism, until men often wrote of him as though even his contemporaries and enemies had looked on him as a man apart. Cf. Verg., *Aen.*, VIII, 670. Hor., *Carm.*, I, 12, 34 f. ; II, 1, 24. Lucan, *passim* (see Haskins's Ed. p. lix). Val. Max., VII, 5, 6. Seneca is never tired of eulogizing him as the ideal *sapiens. E.g. de Const.*, 2 : *adversus vitia civitatis degenerantis, et pessum sua mole sidentis, stetit solus et cadentem rem publicam, quantum modo una retrahi manu poterat, retinuit, donec vel abreptus, vel abstractus, comitem se diu sustentatae ruinae dedit, simulque extincta sunt quae nefas erat dividi, neque enim Cato post libertatem vixit, nec libertas post Catonem.*

victus . . . fasces . . . rapuisse: his defeats at the polls. Cf. Lucan, I, 178 : *rapti fasces pretio.*

For the ideal here, cf. Hor., *Carm.*, III, 2, 17–20.

47. Moessler, following Brouckhusius, holds that this line should be thrown out as the marginal note of some grammarian. But the transition from 46 to 48 — from the fact to the reflection on it — without any connection would be intolerably abrupt. Nor is there anything to prove that another connecting line has been forced out by this one.

dedecoris populo morumque ruina: public disgrace and the overthrow of all moral standards. With *morumque ruina*, Barth cf. Salv. VI, 77 : *nonne eadem (sc. in civitate) et rerum ruina pariter et morum ?*

Anton cf. Ov., *Her.*, XII, 32.

Of the various emendations proposed the most attractive is *dedecus est populi* (Stephanus) which makes the two chiastic pairs of words parallel also in construction.

48–9. There is a suggestion here of Lucan, VII, 264 f. :

> non mihi res agitur, sed vos ut libera sitis
> turba, precor.

homo . . . potestas . . . decus: Cato was not a mere individual, but the incarnation of law and order and the highest ideals of Rome, so that in rejecting and insulting him his countrymen threw away safety and honor as well. There is still no reference (as Moessler thinks) to external conditions. From 39 on Petronius is describing the diseases in the body politic, the excesses abroad which bred them having been stated before.

in uno: in the person of one man. Cf. Lucian, *Iup.*

Trag., 4: τὰ ἡμέτερα ἐν ἑνὶ ἀνδρὶ κινδυνευόμενα (*i.e.*
the continued existence of the gods depends on the
ability of Timocles the Stoic to defend them in argument
against Damis the Epicurean) and contrast Cic., *Cat.*,
I, 5, 11: *non est saepius in uno homine summa salus peric-
litanda rei publicae,* where it means "through the presence of one man."

potestas: de Salas would have this = *libertas* because
of Sen., *de Const.,* 2, *ad. fin.* (see on 45–46) and Lucan, II,
301–3 :

non ante revellar
exanimem quam te complectar, Roma, tuumque
nomen, Libertas, et inanem prosequar umbram.

But while this parallel might instantly strike a com-
mentator, Petronius, if such had been his meaning,
could hardly have depended on *potestas* to convey it to
the general reader.   However, as *potestas* is power limited by law, it refers to the old republican form of gov-
ernment, and so, in a certain sense, does = *libertas.*

perdita: rather passive than active : "ruined," with
"desperate " as a secondary idea.

50. With the thought here cf. Ch. 14, 2.

quid faciunt leges, ubi sola pecunia regnat ?   1.

*   *   *   *   *

ergo iudicium nihil est nisi publica merces.   5.

Pedo Albinov., *El.,* I, 185 :

iura silent, mutaeque tacent sine vindice leges.

Cf. Florus, III, 13, 7 (misfortunes following the Agrarian movement) : *et misera res publica in exitium suum merces erat* (Pithoeus). Val. Max., VII, 6, 4. App., *B. C.*, I, 55. Dio, XLI, 10, 1. Calpurn., I, 51: *ducet captiva triumphos.*

ipsa sui merces: Rome was herself the reward for her own self-destruction. For *merces = praemium*, de Salas, cf. Propert., IV, 11, 71 :

> haec est feminei merces extrema triumphi.

sine vindice praeda: she was plunderer, plundered, and plunder all in one. Where all were criminals or victims, there was no one left to be a champion.

51-52. A metaphor drawn from the sea and its action. The *plebs* is like a neck of land lying between two bodies of water and worn away by the floods that wash over it.

gemino . . . gurgite: Anton takes this to mean luxury and avarice. But these were rather the curses of the wealthy, affecting the *plebs* indirectly only, and in view of *praeterea* it is more natural to refer *gemino . . . gurgite* to what follows : usury and unpaid debts had caught *and* by their progressive action destroyed the people. For *gemino = duo*, cf. 238. Verg., *Aen.*, II, 203 f.; *gemini . . . angues* and III, 305 : *geminas . . . aras.*

plebem: the Mss. read *predam*, which is obviously due to confusion with *praeda*, above. Crusius's emendation, *plebem*, is near to the Mss. and makes excellent sense. The succession of civil wars had reduced great masses of people to desperate poverty. It was to them that

Catiline had addressed his promises, and one of the most difficult problems of Caesar's dictatorship was that of legislation for their relief.   (See Mommsen, *History of Rome*, IV, 523 f.)

deprensam: often used of being overtaken by storm. *E.g.* Verg., *Ge.*, IV, 421 ; *Aen.*, V, 52.   Hor., *Carm.*, II, 16, 2 (*prensus*).   The meaning here is, of course, different.

faenoris . . . usus . . . . aeris: cf. Tac., *Ann.*, VI, 16 : *sane vetus urbi faenebre malum et seditionum discordiarumque creberrima causa. Aes* here = *aes alienum. Faenus* apparently means interest on money borrowed, *usus* that on debts which could not be paid off.

illuvies: the floods which engulf them. Cf. Justin, II, 6 : *aquarum illuvies.* For a similar metaphor, cf. Cic., *Cat.*, II, 10, 21 (of the hopelessly insolvent) : *qui iam pridem premuntur, qui numquam emergunt,* and our own use of "submerged" to describe the lowest social stratum.   Cf. Pers., III, 34 f. of a man morally submerged.

exederat: the ruin wrought by the *faenus* is compared to the erosive and corrosive effects of sea-water. Cf. Tac., *Ann.*, II, 27: *tum primum reperta sunt quae per tot annos rem publicam exedere.*

53. *nulla est certa domus:* an echo of Verg., *Aen.*, VI, 673 : *nulli certa domus,* but with very different meaning, as the latter refers to the idyllic existence of the blessed in Elysium, while this depicts the financial straits of the Romans.   Cf. Sall., *De R. P. Ordinanda.* I, 5, 13: *eos paulatim expulsos agris, inertia atque inopia incertas domos habere subegit.*

nullum . . . corpus: cf. Sall., *Cat.*, 33 : *miseri, egentes, violentia atque crudelitate faeneratorum plerique patriae, sed omnes fama atque fortunis expertes sumus: neque cuiquam nostrum licuit more maiorum lege uti, neque amisso patrimonio liberum corpus habere, tanta saevitia faeneratorum atque praetoris fuit.*

54–55. The spreading corruption is described, first as a wasting disease, then as a ravening beast — or rather, the *tabes* of the first metaphor is in turn made the object of a second metaphor.

tabes: a natural and frequent comparison. Cf. Sall., *Cat.*, 36 : *tanta vis morbi uti tabes plerosque civium animos invaserat. Jug.*, 32 (almost the same words). Livy II, 23, 6. Cicero often compares the Catilinarian conspiracy to a disease. *E.g. Cat.*, I, 13, 31. Cf. Macbeth's words to the Doctor (V, 3, 50 ff.).

tacitis: "secret," "inmost." Cf. Verg., *Aen.*, IV, 67 : *tacitum vivit sub pectore vulnus.*

medullis: lit. "marrow"; here, as often, the vitals.

curis latrantibus: cf. Stat., *Theb.*, II, 338 *magnas latrantia pectora curas.* For other instances of *latrare* in the figurative sense of "worry," "threaten," cf. Enn., *Ann.*, 584 (*Lib. Incert.*, 108). Claud., *In Eutrop.*, II, 486.

56. *detritaque commoda luxu:* recalls 8, but with a difference. *Usu plebeio trita voluptas* means that delights which the masses shared quickly came to seem shabby and commonplace to the rich. The present line refers to fortunes worn away and exhausted by the extravagant demands made on them.

57. *vulneribus reparantur:* cf. "Antony and Cleopatra," IV, 14 : "with a wound I must be cured."

inops audacia tuta est: Dousa, cf. Sall., *Cat.*, 37 : *nam semper in civitate, uis opes nullae sunt, bonis invident, malos extollunt: vetera odere, nova exoptant: odio suarum rerum mutari omnia student: turba atque seditionibus sine cura aluntur, quoniam egestas facile habetur sine damno.* (Cf. the references on 59–60.)

Horace (*Epp.*, II, 2, 26–40) tells the story of a soldier of Lucullus who distinguished himself by gallant conduct after he had lost all his money. Reimbursed, and called upon for another dangerous piece of work :

ibit eo quo vis qui zonam perdidit, inquit.

58. Rome was not only caught in a slough, but so stupefied as to be unconscious of her peril. This was the next stage after that described, 51–52, and would have been the last, had she not been aroused in time to save herself from being completely engulfed. It will be seen that here and in the next two lines the war is represented, not as completing the ruin of Rome, but as a desperate remedy for her condition.

hoc mersam caeno: cf. Ch. 88, 6 : *at nos vino scortisque demersi.* Florus, III, 12, 7 : *illae opes atque divitiae adflixere saeculi mores; mersamque vitiis suis, quasi sentina, rem publicam pessum dedere* (Pithoeus). *P. L. M.*, XLIII, 82 (ascribed to Petronius) :

non satis est quod nos mergit furiosa iuventas ?

(Wernsdorff).

Lactant., VI, 23, 8 : *animas . . . velut in caeni gurgite demersit.* VII, 6, 2. Also Claud., *de Raptu Proserp.*, III, 28 f. Lucr., V, 1008 ; and the references to Cicero and Persius on 51–52.

59–60. Cf. Lucan, I, 182 : *multis utile bellum.* Suet., *Iul.*, 27 : *tum reorum aut obaeratorum, aut prodigae iuventutis subsidium unicum ac promptissimum erat: nisi quos gravior criminum, vel inopiae luxuriaeve vis urgeret, quam ut subveniri posset a se: his plane palam 'bello civili opus esse' dicebat.* Cf. Cic. *Cat.*, II, 9, 20 (of Sulla's veterans) ; III, 10, 25: *lex haec fuit . . . constituta, ut omnes qui salva urbe salvi esse possent, in hostium numero ducerentur.*

sana ratione movere = sanare, by a shock which would startle Rome out of her lethargy. Cf. Cic., *Cat.*, II, 5, 11. Moessler wishes to connect *sana ratione* with *poterant: "ita ut artium vis non re vera esse explorata, sed sanae eorum rationi, quos appellat auctor, exploranda relinqui perhibeatur,"* and further elucidates his point by summarizing the passage as follows : "*Romam accepisti qualis fuisset. iam suscitandae eius potestatem ac vim quibus, praeterquam bello civili, artibus, sanam secutus rationem tribueris?* But this, surely, is to deal with Petronius as a German professor, not a Roman satirist.

libido: the lust of blood.

61–66. The idea contained in these lines was also used with reference to the fate of Pompey and his two sons, in which form it was a favorite with the poets of the Empire. Cf. Mart., V, 74 :

> Pompeios iuvenes Asia atque Europa, sed ipsum
> terra tegit Libyae, si tamen ulla tegit.
> quid mirum toto si spargitur orbe? iacere
> uno non poterat tanta ruina loco.

Octavia, 502–504, 517–524, 827. *Anth. Lat.*, 400–
403. Moessler finds in these lines only a reflection on the
fates of the Triumvirs, and no hint of their parts — especially that of Crassus — in precipitating the war. He
accordingly decides that this was an epigram by Petronius, which has, in some unexplained way, crept into
the poem. But the connection of the Triumvirs with
the war was not only well known to history, but so frequently mentioned in poetry that the mere epithet
duces, 61, would, in this context, be a sufficient re-
minder. Cf. Hor., *Carm.*, II, 1, 1 f. :

> motum ex Metello consule civicum
> bellique causas et vitia et modos.

(Q. Caecilius Metellus Celer was Consul 60 B.C., the year
in which the First Triumvirate was formed.)

Lucan, I., 98 ff.:

> temporis angusti mansit concordia discors,
> paxque fuit non sponte ducum. nam sola futuri
> Crassus erat belli medius mora.   100.
>
> *   *   *   *   *   *
>
>   sic ubi saeva   103.
> arma ducum dirimens miserando funere Crassus
> Assyrias Latio maculavit sanguine Carras,
> Parthica Romanos solverunt damna furores.
> plus illa vobis acie quam creditis actum est,

Arsacidae : bellum victis civile dedistis.
dividitur ferro regnum : populique potentis
quae mare quae terras quae totum continet orbem,
non cepit fortuna duos.

There is nothing unnatural in the brief paragraph, —
especially in a work which lacks the last touches, — if we
take it as introducing the human agents of the struggle,
placed between the undistinguished crowd of mortals,
and the gods who were to share in it. It is possible, however, that Petronius wrote it after the rest of the poem
and inserted it here without taking the trouble to ad-
just it perfectly to its surroundings.

61. *tulerat:* "brought forth." Cf. Hor., *Carm.*, III,
6, 46 f.

> aetas parentum, peior avis, tulit
> nos nequiores.

Tac., *Ann.*, III, 55, 6. *Octavia*, 827.

Fortuna: the first introduction of the power which,
in the succeeding passage, precipitates the war. The
three leaders are her true sons, as is shown by the ex-
tremes of good and ill bestowed on them. Cf. Lucan on
Pompey (see Introd., p. 74).

62. *armorum strue:* "in war's destruction." *Strues*
(*struere*) graphically pictures the slaughter and the
scattered and heaped-up bodies of the fallen, but must
not be taken too exactly, as none of the *tres duces* actually fell on the field of battle.

Erinys: this, and not *Enyo*, seems to be the reading
required by the Mss. But whichever is read, the mean-

ing is the same : "the demon of civil strife." Roman poets were fond of evoking the powers of evil (see on 96 f.), but rarely took the trouble to distinguish carefully between them.

63. *Crassum:* M. Licinius Crassus, the conqueror of Spartacus, killed by the Parthians, 53 B.C., after the annihilation of his army at Carrhae.

Parthus: see on *Romanus,* 1.

habet: "holds," "keeps." Cf. Verg., *Aen.,* I, 556: (te) pontus habet Libyae. IV, 633 :

namque suam (sc. nutricem) patria antiqua cinis ater habebat.

Libyco . . . aequore: on the sands of Egypt. Pompey was murdered at Pelusium, whither he had fled after the battle of Pharsalus, 48 B.C., by the Egyptian general Achillas and the renegade Roman Septimius, formerly one of his own officers. His head was kept for Caesar; his body, cast out of the boat in which he had left his galley, and washed ashore, was given "maimèd rites" of burial by a faithful freedman. His ashes were afterwards transferred to Rome, and nearly two centuries later the little Egyptian tomb was restored by Hadrian. Cf. Lucan, VIII, 536 —. Plut., *Pomp.,* 80 (a detailed and pathetic account). App., B. C., II, 86. Vel. Pat., 2, 53, 3 f.; ending: *tantum in illo viro a se discordante Fortuna, ut cui modo ad victoriam terra defuerat, deesset ad sepulturam. Anth. Gr.,* IX, 402 (Hadrian's epitaph on Pompey) :

τῷ ναοῖς βρίθοντι πόση σπάνις ἔπλετο τύμβου.

Anth. Lat., 404 (corrupt, but to the same purpose). Juvenal, X, 283–288, has some characteristic reflections on his fate.

64. The rhetorical historians speak of Caesar's murder in much the same terms. Vel. Pat., II, 57, 1: *laudandum experientia consilium est Pansae atque Hirtii, qui semper praedixerant Caesari ut principatum armis quaesitum armis teneret. Ille dictitans mori se, quam timeri, malle, dum clementiam quam praestiterat, exspectat, incautus ab ingratis occupatus est.* Florus, IV, 2, 7 ; 95: *sic ille qui terrarum orbem civili sanguine impleverat, tandem ipse sanguine suo curiam implevit.*

66. This conceit of the distribution of weight is characteristic of the tendency of the time to drag in scientific and pseudo-scientific ideas on all occasions. See Introd., p. 23.

gloria: " *pro ambitione et inani studio famae ponitur, quam poetae ut numen a militaribus viris cultam saepe inducunt, quae ad quaevis stimulat et postea hanc mercedem reddit.*" (Burmann.)

reddit: expressive, as it means to render what is due or customary.

67–75. Cf. Verg., *Aen.*, VI, 237 ff. Ov., *Met.*, IV, 432–438. Sen., *Tro.*, 182–184 ; *H. F.*, 664–667, 698–706. Sil. Ital., XII, 120 ff.

67. *est locus:* Verg., *Aen.*, I, 530, and Stat., *Theb.*, II, 32, begin with the same words. The place was the *Phlegraei Campi*, between Vesuvius and Lake Avernus (Vitruv., II, 6, 2. Plin. (see on 68). Diod., IV, 21. Strabo, V, 8, p. 247), so often described by the poets (see preceding note).

hiatu: cf. Verg., *Aen.*, VI, 237 f. :

> spelunca alta fuit vastoque immanis hiatu
> scrupea.

Sil. Ital., XII, 126–128 :

> hinc vicina palus (fama est Acherontis ad undas
> pandere iter) caecas stagnante voragine fauces
> laxat, et horrendos aperit telluris hiatus.

68. *Parthenopen . . . Dicarchidos arva:* Naples and Puteoli. Plin., III 9, 9 : *dein Puteoli colonia Dichae-archia dicti: postque Phlegraei Campi, Acherusia palus Cumis vicina. litore autem Neapolis Chalcidensium, et ipsa Parthenope a tumulo Sirenis appellata.*

69. *Cocyti . . . aqua:* cf. Sil. Ital., XII, 116 f. :

> ast hic Lucrino mansisse vocabula quondam
> Cocyti memorat.

cf. 103 and 278.

70. Cf. Verg., *Aen.*, VI, 240 f. :

> talis sese halitus atris
> faucibus effundens supera ad convexa ferebat.

Sil. Ital., XII, 123 f. (Avernus):

> letale vomebat
> suffuso virus caelo.

71. *Autumno:* probably corrupt. It is a strange word to associate especially with *viret,* and the single *aut* in the sentence suggests that another is hidden in this word. Therefore, while Moessler's *non haec aut pomo*

tellus rubet does not commend itself, it seems probable
that some noun, not referring directly to a season, but
appropriate in sense to *viret*, is concealed in the second
part of *Autumno*, and that the present opposition of
Autumno and *verno . . . cantu* is not the work of the
poet, but the result of an attempt to emend what had
already become corrupt.

72–73. *laetus:* "luxuriant." Cf. the common expression, *laeta seges*.

persona: see Introd., p. 53.

cantu: the song of birds swarming in the under-
growth on their return from the South. Cf Lucr. I,
256:

> frondiferasque novis avibus canere undique silvas.

Most commentators say that the whispering of the
leaves themselves is meant, citing Calpurn., VIII,
30 : *vento garrula pinus*, and Auson., *Epp.*, 29, 13 f. :

> est et arundineis modulatis musica ripis
> cumque suis loquitur tremulum coma pinea ventis.

But on the other hand there is the well-known character
of Avernus (ἄορνος). Cf. Lucr., VI, 738 ff. Verg.,
Aen., VI, 237 ff. Sil. Ital., XII, 123 : (*Avernus*)
formidatus volucri. Strabo, V, p. 244. *Verno*, moreover, is more appropriate to this meaning, as bare twigs
and dry rushes can whisper in the wind too. *Discordi
strepitu* suggests the myriad singing and twittering of
birds of many kinds — ὀρνίθων πετεηνῶν ἔθνεα πολλά
— rather than the unvarying response of the leaves to

the wind. In 57–58, too, where the leaves alone are left, Petronius says *mutoque in litore.*

74. Pliny (*Epp.*, VI, 16, 11), describing the eruption of Vesuvius which destroyed Pompeii (79 A.D.) says: *iam pumices etiam, nigrique et ambusti et fracti igne lapides.* What Petronius pictures here is ground blasted by old eruptions, but yielding in part to wild and irregular growths of vegetation (75).

75. *gaudent:* refers to the abandon with which chaos has seized on the region, admitting no living thing to its domain but the funereal cypresses which struggle up through the heaps of blackened rock. For *gaudere* used of things without sense, cf. Verg., *Ecl.*, IX, 48 : *segetes gauderent frugibus.* Mart., XIII, 16. Plin., *H. N.*, XII, 33 ; XIX, 39, 2.

ferali . . . cupressu: because used at funerals. This custom was probably due to its dark foliage, but was explained by the ancients themselves by its unfruitfulness, and by the fact that, once cut down, it never sprouted again (Serv., *ad Aen.*, VI, 216). For the myth of Cyparissus, who grieved himself to death over the accidental killing of a pet stag, and was changed into a cypress by Apollo, see Ov., *Met.*, X, 106–142.

circum tumulata: ' *tumulorum instar saxa toto campo (id est enim circum) exsurgunt*" (Moessler).

76. *Ditis:* cf. Quintil., I, 6, 34. Serv., *ad Aen.*, VI, 273 : *dicimus autem et hic Dis et hic Ditis.* For similar forms, cf. Petr., Ch. 47, 4 ; and 58, 2 (*Iovis*) ; 62, 13 (*bovis*) ; Acc. (in Prisc., VI, p. 695 K) : *abietem exurat Iovis.*

extulit ora: cf. 272 :

extulit ad superos Stygium caput (Discordia).

77. Cf. Ov., *A. A.*, II, 440 : *summo canet in igne cinis.*
sparsa: a zeugma. With *flammis,* "scorched"
must be understood. Boissier, *L'Opposition sous les
Césars,* p. 245, translates : "*Pluton, . . . le visage noirci
par la flamme des bûchers, la barbe blanche de cendres.*"

78. *volucrem Fortunam:* cf. Hor., *Carm.,* III, 29,
53 f. :

> si celeres quatit
> pinnas.

Sen., *Hipp.,* 1143 : velox Fortuna.
She was represented with wings. Plut., *de Fort. Rom.,*
317 F–318 A, speaks of her laying them aside on the
Palatine (the *Fortuna Augusti*).

79. *Potestas:* cf. Verg., *Aen.,* X, 18 :

o pater, o hominum rerumque aeterna potestas.

In Juv., X, 100 :

an Fidenarum Gabiorumque essa potestas.

the word is used of a civil magistrate (cf. Ital. *po-
destà*). This ascription of unlimited power to Chance is
characteristically Epicurean, but perhaps even more
characteristically poetical. The Stoic Lucan allows
Fortuna to control, or appear to control, most of the
action of the *Pharsalia* (see Haskins's Ed., p. li).

80. This line is omitted by most of the Mss. and by
the First and Second Editions. But ending, as it does,
in a repetition of *potestas,* it is easy to see how it might

have been overlooked by a copyist, while in its favor, as Moessler points out, is its echo of Lucan's *summisque negatum stare diu* (I, 70). Such repetitions, moreover, do not seem to have been as disagreeable to Roman ears as they are to ours. Cf. Lucr., I, 66 f. (*contra . . . contra*). III, 429 f. (*movetur . . . movetur*). V, 680 f. (*noctes . . . noctes*). Verg., *Aen.*, VII, 653 f. (*esset . . . esset*). Lucan, II, 143 f. (*nocentes . . . nocentes*). Sil. Ital., XII, 221 f. (*alter . . . alter*), — all of which can be defended on some rhetorical grounds, or be excused by the lack of *ultima manus*, but nevertheless strike the modern reader unpleasantly.

Fors: cf. Enn., *Ann.*, VI, 197: *Era Fors.* It was the older name of the goddess, afterwards combined with its derivative, *Fors Fortuna*, or *Fortuna* alone.

81. Pithoeus, cf. Menander :

$$\text{Ὦ μεταβολαῖς χαίρουσα παντοιαῖς τύχη.}$$

(Ed. Meinecke, *Incert. Fab.*, 63).

82–83 : cf. Calpurn., I, 84 : *Romanae pondera molis.* Sen., *de Const.*, 2, *vitia civitatis . . . pessum sua mole sidentis.*

perituram: see notes on 19.

84–85. Cf. Liv., *Praefatio*, 4 : *haec nova, quibus iam pridem praevalentis populi vires se ipsae conficiunt.* Propert., III, 13, 60 :

frangitur ipsa suis Roma superba bonis.

Hor., *Epod.*, VII, 9 f. :

> ut secundum vota Parthorum sua
> urbs haec periret dextera?

XVI, 1 f.:

> altera iam teritur bellis civilibus aetas,
> suis et ipsa Roma viribus ruit.

Sen., *Tro.*, 14; *Hipp.*, 481; *Agam.*, 87–89. *Octavia*, 519 f.

struxit opes: cf. Hor., *Carm.*, II, 18, 19: *struis domos.*

86. *luxuriam spoliorum:* Cicero's orations *in Verrem* give us an idea of what these two words cover.

censum in damna furentem: wealth run mad to its own destruction. Cf. Sen., *Controv.*, II, 9 (*pro adoptando, Fabiani Papirii*): *in sua damna validiora;* Sen., *Epp.*, XCV, 26: *nobilem patinam, in quam quicquid apud lautos solet diem ducere, properans in damnum suum popina congesserat* (Barth).

Manil. IV, 11:

> et summum census pretium est effundere censum.

Cf. *per damna*, 36; Ch. 89, 14: *mens semper in damnum potens.*

87–93. The scale on which man was reshaping inanimate nature to serve his ambition or his luxury made a profound impression on thinking Romans. Cf. Sen., *Controv.*, II, 9, 11. Plin., *H. N.*, XXXVI, 1, 1 ff. *lapidum natura restat, hoc est, praecipua morum insania* ... 2. *caedimus hos (montes), trahimusque nihil alia, quam deliciarum causa, quos transcendisse quoque mirum fuit. in portento prope maiores habuere Alpes ab Han-*

nibale exsuperatas . . . nunc ipsae caeduntur in mille genera marmorum. promuntoria aperiuntur mari, et rerum natura agitur in planum. evehimus ea, quae separandis gentibus pro terminis constituta erant, navesque marmorum causa fiunt: ac per fluctus, saevissimam rerum naturae partem, huc illuc portantur iuga . . . caeloque proximae rupes cavantur, ut ibatur glacie.[1] 3. *secum quisque cogitet, cum pretia horum audiat, cum vehi trahique moles videat, quam sine his multorum fuerit beatior vita: ista facere, immo verius pati mortales, quos ob usus, quasve ad voluptates alias, nisi ut inter maculas lapidum iaceant?* Sen., *Thy.*, 455–460; *Hipp.*, 497–499.

87. Cf. Ch. 135, 8:

non Indum fulgebat ebur, quod inhaeserat auro,
nec iam calcato radiabat marmore terra
muneribus delusa suis.

aedificant auro: commentators have seen in this a reference to the Golden House of Nero (Suet., *Nero*, 31); but the use of gold in splendid decorations is repeatedly mentioned by earlier poets. Lucr., II, 23–28. Verg., *Aen.*, I, 726. Hor., *Carm.*, II, 18, 1–5. Manil., V, 508.

ad sidera: cf. Sall., *Cat.*, 12 f.: *operae pretium est, cum domos atque villas cognoveris in urbium modum exaedificatas, visere templa deorum, quae nostri maiores, religiosissimi mortales, fecere.* Sen., *Controv.*, II, 9 (see on 87–93). Sen., *Epp.*, XC, 7.

---

[1] Crystal was believed to be petrified ice.

88. Cf. Sall., *Cat.*, 13 : *nam quid ea memorem, quae nisi eis qui videre nemini credibilia sunt, a privatis compluribus subversos montis, maria constrata esse?* Tibull., II, 3, 45 f. Hor., *Carm.*, III, 1, 33 f. ; *A. P.*, 63–68. Sen., *Thy.*, 459 f.

The harbors at Ostia, the canals connecting the Lucrine Lake and Lake Avernus with the sea, and the moles running out into the water at Baiae, and supporting villas, were all examples of these great constructions. Cf. Verg., *Ge.*, II, 161–164 :

an memorem portus Lucrinoque addita claustra
atque indignatum magnis stridoribus aequor,
Iulia qua ponto longe sonat unda refuso
Tyrrhenoque fretis immittitur aestus Avernis?

(See Suet., *Aug.*, 16.)
Hor., *Carm.*, II, 18, 19–22 :

> struis domos
> marisque Baiis obstrepentis urgues
> summovere litora,
> parum locuples continente ripa.

For Nero's undertakings, cf. Suet., *Nero*, 31. Tac., *Ann.*, XV, 42, 1.

The débris of the great fire at Rome was shipped down the Tiber to fill in the marshes about Ostia. The description of the villa of Pollius Felix at Surrentum (Stat., *Silv.*, II, 2) gives an idea of the scale on which private constructions were carried out. Cf. also Sen., *Excerpt. Controv.*, V, 5, pt. 1.

On the subject of fish-ponds, cf. Varro, *R. R.*, III, 17, 2 ff. Colum., VIII, 16 f.

89. *rebellant:* the subject understood is *Romani*, as with *aedificant*, 87. Cf. Tac., *Ann.*, XV, 42, 1 (of Nero's engineers) : *ingenium et audacia erat etiam quae natura denegavisset per artem temptare.*

90. *mea regna:* cf. *Il.*, 20, 61–65 :

ἔδεισεν δ᾽ ὑπένερθεν ἄναξ ἐνέρων, Ἀϊδωνεύς,
δείσας δ᾽ ἐκ θρόνου ἆλτο, καὶ ἴαχε, μή οἱ ὕπερθε
γαῖαν ἀναρρήξειε Ποσειδάων ἐνοσίχθων,
οἰκία δὲ θνητοῖσι καὶ ἀθανάτοισι φανείη
σμερδαλέ᾽, εὐρώεντα, τάτε στυγέουσι θεοί περ.

91–92. *(perfossa)* . . . *molibus insanis:* "(hollowed) by the removal of enormous masses of rock." Cf. Sen., *Epp.*, XC, 25 : *quid (loquar) lapideas moles . . . quibus porticus et capacia populorum tecta suscipimus?*

insanis: means not only "enormous," but "extravagant." Cf. Hor., *Serm.*, II, 2, 5 :

cum stupet insanis acies fulgoribus.

montibus haustis antra gemunt: the mountains are drained of their marble, as though it were only so much water to be dipped out, and the subterranean caverns — *Dis* speaks from his own point of view — rumble and groan as the attack comes nearer and their walls grow thinner.

For *gemunt*, cf. Val. Flacc., VI, 168 f. :

ipse rotis gemit intus ager, tremebundaque pulsu nutat humus.

Claud., III *Cons Hon.*, 196 :

ignifluisque gemit Lipare fumosa cavernis.

Trag. reads *austris;* Moessler, *montibus haustis claustra gemunt:* *"de moenibus . . . Orci, excisione montium concussis ac rimas agentibus."*

vanos . . . usus: useless uses. *Varius* is so common an epithet of marble (*e.g.* Hor., *Serm.*, II, 4, 83 :

ten lapides varios lutulenta radere palma ?

Sen., *Controv.*, II, 9 : *varius ille . . . lapis.* Sen., *Thy.*, 647 :

variis columnae nobiles maculis)

that at first sight one is tempted to adopt it here. But the weight of Mss. evidence is in favor of *vanos* (with the slight change of *usus* for *usum,* Delbenius), and from the point of view of style *vanos lapis invenit usus* is distinctly better than *varius lapis invenit usum.*

Moessler would have *lapis* = gems, which are not in question here.

93. Cf. Sen., *Oed.*, 570 f. ; *Thy.*, 804–806 ; *H. F.*, 50–52, 55 f., 282 f., 566–568. *inferni manes:* the shades of the dead.

caelum: includes, beside the sky, sunlight, and the open air, which were often identified in the minds of the ancients. Cf. Verg., *Aen.*, III, 600 : *caeli spirabile lumen.*

sperare fatentur: the hope of enjoying the light and air once more had grown so strong in the shades that

they were emboldened to declare it — a sure sign that
they were on the verge of rebellion against their tyrant,
believing his power to be threatened.   The dead never
ceased to yearn for the air which they no longer breathed,
and the sun to which they had said farewell (cf. *Od.*, XI,
488 ff.   Verg., *Aen.*, VI, 436 f.   The heroes of Greek
tragedy regularly bid farewell to the sun before their
deaths).   The powers of Hades, on the other hand,
loved darkness and hated light (cf. Ov., *Met.*, II, 260 f. ;
V, 356, and see notes to 90, above).   The shades, it is
true, are commonly represented as dreading a sudden
flood of sunshine (*e.g.* Verg., *Aen.*, VIII, 246. Ov., *Met.*,
V, 358.   Sen., *H. F.*, 292 f. ;   Sil. Ital., XII, 129), as
would anyone long confined in darkness, but that would
not prevent their hailing with joy the prospect of an
ultimate release and return to it.

fatentur: is not uncommonly used to mean "declare,"
with only a secondary idea of some motive for reticence
(*e.g.* Juv., III, 59 ;   X, 172 ;   XV, 132).   Here it is sufficiently explained by the fact that such an admission
would be considered seditious by *Dis.*

In support of the reading *iubentur*, one striking ver-
bal parallel is cited : *quid me caelum sperare iubebas?*
(Verg., *Ge.*, IV, 325), but in the face of the overwhelm-
ing majority of Mss. in favor of *fatentur* — a reading
satisfactory in itself — this is not sufficient reason for
adopting it.

Seneca, it may be noted, is very fond, in his tragedies,
of references to breaking open the House of Hades, *e.g.*
Oed., 570 f. ;   *Thy.*, 804–806 ;   *H. F.*, 50 ff., 566–568.

94. *in proelia, i.e.* change to a look suitable for battle.

95. *cie:* cf. 135.

funera: used for the dead who were to swell the number of his subjects.

96-97. *Dis* bathes his face, Tisiphone her whole body, in the blood of the slain. In 120 she also devours their flesh.

mea: Dis finds the fiend a creature after his own heart.

sitientis: "parched."

perluit: cf. Ov., *Met.*, III, 173; IV, 310.

The Furies were sometimes limited to three: Allecto, Megaera, and Tisiphone, the last being the most terrible. The Roman writers always represent them under their most loathsome aspect, never as the idealized Eumenides of Athens.

98. *Sullanus . . . ensis:* the sword of Sulla. The figurative language is used with quite modern feeling.

bibit: cf. Verg., *Aen.*, II, 600:

iam flammae tulerint inimicus et hauserit ensis.

XI, 804 (hasta):

haesit virgineumque alte bibit acta cruorem.

Ov., *Tr.*, III, 11, 57. Sen., *de Clem.* I, 12: *quis . . . umquam tyrannus tam avide humanum sanguinem bibit, quam ille qui septem milia civium Romanorum contrucidare iussit (i.e.* Sulla)?

The massacres of Sulla had set, as it were, a standard in slaughter, and the Roman mind always reverted to them in times of civil peril. Cf., *e.g.*, Cic., *Cat.*, II, 9, 20. Caesar (in Cic., *ad Atticum*, IX, 7, c) : *L. Sullam, quem imitaturus non sum.* Lucan, I, 580 ff., makes the shades of Marius and Sulla rise to give warning of the impending struggle.

horrida tellus: *horrida* is proleptic, referring to the *fruges* of the next line. Anton says, *horrens aristis*, and cf. Verg., *Ge.*, III, 198 f. :

> tum segetes altae campique natantes
> lenibus horrescunt flatibus.

Burmann, who omits *et*, against the Mss., recommends *sordida*, i.e. *madefacta sanguine belli*, to restore the meter.

99. *nutritos sanguine fruges:* this unpleasant idea was a familiar one to the ancients. Cf. Verg., *Ge.*, I, 491 f. Ov., *Her.*, I, 1, 53 f. :

iam seges est ubi Troia fuit, resecandaque falce
  luxuriat Phrygio sanguine pinguis humus.

Plut., *Marius*, 21. Serv., *ad Aen.*, XII, 119.

100. This line consists of two Vergilian hemistichs. Cf. Verg., *Aen.*, II, 790; VI, 628; VII, 323; XII, 81; 441; VIII, 164; and I, 408. Petr., Ch. 61, 5. For similar expressions, cf. Verg., *Aen.*, I, 408. Ov., *Met.*, VI, 447 f. Livy, III, 61, 7; VII, 33, 11.

The hand-clasp was intended as the pledge of their compact.

101. *Dis* apparently fails to clasp the hand of *Fortuna*, but the effort opens a new fissure in the ground where the interview is taking place. His failure is

probably due to the fickle and elusive character of the goddess, who slips from his grasp as ghosts from the hands of men (cf. *Il.*, XXIII, 99 f.; *Od.*, XI, 253 ff. Verg., *Aen.*, II, 792 ff.). The rending of the earth shows the tremendous power in every motion the god makes.

rupto tellurem solvit hiatu: cf. Sen., *Thy.*, 88 : *tellure rupta.* The same words, *Octavia*, 135, 595. 728 f. :

> diducta subito patuit ingenti mihi
> tellus hiatu.

102. *Fortuna levi . . . pectore:* cf. 244 : *Fortuna levis.*

103. *Cocyti penetralia:* the regions beyond Cocytus.

104. See Introd., p. 65.

105. *vota tibi cedent:* a majority of Mss. read *mihi*, which Anton adopts on the ground that *Fortuna* is thus made subordinate to *Dis.* "*I am, quod optavi, eveniet.*" But this subordination to *Dis* is not in keeping with his manner of addressing her in 79, or with the general tone of his appeal (Introd., p. 64.) *Tibi*, which makes *cedent* an authoritative promise, is more vigorous, and accords better with her function in the poem.

For the use of *cedent*, cf. Florus, III, 1, 2 : *citra spem omnium Fortuna cessit.* Suet., *Aug.*, 91: *cessitque res prospere.* (Anton.) Contrast Ch. 82, 5, 2 : *quem sua vota premunt.*

rebellat: Erhard proposed *rebullit*, suggesting the physical effect of anger, and Reiske followed him. But Petronius uses *rebellare* freely. Cf. 89, 287. Cf. also Sen., *Epp.*, LXIX, 4 : *cito rebellat affectus* (Anton).

M

106. *-que:* Latin frequently has "and" where English requires "or" or "nor." Cf. Verg., *Aen.*, II, 36 f.

107. *Romanis arcibus:* the hills of Rome, with special reference to the Palatine — once walled off by itself, the nucleus of the later city — and the Capitoline, on one summit of which was the *Arx.* Moessler cf. Verg., *Ge.*, II, 172 :

> in bellum avertis Romanis arcibus Indum.

Aen., IV, 234 :
> Ascanione pater Romanas invidet arces?

X, 11–13 :

> adveniet iustum pugnae, ne arcessite, tempus,
> cum fera Karthago Romanis arcibus olim
> exitium magnum atque Alpis immittet apertas.

odi: cf. Florus: *invidens Fortuna,* etc. (quoted on 1–60).

108. *muneribusque meis irascor:* cf. Ch. 135, 8, 3 : *muneribus delusa suis.*

destruet: cf. *cedent,* 105. *Fortuna* continues in the same tone of authority.

109. *idem . . . deus:* Mars, the father of Romulus and Remus, and patron of the city. Cf. Verg., *Aen.*, I, 276 f. : *Mavortia . . . moenia.* Cf. Neptune's part in the destruction of Troy, which he had helped to build, Verg., *Aen.*, II, 608 ff. ; III, 3 : *Neptunia Troia.*

110. *cremare viros:* cf. Verg., *Aen.*, VII, 295 f. :

> num incensa cremavit
> Troia viros ? (Moessler.)

Editors who have found difficulty with the expression have suggested *armare* (Gronovius), *caede creare* (Reiske), *ciere, gregare* (Moessler), all far less vigorous than the original.

sanguine pascere luxum: cf. 56 f. The degenerate Romans are to get what they want — and deserve. Some editors refer this to the amassing of fortunes based on plunder and confiscation, as in the days of Sulla, but *Fortuna* is here thinking only of the work of destruction, and not of the survivors.

111–112. *cerno:* frequently used to introduce a prophecy or vision. Cf., *e.g.*, Cic., *Cat.*, IV, 6, 11: *cerno animo sepulta in patria miseros atque insepultos acervos civium.* Verg., *Aen.*, VI, 87 ; VII, 68. Sil. Ital., I, 126 and 137. The epic poets frequently used this device to introduce matter lying outside the scope of the narrative, or to anticipate some particularly impressive event. Cf. Verg., *Aen.*, I, 257 ff. ; VI, 756 ff. Sil. Ital., VIII, 661 ff. (for Lucan, see Introd., p. 76). It also found its way into later dramatic poetry (*e.g.* Shakspere, *Henry VIII*, V; 5), where its abuse was cleverly satirized by Sheridan, *The Critic*, II, 2 : "The Spanish fleet thou canst not see," etc.

gemina . . . morte: the dead of Philippi and Pharsalus (*Thessaliae . . . rogos*).

stratos: Moessler, cf. Sil. Ital., IX, 39 :

> stratis deleto milite campis.

Philippos Thessaliaeque rogos: Pharsalus and Philippi. The violation of chronological order is not to be insisted on, as the names of the two battles, and also of the regions where they were fought, Thessaly and Macedon (Emathia), had come to be used interchangeably in referring to them. Cf., *e.g.*, Florus, IV, 2, 43: *sic praecipitantibus fatis proelio sumpta est Thessalia, et Philippicis campis urbis, imperii, generis· humani fata commissa sunt.* Ov., *Met.*, XV, 823 f. (of Augustus):

Pharsalia sentiet illum
Emathiaque iterum madefient caede Philippi.

Lucan, VII, 847 ff.; IX, 271. Juv., VIII, 242 f. (Pharsalus). Verg., *Ge.*, I, 489–492. Lucan, I, 680 and 695; VII, 427 (Philippi). The apostrophe to Brutus, Lucan, VII, 591 f.:

nec tibi fatales admoveris ante Philippos,
Thessalia periture tua.

means: "in a Thessaly of your own," *i.e.* in a region which will be to you what Thessaly has been to Pompey. In the closing passage of Book VII (728 ff.) Lucan uses *Thessalia, Emathia*, and even *Threicia* of the same region.

funera gentis Hiberae: Caesar's two Spanish campaigns; against Pompey's lieutenants, Petreius and Afranius (49), and against his sons (45). Munda, which ended the latter, was the last of Caesar's battles.

Sil. Ital. associates Munda and Philippi (III, 400):

et Munda, Emathios Italis paritura labores.

With the brief yet highly effective descriptive touches in these two lines, contrast Lucan, VII, 787–846, where he enlarges *ad nauseam* on the horrors of the battle-field.

113. Some editors have attempted to find a place for this line elsewhere, not noticing that its function here is to show that the vision is growing stronger and clearer. At first *Fortuna* sees only undistinguished masses — the panorama of the battle-field, but in 115 she distinguishes individuals (*timentes*), and between the two, as though she were actually coming nearer to the scenes which she describes, the noise of battle begins to reach her ears. Cf. the progressive description of the approaching army, Aesch., *Sept.*, 78 ff.

trepidantes: "excited," "eager," but without the accessory idea of hurried motion which commonly belongs to it in this sense. There is, of course, no notion of fear involved.

114. *Libyae . . . Nile:* for the collocation, cf. Lucan, X, 328 :

qui Libyae te, Nile, negant.

Libyae here = Egyptian. Cf. 63.

gementia castra: camps full of confusion and anguish. Throughout this vision it is the vanquished and the sufferers that *Fortuna* sees.

The reference here is to Caesar's campaigns about the Nile, and possibly also those against Cato and Juba (48–46 B.C.).

115. The battle of Actium was fought near the promontory of that name, in the Ambracian gulf, on

the west coast of Greece, 31 B.C. Octavianus afterwards paid splendid honors to Apollo, one of whose
shrines stood on the promontory, and to whose divine
aid he declared his victory due (Dio, LI, 1). This
battle, decisive for the future of Rome and of the world,
made a profound impression upon the minds of men,
and contemporary writers speak of it as of another
Salamis — as, in some sort, it was. Cf. Verg., *Aen.*,
VIII, 675–728. Hor., *Carm.*, I, 37 ; *Epod.*, 9. Propert.,
IV, 6. Ov., *F.*, I, 709–712.

timentes: substantive : the enemy appalled by the
vision of Apollo in his wrath. Cf. Verg., *Aen.*, VIII,
704–708 :

> Actius haec cernens arcum intendebat Apollo
> desuper : omnis eo terrore Aegyptus et Indi,
> omnis Arabs, omnes vertebant terga Sabaei ;
> ipsa videbatur ventis regina vocatis
> vela dare et laxos iam iamque immittere funis.

With this cf. *Il.*, I, 44 ff., to which Propertius refers
specifically in the poem mentioned above, ll. 33 f. :

> sed quali aspexit Pelopeum Agamemnona vultu,
> egessitque avidis Dorica castra rogis.

It often happens in Latin poetry that a description
will suggest as its inspiration, not the poet's own vision,
but some earlier poem or work of art. (Cf. Byron's
dying gladiator, *Childe Harold*, IV.)˙ Thus Petronius
here clearly had Vergil in mind, as Vergil and Propertius
had looked back to Homer.

116. *Fortuna* is commanding *Dis*.
pande: cf. *Octavia*, 134 f. :

> aut Stygios sinus
> tellure rupta pande.

Sen., *H. O.*, 950 : *laxate manes* (cf. Lucan, III, 17 ; see Introd., p. 77) Sil. Ital., IX, 250 f. :

> pallenti laetus in unda
> laxabat sedem venturis portitor umbris.

sitientia regna: refers to 96 ff. For this reason Crusius wished to read *cruorem* at the end of the line : "realms th rsting for the blood of the world," an emendation as awkward as it is unnecessary.

117. *accerse:* see Introd., p. 48, and l. 158.

navita: the archaic form is common in poetry. Cf. Verg., *Aen.*, VI, 315. Tibull., I, 10, 36. Sen., *Oed.*, 166–170 (all of Charon).

Porthmeus: cf. Eurip., *Alc.*, 253 : νεκύων δὲ πορθμεύς. Juv., III, 266 : *porthmea* (both of Charon).

118. *simulacra virum:* Sil. Ital. uses the same words in XIII, 650, of the shades of Scipio's ancestors. *Simulacrum* is more commonly used of phantoms appearing to men, but cf. Serv., *ad Aen.*, IV, 654 : *esse quoddam simulacrum, quod ad nostri corporis effigiem pictum, inferos petit.* He adds that the poets use *umbra* and *simulacrum* without distinction. *Cf.* Ov., *Met.*, IV, 434 f.

cumba : the *cumba sutilis* of Vergil (*Aen.*, VI, 413 f.).

119. *tuque:* Fortuna apostrophizes Tisiphone, whom *Dis* had mentioned, 97.

120. *pallida Tisiphone:* cf. Verg., *Ge.*, III, 552; *Aen.*, X, 761. Her pallor denotes ferocity and rapacity. Cf. Verg., *Aen.*, III, 217 f. (the Harpies) : *pallida semper | ora fame.* Ov., *Met.*, II, 775 (*Invidia*): *pallor in ore sedet.*

concisaque vulnera mande: cf. Verg., *Aen.*, III, 626 f. (of Polyphemus) :

vidi atro cum membra fluentia tabo
manderet et tepidi tremerent sub dentibus artus.
Ov., *Met.*, XV, 91 ff.:

scilicet in tantis opibus, quas optima matrum
Terra creat, nil te nisi tristia mandere saevo
vulnera dente iuvat ritusque referre Cyclopum ?

Petronius's three words are exactly parallel in feeling to these longer passages, and present a vivid picture of the Fury's ghoulish meal.

121. Cf. *Octavia*, 505 f. :

quantum cruorem Roma tunc vidit sui
lacerata toties !

122. The action changes with dramatic suddenness. Jupiter begins to play his part, and the Lord of Shadows hides from the glare of his lightnings.

With this and the next line cf. Stat., *Theb.*, I, 353 f. :

nec non abrupta tremescunt
fulgura.

123. The cloud quivers as it is rent, the forked lightning is shot out and then cut off from its source.

124. *pater:* "lord." Cf. Vergil's use of *pater Aeneas* when authority, not age, is the point.

gremioque reducto | telluris: drawing the earth (represented as a mantle) together, so as to cover the chasm through which he ascended, 76 ; perhaps also that mentioned in 101.

125. *fraternos . . . ictus:* Jove's thunderbolts.

126. *clades:* as well as *venturaque damna,* refers to the future.

127. Latin literature abounds in tales of prodigies seen in times of national peril. Livy records them conscientiously, remarking, however, that it was perhaps because people were looking for them that they found so many. Cic., *Cat.,* III, 8, 18 f., enumerates those which foretold the great conspiracy. Caesar himself, *B. C.,* III, 105, tells of the portents which were said to have marked the day of Pharsalus. Vergil, *Ge.,* I, 466–488, has a striking passage on those which followed his assassination (cf. Ov., *Met.,* XV, 783 ff., on those which preceded it). For the phenomena to which Petronius refers here, cf. App., *B. C.,* II, 36 :

Τέρατά τε αὐτοῖς ἐπέπιπτε πολλὰ, καὶ σημεῖα οὐράνια, αἷμά τε γὰρ ἔδοξεν ὁ θεὸς ὗσαι. . . . ἄλλα τε πολλὰ δυσχερῆ προσήμαινε τὴν ἐς ἀεὶ τῆς πολιτείας ἀναίρεσίν τε καὶ μεταβολήν.

Petronius's account follows Lucan's most closely (see Introd., p. 77 ff.), but is really a selection from the whole body of tales of such miraculous occurrences.

Shakspere, in *Julius Caesar* and *Macbeth,* has made significant use of similar material.

"Auratus coniicit forte talem versum subsequi debuisse :
nostrum quadriiugi scandens sol aethera curru."

(Anton.)

An excellent example of the way in which the old commentators displayed their learning and ingenuity at
the expense of the poet.

128. *deformis Titan :* the sun, made hideous by the
change in form and color which ushered in the eclipse.
Vergil, *Ge.*, I, 463–468, says of the sun :

> solem quis dicere falsum
> audeat ? ille etiam caecos instare tumultus
> saepe monet fraudemque et operta tumescere bella.
> ille etiam extincto miseratus Caesare Romam,
> cum caput obscura nitidum ferrugine texit
> impiaque aeternum timuerunt saecula noctem.

Titan : Hyperion, the older sun-god, was one of the
Titans. Apollo is sometimes epresented as his son.
Cf. *Titania* for Diana, Ov., *Met.*, III, 173.

129. The emendation *spectare* (Buecheler) seems
necessary. *Sperare putares* implies that the sun is not
yet looking forward to the strife, thus reversing the
obvious meaning of the author. The sun and moon
veil their faces :

> " As if they already stood aghast
> At the bloody work they would look upon."

130. *Cynthia :* the moon, from Mt. Cynthus, on
Delos, where Apollo and Diana were born.

131–132. *rupta . . . iuga:* cf. Verg., *Ge.*, I, 473 :

insolitis tremuerunt motibus Alpes.

Stat., *Theb.*, I, 364 :

saxa iugis fugientia ruptis.

Sen., *Phoen.*, 674 f.

With these lines and 133, cf. Liv., XXII, 5, 8 : *motum terrae qui . . . avertit . . . cursu rapidos amnis . . . montes lapsu ingenti proruit.*

montis : like ὄρος, *mons* may mean a range of mountains as well as a single peak. Cf. *mons Appenninus.*

133. (*nec vaga passim*) *flumina,* etc., appears to be an expansion of the familiar *sistunt amnes* (cf., *e.g.,* Verg., *Ge.*, I, 479 ; *Aen.*, IV, 489), one of the commonest of prodigies, but the expression is involved and obscure, the relation of the parts to the whole and each other difficult to discover. The most probable interpretation is : "and the rivers, no longer spreading far and wide, crept feebly along their beds." But even here the difficulty remains that the words *vaga passim,* which in themselves suggest an opposition to *per notas ripas,* are made to mean no more than the free movement of the full current, for *morientia* is, of course, contrasted with the normal state of things, not with anything unusual, such as a flood. The emendation *torrentia* (Reichardt. Cf. Verg., *Ecl.*, VII, 52 : *torrentia flumina ripas*) is good, but so long as the received text can be explained by allowing for a little, not excessive, carelessness, it is better to adhere to it.

For *morientia*, cf. Manil., IV, 625 :

> litora Niliacis iterum morientia ripis.

"the coast-line losing itself in the banks (*i.e.* mouths) of the Nile."

notas ripas: cf. Hor., *Carm.*, IV, 2, 6 (Anton).

134–136. *armorum strepitu:* a common omen of war or other peril. Cf. Verg., *Ge.*, I, 474 f. :

> armorum sonitum toto Germania caelo
> audiit.

Tibull., II, 5, 73. Ov., *Met.*, XV, 783–785. Stat., *Theb.*, III, 423. Avien., *Descr. Orb. Terr.*, 1374. Caes., *B. C.*, III, 105, 4. Cic., *de Harusp. Resp.*, 10. *Val. Max.*, I, 6, 12. Dio, XXXIX, 20, 2.

tuba . . . tremefacta ciet: cf. 271 and German *schmettern* used of the sound of the trumpet. The many strange readings found in the Mss. or supplied by conjecture have inspired still stranger explanations. Perhaps the wildest is *sideribus trinis* or *tribus acta*, in which Burmann saw an allusion to the Triumvirate. He compared Florus, III, 21, 3 : *tribus . . . sideribus agitatum est*, where, however, the reference is to successive stages of the war between Marius and Sulla, marked by increasing ferocity.

sideribus: from the heavens.

voratur: cf. Hor., *Carm.*, III, 4, 75 :

> nec peredit
> impositam celer ignis Aetnen.

App. Verg., Aetna, 113.

ignibus insolitis: cf. 180, Ch. 136, 6, 5 : *planctibus insolitis.* Verg., *Ge.*, I, 475: *insolitis . . . motibus.*

For descriptions of Aetna in eruption, cf. Verg., *Ge.*, I, 471–473 ; *Aen.*, III, 571–582.

in aethera fulmina: a daring expression, depicting the violence of the eruption, which seemed to reverse the order of nature, and dart lightnings from earth to heaven.

137–138. Cf. Verg., *Ge.*, I, 476 ff. :

> vox quoque per lucos vulgo exaudita silentis
> ingens, et simulacra modis pallentia miris
> visa sub obscurum noctis.

Sen., *Thy.*, 671 f. ; Stat., *Theb.*, I, 36 f. :

> tumulisque carentia regum
> funera.

and VII, 409.

Anton, cf. Lactant., II, 2, 6.

stridore: it has been pointed out that this word is regularly applied to the sound supposed to be made by ghosts. Cf. Acc., *Alc.* (Prisc., p. 867 P).

> cum strideret retracta rursus inferis.

Stat., *Theb.*, IX, 299 :

> stridebit vestros Tydeus inhumatus ad ignes.

Lucan, VI, 623 (see Introd., p. 80). As a charm to raise the dead, Tibull., I, 2, 47.

It will be observed that Petronius here brings upon the scene the shades both of the duly buried, and the unburied, dead. The latter would be by far the more malignant, but the presence of the former would be the greater prodigy.

139. *incendia:* the blazing tail of the comet. Cf. Verg., *Ge.*, I, 486 f. :

> non alias caelo ceciderunt plura sereno
> fulgura nec diri totiens arsere cometae.

Ov., *Met.*, XV, 787. Claud., *Bell. Get.*, 241 ff. (Anton).

140. Blood falling in rain or gushing from springs is another frequently recurring portent. Cf. Verg., *Ge.*, I, 485. Ov., *Met.*, XV, 788. Stat., *Theb.*, VII, 408. Claud., *in Eutrop.*, I, 4 ff. :

> nimboque minacem
> sanguineo rubuisse Iovem. puteosque cruore
> mutatos.

App. (quoted on 127).

rubens: the Mss. are almost unanimous in favor of *recens*. But *recens* makes no sense except as a transferred epithet, — for "fresh blood," — and even there it seems unduly forced. *Rubens*, on the other hand, has, as Anton points out, the support of Claudian, quoted above, and is strikingly appropriate. It might have been corrupted to *repens* at a very early period, and this in turn corrected to *recens*.

descendit Iuppiter imbre: cf. Verg., *Ecl.*, VII, 60 :

> Iuppiter et laeto descendet plurimus imbre.

Jupiter here appears in the original character of the Sky. Cf. Hor., quoted on 148, and App., on 127.

141. *solvit:* "performed" as an official duty.

142. *moras:* his hesitation about beginning the war, cf. 158 f.

vindictaeque actus amore: cf. Florus, IV, 2, 17 : *his* (the acts of the Senate) *Caesar agitatus, statuit praemia armorum armis defendere.* But see notes on 158.

143. Gaul had been finally "pacified" some time before the civil war began (cf. Florus, IV, 2, 23 : *nihil hostile erat in Gallia: pacem ipse fecerat*), but Petronius, as a poet, naturally ignores the last uneventful months of Caesar's proconsulship, and the fruitless negotiations with the Senate which occupied the close of 50 B.C. By a further poetic license he represents the Alps, and not the Rubicon, as the barrier which Caesar crossed as his first overt act of war.

proiecit: the regular word for throwing anything away. In military language it means "ground arms," a sense to which the author has not adhered in this line.

144–145. With the following description cf. Sil. Ital., III, 479–493 :

cuncta gelu canaque aeternum grandine tecta
atque aevi glacie cohibent : riget ardua montis
aetherii facies ; surgentique obvia Phoebo,
duratas nescit flammis mollire pruinas.
quantum Tartareus regni pallentis hiatus
ad manes imos atque atrae stagna paludis
a supera tellure patet ; tam longa per auras
erigitur tellus, et caelum intercipit umbra.
nullum ver usquam, nullique aestatis honores.
sola iugis habitat diris, sedesque tuetur

perpetuas, deformis hiems : illa undique nubes
huc atras agit et mixtos cum grandine nimbos.   490.

*   *   *   *   *   *

abeuntque in nubila montes.   493.

IV, 742–746 :

protinus aerii praeceps rapit aggere montis.
horrebat glacie saxa inter lubrica, summo
piniferum caelo miscens caput, Appenninus.
condiderat nix alta trabes, et vertice celso
canus apex structa surgebat ad astra pruina.

Alpibus aeriis: cf. Verg., *Ge.*, III, 474 : *aerias Alpes.*
Ov., *Met.*, II, 226 : *aeriaeque Alpes.* Lucan, I, 689 :
aeriam Pyrenen.

Graio numine pulsae: "the rocks [once] trodden by
the Greek divinity." *Pulsae* here = *calcatae.* See on
152. Reiske's emendation, while very slight, improves
the line greatly. *Graio nomine pulsae . . . rupes*
would mean : "the weather-beaten rocks (cf. Verg.,
Aen., IV, 249), by name *Graiae*," but the construction
is grievously strained. *Graio nomine pulso*, etc. :
"*Alpes Graiarum nomine amisso magis descendunt in
planitiem, et maritimae vocari incipiunt*" (Wernsdorff)
may be right, but *pellere* seems too strong for the
meaning attached to it.

The *Alpes Graiae* were supposed to take their name
from Hercules, the first traveler to cross them (cf.
Nepos, *Han.*, III, 4), but the name was probably of
Celtic origin, and certainly had nothing to do with
Greece.

146. *est locus:* cf. 67.

Herculis aris sacer: in the maritime Alps, near the present Monaco. Cf. Sil. Ital., I, 585 f. :

> Herculei ponto coepere exsistere colles,
> et nebulosa iugis attollere saxa Monoeci.

Verg., *Aen.*, VI, 830 f.

147. *claudit:* "blocks."

vertice tollit: sc. se. Verg., *Aen.*, XII, 703. :

> vertice se attollens pater Appenninus ad auras.

148. *caelum illic cecidisse:* because of the accumulated masses of snow. Cf. Hor., *Epod.*, XIII, 1 f. :

> imbres
> nivesque deducunt Iovem.

Also because, to one looking up at the heights, the sky appears to rest upon them.

solis adulti: "the blazing sun," at midday or in summer. Cf. Sen., *H. O.*, 1289 f. :

> vincitque faces
> solis adulti glaciale iubar.

Apul., *Met.*, XI, 24 : *flammis adulta fax.*

Cf. also Sen., *Med.*, 589 ff. :

> aut ubi rivos nivibus solutis
> sole iam forti, medioque vere
> tabuit Haemus.

149. *mansuescit:* "grows soft," "melts."

150. *glacie concreta rigent:* cf. 200 : *concreta gelu.*

N

Verg., *Aen.* IV, 251 (Atlas) : *glacie riget horrida barba.*
Liv., XXI, 36, 8 : *alte concreta glacie.* Stat., *Theb.*,
III, 672 : *exuti concreto frigore montes.* Neither
riget nor *rigens* will agree with *concreta* (neuter plural),
but *rigent* (*sc. omnia*) solves the difficulty, the change
of subject being perfectly natural.

151. Cf. 147. Cf. Verg., *Aen.*, IV, 247 (Atlas) :

> caelum qui vertice fulcit.

umeris minitantibus: towering threateningly into
the sky. Cf. Verg., *Aen.*, I, 162 f. : *minantur in caelum
scopuli.*
Sidon. Apoll., *C.*, V, 511 :

> Alpes marmoreas, atque occurrentia iuncto
> saxa polo.

orbem: the heavenly sphere, supported by Atlas.
152. *calcavit . . . iuga:* cf. Sil. Ital., XI, 217 f. (of
Hannibal) :

> cui patuere Alpes, saxa impellentia caelum
> atque uni calcata deo.

XVII, 319 f. :

> turmae, vidi certantia caelo
> quas iuga calcantes, summas volitare per Alpes ?

Calcare is used because the crossing of the Alps is
thought of as a remarkable feat ; the trampling under
foot of what should have been an insurmountable
barrier. See on 87–93 (Pliny). Cf. Sen., *Hipp.*, 234 f.
milite: "soldiery." So often in poetry. Cf. Verg.

Aen., II, 495 : *loca milite complent*, and Sil. Ital. (quoted on 111–112 and 203).

laeto: Caesar (*B. C.*, I, 7) speaks of the loyal response of the Thirteenth Legion to his speech at Ravenna : *conclamant . . . milites . . . sese paratos esse imperatoris sui tribunorumque plebis iniurias defendere*, but avoids anything which might suggest unseemly eagerness on their part.

153. *optavitque locum:* cf. Verg., *Aen.*, III, 109 : (*Teucrus*) *optavit locum regno*. The ordinary military term was *locum castris deligere* (*e.g.* Caes., *B. G.*, II, 18). Moessler reads *purgavitque* on the strength of Liv., XXI, 37, 1 (of Hannibal's passage of the Alps) : *castra in iuga posita, aegerrime ad id ipsum loco purgato, tantum nivis fodiendum atque egerendum fuit*. But the author is not insisting upon the difficulties of the way here as in 185 ff., and *optavit* is not only nearer the Mss. but more natural. A Roman commander would, of course, have made the selection of a camping-ground the first consideration at the end of a march (though he would not necessarily attend to it himself), but a man in Caesar's mood, looking down on the land which had disowned him and now lay at his mercy, would hardly wait the leisure of the snow-shoveling squad to give rein to his feelings.

154. Cf. Liv., XXI, 35, 8: *praegressus signa Hannibal in promuntorio quodam, unde longe ac late prospectus erat, consistere iussis militibus Italiam ostentat subiectosque Alpinis montibus circumpadanos campos, moeniaque eos tum transcendere non Italiae modo sed etiam urbis Romanae*.

Sil. Ital., III, 418 : *late prospectat Iberos.*

155. *intentans cum voce manus ad sidera:* the regular attitude of prayer among the ancients. Cf., *e.g., Il.,* I, 450 :

τοῖσιν δὲ Χρύσης μεγάλ᾽ εὔχετο χεῖρας ἀνασχών.

Verg., *Aen.,* II, 687 f. :

at pater Anchises oculos ad sidera laetus .
extulit et caelo palmas cum voce tetendit.

X, 667 :

et duplices cum voce manus ad sidera tendit.

Ov., *Met.,* VI, 368 ; and the phrase *manus supinae* (Verg., *Aen.,* III, 176 f. Hor., *Carm.,* III, 23, 1). It was also the attitude of the worshiping Hebrew (Ps. xxviii., 2 ; lxiii., 4 ; lxxxviii., 9 ; cxli., 2).

This use of *intentans* instead of *tendens* or *intendens* seems to be without parallel in Latin literature. *Intentare manus in aliquid* is used of threatening gestures, *e.g. in oculos,* Petr., Ch. 9, 6 ; 95, 8 ; 108, 5. For this reason de Salas saw in the line a defiance hurled at the gods from the vantage-ground of the Alpine summit, a view hardly to be reconciled with what follows. O*thers, following Trag., have read *intendens.* It may b. assumed, however, that Petronius, following the tendency of the Plebeian Latin of which he had used so much in his narrative, substituted a stronger word for the one regularly employed in this phrase.

156-176. This speech, delivered at the top of the Alpine pass, corresponds to the one actually made at

Ravenna (or possibly Ariminum) in January, 49, when the news of the flight of the Tribunes reached Caesar (see on 152 and 288 f.). For his own account of the Ravenna speech, see *B. C.*, I, 7. Before Pharsalus he said :

differendum est iter in praesentia nobis et de proelio cogitandum, sicut semper depoposcimus. animo sumus ad dimicandum parati; non facilę occasionem postea reperiemus (III, 85).

and before giving the order to charge :

commemoravit testibus se militibus uti posse, quanto studio pacem petisset . . . neque se umquam abuti militum sanguine neque rem publicam alterutro exercitu privare voluisse (90).

For Lucan's version of these speeches, see Introd., p. 80 ff.

156. *Saturnia Tellus:* a very ancient and therefore very solemn form of address. Varro, *L. L.*, V, 7, 42, says that the *Capitolium* was early called *Mons Saturnius, et ab eo late Saturniam terram, ut etiam Ennius appellat* (see below). Cf. Festus, p. 322. Enn., *Ann.*, I, 25. Ov., *F.*, V, 625. Vergil uses the epithet repeatedly, most impressively, *Ge.*, II, 173 f. :

> salve magna parens frugum, Saturnia tellus,
> magna virum !

Caesar's manner of addressing his country shows *pietas*, not the feelings of a ruthless invader. Lucan also does him this grace. Cf. I, 199 ff. (see Introd., p. 80).

157. *onerata: ornata, honestata* (Erhard). Plays on *honos* and *onus* are frequent in Latin. Cf. Liv., XXII, 30, 4 : *plebeiscitum, quo oneratus sum magis quam honoratus.* Ov., *Her.*, IX, 31. Varro, *L. L.*, V, 10, 73. Auson., *Protrept*, 97 ff. Sidon. Apoll., *Epp.*, VII, 9, 7. Rutil. Lup., I, 3. Cf. also the Ms. reading *sub honore* in 118. See p. 248.

triumphis: is not used in the technical sense, as Caesar celebrated no triumphs until after the civil war (in 46 and 45), but refers to his victorious campaigns in Gaul and the *supplicationes* decreed by the Senate *ex litteris Caesaris* (*B. G.*, II, 35 ; VII, 90). Cf. Cic., *de Prov. Cons.*, X, 24 : *C. Caesari supplicationes decrevistis, numero, ut nemini uno ex bello ; honore ut omnino nemini.* Suet., *Iul.*, 24. See on 163.

158. *testor:* most editors read *te* in 156 to supply an object. But the change from the Mss. reading is unnecessary, as is shown by other cases of *testor* used absolutely. *E.g.* Verg., *Aen.*, II, 431 f.:

> Iliaci cineres et flamma extrema meorum,
> testor in occasu vestro nec tela nec ullas
> vitavisse vices Danaum.

Lucan, VII, 91 f. :

testor, Roma, tamen : Magnum, quo cuncta perirent accepisse diem.

So also μαρτύρομαι : Thuc., VI, 80, 3. Lucian, *Timon*, 46 (160).

acies: loosely used for "battles," as the meaning of

triumphus is stretched in 157 and 163, and that of *tropaeum* in 172. See Introd., p. 51.

invitum: Caesar always maintained that the war was forced upon him. Cf. *B. C.*, III, 90 (see on 156–176). Looking at the dead after Pharsalus, he said to those about him : *hoc voluerunt. tantis rebus gestis C. Caesar condemnatus essem, nisi ab exercitu auxilium petissem* (Suet., *Iul.*, 30, quoting from Asinius Pollio, who was present at the time. Cf. Plut., *Caes.*, 46). His moderation both during the war and afterwards, often in the face of extreme provocation, is a strong proof of his sincerity. Cf. also Hirtius, Book VIII of the *Bell. Gall.*, the closing sentence : *Caesar omnia patienda esse statuit quoad sibi spes aliqua relinqueretur iure potius disceptandi quam belligerandi.*

accersere: though found in a minority of the Mss., is undoubtedly to be preferred to the more formal *arcessere* here as in 117. The real Caesar always used *arcessere* in his writings, as does Vergil, *Aen.*, X, 11 :

adveniet iustum pugnae (ne arcessite) tempus.

But Petronius has *accersere* throughout his prose (Chs. 37, 101, 102, 139), and as it is also Lucan's choice (I, 166; IV, 484; VII, 252: the last in Caesar's speech at Pharsalus), there is every reason to believe that it was used here as well.

159. *ferre manus:* cf. Verg., *Aen.*, V, 402 f.:

Eryx in proelia suetus
ferre manum.   (Anton.)

But *manus* is here modified by *invitas*, and the expression has not the same stereotyped appearance as the Vergilian phrase, which is probably a bit of sporting language.

vulnere: the injustice with which he had been treated. As the end of his term of office in Gaul approached, the Senate refused to allow him to stand for the consulship unless he made his canvass in person, a requirement which involved disbanding his troops without a triumph, and putting himself at the mercy of his enemies by returning to Rome as a private citizen; and all this in violation of promises which had been made to him. Not content with this, the Senate finally ordered him to disband his army without waiting for the arrival of his successor in office, on pain of being declared a rebel. When, following this decree, the Tribunes who had been expelled from Rome for attempting to veto it took refuge with him (see on 288 f.), he crossed the Rubicon and commenced hostilities.

160. *pulsus:* Caesar does not speak by the card. He was not cast out, but shut out, or rather his return was made to depend upon conditions which it would have been suicidal to accept (see on 159, and his own words quoted on 158).

urbe mea: cf. 166 and Lucan's *Caesar ubique tuus . . . miles* (see Introd., p. 80).

Rhenum . . . tinguo: cf. Ov., *Tr.*, IV, 2, 42:

decolor ipse suo sanguine Rhenus erit.

Caesar's words are literally true, as after the defeat of

Ariovistus in 58, and again after that of the Usipetes and
Tencteri in 55, the routed Germans had been driven by
thousands into the Rhine. But the words are meant to
cover, not only these battles, but all his successes against
the Germans. Petronius mentions them again in 163
and 214, throwing the emphasis on this part of Caesar's
work, although the battle had really been against the
Gauls. This is but natural in a poet of his times, for
Gaul, the terror of the Republic (see on 161) soon
became a loyal member of the Empire, while Germany,
in spite of hollow triumphs and high-sounding titles
bestowed on those who had crossed her borders and lived
to tell the tale, loomed ever more formidable on the
horizon.

With *sanguine tinguo* cf. 294.

161. *iterum:* referring to the sack of Rome by the
Gauls in 390 B.C. Until Caesar completed his conquest,
the fear of another Gallic invasion was never far from
Roman thoughts. Hence the enthusiasm which his
victories aroused and the unprecedented honors voted
him by the Senate, in spite of his many bitter enemies
among its members (see on 157). Cf. Cic., *de Prov.
Cons.*, 13 f.: *nemo sapienter de re publica nostra cogita-
vit iam inde a principio huius imperi, quin Galliam
maxime timendam huic imperio putaret . . . restitimus
semper lacessiti. nunc denique est perfectum ut imperi
nostri terrarumque illarum idem esset extremum. Alpibus Italiam munierat antea natura non sine aliquo divino
numine; nam si ille aditus Gallorum immanitati multi-
tudinique patuisset numquam haec urbs summo imperio*

domicilium ac sedem praebuisset. quae iam licet con-
sidant, nihil est enim ultra illam altitudinem montium
usque ad Oceanum quod sit Italiae pertimescendum. Cf.
App., *B. C.*, II, 41 (quoted on 292); Lucan I, 307 f.
(Introd., p. 81).

162. *Alpibus excludo:* keep them on their own
ground, behind the barrier of the Alps.

vincendo certior exul: for similar paradoxes, cf. Hor.,
Carm., III, 5, 48 : *egregius exul* (Regulus). Lucan, VII,
256 : *vetitos remeare triumphos.* Sen., *H. F.*, 249:
orbe defenso caret.

163. Cf. Cic., *Marcell.*, 28 : *obstupescent posteri certe*
imperia, provincias, Rhenum, Oceanum, Nilum, pugnas
innumerabiles, incredibiles victorias, monumenta, munera,
triumphos audientes et legentes tuos.

sanguine Germano: see on 160, 214.

sexagintaque triumphis: "a hundred battles." *Sexa-*
ginta is used as a round number (see Wölflin, *Das Duo-*
decimalsystem, Archiv, IX, 537–599). Cf. Cic., *Deiot.*,
4, 12 : *itaque Cn. Pompeii bella, victorias, triumphos,*
consulatus, admirantes numerabamus, tuos enumerare
non possumus. Historians give Caesar's victories over
foreign enemies as upwards of 50 (Solin., I, 100 f. Plin.,
H. N., VII, 25. Plut., *Caes.*, 15).

164. *esse nocens coepi:* I began to appear guilty at
Rome. For the form of expression, see Introd., p. 43.

gloria: Caesar's greatness.

165. *bella vident:* anticipate war, *i.e.* fear that Caesar
will commit some violence against the state unless his
power is broken. It was with this fear as an excuse that

the Senate forced upon Caesar the war which destroyed its power forever.

mercedibus emptae: the old commentators referred this to Pompey's foreign troops, citing App., *B. C.*, II, 34 and 74. Also Lucan, X, 407 f. :

> nulla fides pietasque viris qui castra sequuntur
> venalesque manus. ibi fas, ubi maxima merces.

But, as the next line clearly shows, the reference is to the mongrel *populus*, ready to sell their votes to the highest bidder. Cf. 39 above : *emptique Quirites*, and Lucan, I, 314, where Caesar at Ariminum calls Pompey's partisans *empti clientes*.

166. *viles operae:* for the adjective, cf. Lucan, V, 263 : *viles animas. Operae* was employed euphemistically for men engaged in dishonest political work. Cf. Cic., *Phil.*, I, 9, 22 : *operas mercennarias. Pro Sest.*, 17, 38 : *erat mihi contentio cum operis conductis et ad diripiendam urbem concitatis.* Suet., *Aug.*, 3 : *divisores operasque campestres.* It could not properly be applied to foreign troops or to the class referred to in Caes., *B. C.*, I, 3 : *omnes amici consulum, necessarii Pompeii atque eorum qui veteres inimicitias cum Caesare gerebant in senatum coguntur.* (Anton.)

quorum . . . noverca: these words, inappropriate in the mouth of the democratic leader Caesar, are imitated from the younger Scipio's famous rebuke to the angry populace : *taceant, quibus Italia noverca est . . . non efficietis ut solutos verear quos alligatos adduxi.* (Val. Max., VI, 2, 3.) Cf. Vell. Pat., II, 4, 4. Plut.,

Apophtheg., p. 201 F. *De Viris Illustr.* (ascribed to Aurel. Victor), LVIII, 8. · In Plato, *Menex.*, p. 237 B, occur the words : αὐτόχθονας, καὶ τῷ ὄντι ἐν πατρίδι οἰκοῦντας καὶ ζῶντας, καὶ τρεφομένους οὐχ ὑπὸ μητρυιᾶς, ὡς οἱ ἄλλοι, ἀλλ' ὑπὸ μητρὸς, τῆς χώρας ἐν ᾗ ᾤκουν.

(P. Wesseling.)

quorum: agrees with the sense of *operae; emptae*, 165, with its grammatical gender.

mea Roma: love of country and pride of birth speak together in this possessive.

167. *sine vindice:* with impunity.

168. *(dextram) vinciet:* cf. Sil. Ital., II, 48 (Hannibal to his soldiers on the demand of the Roman envoys) :

(me) evincta lacerandum tradite dextra.

dextram refers to the custom of handcuffing a prisoner to his guard. Cf. Stat., *Theb.*, XII, 460 : *dextras* . . . *insertare catenis.* Sen., *de Tranq. Animi*, 10, 2 f.

ignavus: perhaps a thrust at Pompey, as no longer fit for war. Cf. Lucan, I, 311 ff.

ite furentes: cf. Lucan, X, 393 : *ite feroces.* Moessler objects that *furentes* is not in keeping with Caesar's character. But it is in no way at odds with the conventional picture of him, with its mixture of demigod and Cyclops. Lucan's Caesar ranges freely from lofty chivalry to brutal savagery. Moreover, the word, as Anton remarks, is so commonly applied to fighting men that it becomes a mere conventional epithet. Cf. Lucan, II, 439: *Caesar in arma furens.* Verg., *Aen.*, I, 491; IV, 42 f. Stat., *Theb.*, VI, 788; XII, 763. Val. Flacc., I, 144.

169. *mei comites* = the *commilitones* with which Caesar addressed his men (Suet., *Iul.*, 67).

causam dicite ferro: cf. Ch. 112, 6 : (*militem*) *gladio ius dicturum ignaviae suae.*

causam dicere: the technical phrase for pleading a case is here used ironically by Caesar, who had been forced to appeal to the sword and who realized fully the truth of the saying : *silent leges inter arma* (Cic., *pro Mil.*, IV, 11). Cf. Plut., *Caes.*, 35 : οὐκ ἔφη τὸν αὐτὸν ὅπλων καὶ νόμων καιρὸν εἶναι (see on 292). Cf. also Plut., *Pomp.*, 10. The expression was perhaps suggested by the anecdote found in Plut., *Caes.*, 29, of officers sent from Cisalpine Gaul to represent Caesar's claims before the Senate : λέγεται τινὰ τῶν ἀφιγμένων παρ᾽αὐτοῦ ταξιαρχῶν, . . . πυθόμενον, ὡς οὐ δίδωσιν ἡ γερουσία Καίσαρι χρόνον τῆς ἀρχῆς· Ἀλλ᾽ αὕτη, φάναι, δώσει· κρούσαντα τῃ χειρὶ τὴν λαβὴν τῆς μαχαίρας. (Also *Pomp.*, 58.) Cf. App., *B. C.*, II, 25, where the retort is ascribed to Caesar himself. Suet., *Aug.*, 26, and Dio, XLVI, 43, tell it of the officers of Octavianus. Cf. also Caesar's forcible entrance into the Treasury at Rome (see on 292).

170. *crimen:* the charge or charges which would be brought against Caesar by his enemies if he returned to Rome as a private citizen. His fall would not only deprive his men of their promised rewards, but expose them to punishment as his accomplices.

vocat: sc. *in periculum* or *in iudicium.*

171. *reddenda est gratia:* for the commoner *gratiam referre.*

172. *non solus vici:* cf. Caes., *B. G.*, I, 40 : *Cimbris et Teutonis a C. Mario pulsis, non minorem laudem exercitus quam ipse imperator meritus vi ebatur.*

Lucan, VII, 264 f. (Introd., p. 83).

Caesar was always most generous in recognizing the services of his officers and men.

poena: cf. Lucan, VII, 303 (Introd., p. 84).

tropaeis: "victories." Cf. *triumphis*, 157 and 163.

173. *sordes:* lit. "dirt," then used of the mourning assumed by persons arraigned on a serious charge, which etiquette decreed should be as shabby and squalid as possible, the whole custom running directly counter to our notions of self-respecting conduct. Cf. Cic., *pro Clu.*, 18, *praesto est mulier . . . crudelis, . . . squalore huius et sordibus laetatur.*

meruit: the regular word for military service, forms an effective contrast with *sordes.* The service which should have led to a triumph threatens to lead to disgrace.

174. *iudice . . . alea:* based on the story of Caesar's words at the Rubicon : *eatur, inquit, quo deorum ostenta et inimicorum iniquitas vocat. iacta est alea.* (Suet., *Iul.*, 32. Cf. Plut., *Caes.*, 32. App., *B. C.*, II, 35). Cf. Lucan, VI, 6–8 (Caesar at Dyrrachium) :

> funestam mundo votis petit omnibus horam
> in casum quae cuncta ferat : placet alea fati
> alterutrum mersura caput.

VI, 603 : *alea fati.* At the Rubicon he makes Caesar say :

te, Fortuna, sequor. procul hinc iam foedera sunto
credidimus fatis. utendum est iudice bello.   (I, 226 f.)

sumite bellum: cf. 283. Ch. 89, 62 : *bellumque
sumunt.* Florus, IV, 12, 24 : *hoc velut sacramento sump-
serant bellum.* Shakspere, *Twelfth Night*, V, 1 : "Take
thy fortunes up."

175. *temptate:* cf. Ch. 89, 58 : *temptant in armis se
duces.* (Burmann.)

causa peracta est: "my case is won," legal language
again. Cf. Ch. 137, 9, 6 :

> et peragat causas, sitque Catone prior.

Cic., *Sest.*, 87. Hor., *Serm.*, I, 10, 26. Ascon., *in Mil.*,
47, 95.   In the language of the arena, *peractum est*
meant just the opposite of this : "it's all up" *sc.* with
the defeated gladiator. Seneca is inordinately fond of
the phrase in this sense, putting it into the mouths of
many of his tragic heroes and heroines.

176. With the lofty confidence here expressed, cf. the
latter part of the speech by which Caesar brought his
panic-stricken and mutinous soldiers to their senses on
the eve of his campaign against Ariovistus (*B. G.*, I, 40).

177. *personuit:* for a more reasonable use of the word,
cf. Claud., *de Bell. Get.*, 450 f. :

> ipso Roma die (nec adhuc ostenditur auctor)
> personuit venisse ducem.

Delphicus ales: either the raven or the falcon, both of
which were sacred to Apollo. For the former, cf. Ov.,
Met., II, 544 ff. : for the latter, *Od.*, XV, 525 f.

178. *omina . . . dedit:* in such expressions as this
do = facio and represents the survival of a verb akin to
τίθημι.   It is used in a great many phrases by Lucretius
and Vergil (see Munro's note to Lucr., IV, 41).
Sometimes in a given phrase *facere* and *dare* are inter-
changeable, as with *potestatem,* to give permission or
opportunity.

pepulitque . . . auras: part of the omens, which were
derived from both the movements and the cries of birds.
Cf. Eurip., *Hipp.,* 1058 f.; and Soph., *O. T.,* 965 f.
Verg., *Aen.,* III, 361 :

> et volucrum linguas et praepetis omina pennae.

de Salas, cf. Suet., *Vitell.,* 9 : *praemisso agmini laetum
evenit auspicium; siquidem a parte dextra repente aquila
advolavit,* and *Claud.,* 7.

With the omen of the bird, confirmed by manifesta-
tions on the left, cf. Cic., *Div.,* I, 48 (a poetical fragment
on Marius, who sees an eagle kill a serpent) :

> hanc ubi praepetibus pinnis lapsuque volantem
> conspexit Marius, divini numinis augur,
> faustaque signa suae laudis reditusque notavit,
> partibus intonuit caeli pater ipse sinistris :
> sic aquilae clarum firmavit Iuppiter omen.

179–180. *horrendi nemoris:* a grove of awful sanctity.
Petronius has forgotten that his hero is among the
eternal snows.

de parte sinistra: the Romans, contrary to the

Greeks, generally regarded omens from the left as favorable. Cf. Enn., *Fr.*, 527 :

> tum tonuit laevum bene tempestate serena.

Cic., *Div.*, II, 39. Dion. Hal., II, 5. Nonius, p. 51 M. Donat., *ad Aen.*, II, 693. In poetry, however, the Greek view is sometimes adopted without warning. *E.g.* contrast Verg., *Aen.*, II, 54 and 693.

insolitae voces: cf. the story of Aius Locutius or Loquens, Cic., *Div.*, II, 32, 69. For the adjective, cf. 136.

flamma . . . sequenti: of course merely the harmless appearance of fire, as in Verg., *Aen.*, II, 680 ff. Liv., I, 39, 1–2.

181–182. *nitor Phoebi:* the shining face of the sun. *laetior:* more brilliant than usual. Cf. Verg., *Aen.*, I, 228 f. : *tristior . . . adloquitur Venus. Latior,* the reading of most of the Mss., is not only flat, but tautological with *vulgato . . . orbe,* "with disc fully revealed," and *crevit,* "appeared larger than usual."

183. *Mavortia signa: signa militaria.*

184. de Salas, cf. Sil. Ital., III, 516 f. :

> rumpit inaccessos aditus, atque ardua primus
> exsuperat.

Four readings may be derived from the Mss. : *insolito gressu . . . ausus; insolitos gressus . . . ausu; insolito gressus . . . ausu;* and *insolitos gressu . . . ausus.* The first two give undue emphasis to *gressus* or *gressu.* In the third, *gressus ausu occupare* is an inversion which weakens instead of strengthening the line. The last form, however, restores things to their proper balance :

o

Caesar, striding ahead, takes the initiative in this un-
accustomed enterprise (civil war). *Gressu prior occupat* belong together. *Gressu prior* describes Caesar's
impetuous action. *Prior occupat* — the adjective
"squints" — is like Vergil's: *occupat Aeneas aditum*
(*Aen.*, VI, 424), and refers to his anticipating the action
of the other party. In this sense *occupo* = φθάνω,
which is also at times strengthened by the addition of
πρῶτος (*e.g.* Xen., *An.*, III, 4, 20).

185–186. *vincta . . . humus:* cf. *nimbos . . . ligatos*, 187, and *undarum vincula*, 188.

pruina: cf. Sil. Ital. (quoted on 144–145).

non pugnavit . . . quievit: the ice remains firm and
quiet, in contrast to what follows. "Offered no
resistance" at first seems strange in this connection,
but as a matter of fact it is when the ice breaks that
the struggle commences and progress is impeded. *Mitique horrore* contrasts the slight "scrunching" sound
made by marching over the firm crust with the noise of
cracking ice and falling bodies which follows.

187 ff. On the relation of this passage to Liv., XXI,
35–36 and 58, see Introd., p. 38. Cf. 35, 12:

omnis enim ferme via praeceps, angusta, lubrica erat,
ut neque sustinere se a lapsu possent, nec, qui paulum
titubassent, haerere adflicti vestigio suo, aliique super alios
et iumenta in homines occiderent. 36, 6 ff. : *ut vero tot*
hominum iumentorumque incessu dilapsa est (nix), per
nudam infra glaciem fluentemque tabem liquescentis nivis
ingrediebantur. taetra ibi luctatio erat lubrica glacie non

recipiente vestigium et in prono citius pedes fallent? . . .
ita in levi tantum glacie tabidaque nive volutabantur.
iumenta secabant interdum etiam infimam ingredientia
nivem, et prolapsa iactandis gravius in conitendo ungulis
penitus perfringebant, ut pleraque velut pedica capta
haererent in dura et alte concreta glacie. 58, 3 ff. : *vento*
mixtus imber cum ferretur in ipsa ora . . . tum vero
ingenti sono caelum strepere et inter horrendos fragores
micare ignes . . . tandem effuso imbre, cum `eo magis
accensa vis venti esset . . . et mox aqua levata vento cum
super gelida montium iuga concreta esset, tantum nivosae
grandinis deiecit ut omnibus omissis procumberent homi-
nes. Sil. Ital., III, 547 ff. :

> mutatur iam forma locis. hic sanguine multo
> infectae rubuere nives: hic nescia vinci
> paulatim glacies cedit tepefacta cruore ;
> dumque premit sonipes duro vestigia cornu
> ungula perfossis haesit comprensa pruinis.
> nec pestis lapsus simplex : abscissa relinquunt
> membra gelu ; fractosque asper rigor amputat artus.

IV, 749–752 :

> scandunt praerupti nimbosa cacumina saxi ;
> nec superasse iugum finit mulcetve laborem.
> plana natant, putrique gelu liquentibus undis
> invia limosa restagnant arva palude.

187. *nimbos . . . ligatos:* ice.

188. *pavidus:* an important word. The horses
have been frightened by finding themselves on treach-

erous ground, and their plunging and trampling increases the strain on the ice (cf. Liv. on 187 ff.).

undarum vincula: frozen streams which the army is crossing. The author's topography is not consistent.

189. *incaluere:* melted. Cf. *tepefacta,* Sil. Ital., (quoted on 187 ff.).

flumina: apparently cascades fed by the melting snows, not the streams indicated in 188.

190–193. The expression here is obscure and the idea fantastic. Petronius appears to mean that for a short time the melting snow and ice ran down in streams, then froze with miraculous suddenness into irregular masses more difficult to cross than the former smooth and slippery surface.

190. *iussa:* as though by divine command. Anton cf. Lucan, X, 216 f.: *Oceanus . . . iussus adest.* Things so described are, of course, represented as in a vassal state.

191. *vincta . . . ruina:* the frozen torrent. Moessler cf. Lucan, VI, 348 f.: *subitaeque ruinam | sensit aquae Nereus.*

stupuere: hung motionless.

192. *paulo ante:* modifying *lues* and opposed to *iam* (cf. the Greek οἱ τότε ἄνθρωποι). "What was recently flowing freely was now hard and solid."

lues: the melted snow and ice.

concidenda: this was no half-frozen slush, but solid ice which would yield only to edged tools.

193. *male fida prius:* treacherous before: its present state was worse. Cf. Verg., *Aen.,* II, 23: *statio*

male fida carinis. Anton, cf. Florus, III, 4, 5 : *dum perfidum glacie flumen equitatur.*

vestigia lusit: refused a foothold.

194. *turmae:* includes the horses.

195. *congesta strue . . . iacebant:* lay in heaps. *Strue* represents the state, *iacebant* its continuance also.

deplorata: past hope of rising again. *Deplorare* was used of wailing over the dead, and thence transferred to anything given up for lost. Cf. 227.

196. *rigido . . . flamine:* cf. Shelley's "frozen wind" ("A Widow Bird").

197. *rupti turbine venti:* Anton, cf. Verg., *Aen.*, II, 416 :

> adversi rupto ceu quondam turbine venti.

Here the epithet is transferred. Some Mss. give *rupto*, but *rupti* is to be preferred, not only as the better attested, but as the *difficilior lectio.*

198. *confractum grandine caelum:* the sky shattered into hail.

199–200. *nubes ruptae* and *unda* suggest a heavy downpour of rain; but, as *concreta gelu* and *nive* (201) show, snow, or possibly sleet, must be meant.

super arma. See Introd., p. 54.

concreta gelu: cf. 150, *glacie concreta.*

201–202. *victa*, etc. : the earth and the frozen rivers were buried under the snow, and the sky hidden by the storm. Cf. *Laudes. Herc.*, 125 f.:

> solque licet glaciali frigore victus
> abstrusum mundo claudat iubar.

203. *nondum Caesar erat: sc. victus:* with the following picture of the indomitable Caesar, cf. Sil. Ital., III, 500 ff. (Hannibal crossing the Alps):

at miles dubio tardat vestigia gressu
impia ceu sacros in fines arma per orbem
(natura prohibente) ferant, divisque repugnent.
contra quae ductor: non Alpibus ille nec ullo
turbatus terrore loci; sed languida monstris
corda virum fovet hortando, revocatque vigorem.

magnam . . . hastam: cf. the *ingens hasta* of Mars, 268. Caesar is here endowed with one of his attributes. Cf. Lucan, VII, 567 ff., where Caesar at Phàrsalus is compared to Mars and Bellona.

204. With this imaginary picture cf. Caesar's own account of his crossing of the snow-covered Cévennes in midwinter, 51: *etsi mons Cebenna . . . durissimo tempore anni altissima nive iter impediebat, tamen discussa nive in altitudinem pedum sex atque ita viis patefactis, summo militum sudore ad fines Arvernorum pervenit . . . ne singulari quidem umquam homini eo tempore anni semitae patuerant.* (B. G., VII, 8.)

horrida . . . arva: fields where the snow crust had been broken.

securis . . . gressibus: as confident as if he were on even ground.

205–206. *Caucasea . . . arce:* the Caucasus was the scene of Prometheus's punishment until Heracles liberated him. Cf. Aesch., *Prom.,* 871 ff.

arduus: Vergil applies this term to the Cyclops, *Aen.,* III, 619.

Amphitryoniades: cf. Catull., LXVIII, 112 (de Salas) ; and Stat., *Theb.*, I, 486. Cf. also 270 and note. Sil. Ital., III, 496–499 :

> primus inexpertas adiit Tirynthius arces.
> scindentem nubes, frangentemque ardua montis
> spectarunt Superi, longisque ab origine saeclis
> intemerata gradu magna vi saxa domantem.

(For the lines which follow, see on 203.)

torvo Iuppiter ore: Jupiter in his wrath.

207. Cf. *Il.*, I, 44 :

> βῆ δὲ κατ' Οὐλύμποιο καρήνων χωόμενος κῆρ.

Lucan, VII, 144 ff., compares the preparations for Pharsalus to those for the battle of the gods and giants (Hes., *Theog.*, 664 ff.).

208. *disiecit:* cf. Verg., *Ge.*, I, 283 (the giants attempt to scale heaven) :

> ter pater exstructos disiecit fulmine montis.

209. Moessler is certainly right in referring this line to the descent from the Alps. Cf. *arce*, 205; Grat., *Cyneg.*, 524 : *Aetnaeas . . . arces. Tumidas*, moreover, applied to fortifications, would be inflated language indeed. *deprimit* = "descend," with the additional idea of difficulty overcome, and so of mastery. Moessler extends the meaning of the phrase to include the capture of Ariminum and the other towns on the march to Rome, but this is doubtful, as *Fama*, below, knows nothing of it.

210–211. With this episode cf. Sil. Ital., IV, 1-9 :

Fama per Ausonias turbatas spargitur urbes
nubiferos montes et saxa minantia caelo
accepisse iugum, Poenosque per invia vectos,
aemulaque Herculei iactantem facta laboris
descendisse ducem. diros canit improba motus
et gliscit gressu volucrique citatior Euro
terrificis quatit attonitas rumoribus arces.
astruit auditis, docilis per inania rerum
pascere rumorem vulgi, pavor.

motis conterrita pinnis: startled *and* flapping her
wings. The words contain an echo of Verg., *Aen.*, V,
215 : *plausumque exterrita pinnis (dat.).* Cf. Ov.,
Met., II, 547 ff. : *motis | consequitur pinnis . . . cornix.*

Moessler argues that *pinnis* = *arcibus,* and should
be construed as Ablative of Means with *conterrita:*
"frightened by the capture of the towns," *i.e.* the destruction of the fortifications. The word-order, he
thinks, is against construing the ablative with *volat.*
In support of this view might be cited Sen., *Tro.*, 1074 .

summisque pinnis arbiter belli sedens.

but Vergil's description had fixed *Fama* in the Roman
mind as a winged creature, so that if Petronius had
written the words with the meaning given by Moessler
in mind he would simply have laid himself open to
misunderstanding. Nor does it strain the Latin as
much to take *motis . . . pinnis* as an Ablative of

Manner with *volat*, as to make *motis* describe the capture or destruction of fortifications. *Conterrita* shows that *Fama* herself shares the emotions with which she inspires others.

Fama volat: also the opening words of Verg., *Aen.*, III, 121. For the picture here cf. *Aen.*, IV, 184–187:

nocte volat caeli medio terraeque per umbram,
stridens, nec dulci declinat lumina somno.
luce sedet custos aut summi culmine tecti
turribus aut altis, et magnas territat urbes.

Also VII, 512 (Allecto). Stat., *Theb.*, I, 123 f.; II, 208 f.:

Thebas
insilit et totis perfundit moenia pennis.

Palati: the cradle of Rome, and destined to be the site of the imperial residence.

212. Cf. Stat., *Theb.*, III, 423: *armorum tonitru ferit.* Sil. Ital., IV, 7 (quoted on 210).

Romano tonitru . . . omnia signa: "the Roman thunderbolt" is the news of civil war, the *signa* the statues of the gods, including, by synecdoche, their temples. But the line is awkward and unsatisfactory. Bouhier read *Romanos*, to which Buecheler suggests adding *obvia*, joining *obvia signa* to what follows as the first item of the bad news. There is no authority for adopting this, but it is certainly the more satisfactory version of the line.

213. *iam classes fluitare mari:* his fleets were already at sea. For the verb, cf. 281. Stat., *Theb.*, VII, 808:

bellum fluitans = navale. (Anton.) In Florus, II, 2, 32 :
cum Punicae . . . frustrarentur et fluitarent, it means
"were scattered, drifting."

Fama is exaggerating. Caesar was always weak in
sea power.

With this and the following line cf. Caes., *B. C.,* I, 14 :
*Caesar enim adventare iam iamque et adesse eius equites
falso nuntiabantur.*

213–214. Cf. Lucan, II, 439 ff. (see on 291), 534–536 :

ardent Hesperii saevis populatibus agri :
Gallica per gelidas rabies effunditur Alpes :
iam tetigit sanguis pollutos Caesaris enses.

214. *fervere:* "swarm." For scansion, see Introd., p. 61.

Germano . . . sanguine: cf. 163. German blood is,
of course, meant in both places, but the ominous play
on words (*germanus* = fraternal) would have had its
effect. So the soldiers of Lepidus and Plancus, who
had both caused their brothers to be proscribed,
chanted at their triumph :

de germanis non de Gallis duo triumphant consules.

(Vell. Pat., II, 67.) Cf. Cic., *Phil.,* XI, 6, 14 : *nisi
forte iure germanum Cimber occidit.*

215. Throughout Italy people expected a renewal of
the scenes of the last civil war. Caesar was an object
of terror until his generous conduct at Corfinium (*B. C.,*
I, 22 f.) relieved men's apprehension. See on 98.

totaque bella: all the horrors of war, summing up
arma, cruor, caedes, incendia.

216. *pulsata tumultu:* smitten with panic. Cf. Petr., *Fr.*, XXVIII (Buecheler), 3:

subitis rumoribus oppida pulsat.

Caes., *B. C.*, I, 14: *quibus rebus Romam nuntiatis tantus repente terror invasit,* etc.

217. Cf. Verg., *Aen.*, II, 39:

scinditur incertum studia in contraria vulgus.

Moessler reads *per dubias* because three possibilities are mentioned below (218–219). This makes a smoother reading than that of the Mss., where *sunt* has to be understood with *pulsata . . . pectora,* but the argument for it is not conclusive, as *duas* might not unnaturally refer only to the counsels of the panic-stricken, those who wish to fight being introduced as an afterthought.

218 ff. With the following, cf. Dio, XLI, 7 f.: οἵ τε γὰρ ἐξιόντες (ἦσαν δὲ πάντες ὡς εἰπεῖν οἱ πρῶτοι καὶ τῆς βουλῆς καὶ τῆς ἱππάδος καὶ προσέτι καὶ τὸ τοῦ ὁμίλου) λόγῳ μὲν ἐπὶ πολέμῳ ἀφωρμῶντο, ἔργῳ δὲ τὰ τῶν ἑαλωκότων ἔπασχον. τήν τε γὰρ πατρίδα καὶ τὰς ἐν αὐτῇ διατριβὰς ἐκλιπεῖν καὶ τὰ ἀλλότρια τείχη οἰκειότερα τῶν σφετέρων νομίζειν ἀναγκαζόμενοι δεινῶς ἐλυποῦντο. . . . ὥστε καὶ ἐς ἀμφίβολον καὶ ταῖς γνώμαις καὶ ταῖς εὐχαῖς ταῖς τε ἐλπίσι καθιστάμενοι τοῖς τε σώμασιν ἅμα ἀπὸ τῶν οἰκειοτάτων σφίσιν ἀπεσπῶντο καὶ τὰς ψυχὰς δίχα διῃροῦντο . . . οἱ δ' ὑπολειπόμενοι . . . ἐν τῇ ἐξουσίᾳ τοῦ τῆς πόλεως κρατήσοντος ἐσόμενοι . . . ὑπὸ τοῦ φόβου καὶ τῶν ὕβρεων καὶ τῶν σφαγῶν ὡς καὶ γιγνομένων ἤδη ἐταλαιπώρουν. Cf. also Caes., *B. C.*, I, 14 (see on 216).

218. Throughout this passage there are many touches which show that Petronius is thinking less of Rome than of Troy (see on 115). Here, for instance, he would scarcely have mentioned flight by sea but for the memory of Aeneas and his followers.

219. Commentators have given themselves a great deal of trouble over this line, and offered all manner of unintelligible readings by way of improvement, but except for a little excusable abruptness, there is no difficulty with it at all. The most terrified of the *émigrés*, feeling themselves unsafe on the same ground with Caesar, take to the water, preferring the perils of the deep to the chance of encountering the terrible foe. To appreciate the full force of *patria pontus iam tutior*, we must remember that the Romans had an inveterate dread of blue water, the abode, to them, of shipwreck, squalls, seasickness, and horrors without number. From this topic Petronius turns sharply to that of the party which favored resistance.

220. (*arma*) *temptare:* cf. 175 : *temptate manus.* The reading *temptata* is vigorous and well attested, but the abrupt change of construction in *uti* renders it doubtful.

fatis . . . *uti:* cf. Lucan, I, 227 : *utendum est iudice bello.* Verg., *Aen.*, XII, 932 : *utere sorte tua.*

221. A miserable line, which adds nothing to the passage and fails to justify itself. Moessler is probably right in this belief that it is an interpolation, composed of a marginal note : *quantum* . . . *fugit*, and *ocior ipse*, added to fill out the meter and connect the line with what follows. Without it 220 and 222 fit together perfectly.

222. *motus:* the conflicting currents of excitement.

miserabile visu: another Vergilian phrase (see on 100). Cf. Verg., *Aen.*, I, 111.

223. *mens icta:* cf. *pulsata tumultu pectora*, 216 f. Ch. 100, 5: *tam inexpectato ictus sono* (Anton). Corn. Sev., *Fr. de Morte Ciceronis*, 10 f.:

> ictaque luctu
> conticuit Latiae tristis facundia linguae.

deserta . . . urbe: is carried away, leaving the city empty.

224. *gaudet Roma fuga:* Rome — identified with her citizens — gives herself up without restraint to flight (cf. *gaudet*, 75). In the same way we speak of " embracing" a faith, cause, opportunity, etc., without necessarily implying any affection for it.

debellatique Quirites: ironical, as they had been conquered without a blow.

225. Cf. *Octavia*, 509–511. Sil. Ital., IV, 26–31 (quoted on 230–231).

226. With this part of the description cf. Verg., *Aen.*, II, 486–490. Liv., I, 29.

227–228. *deploratum . . . limen.*, cf. 195. The opposite of *maerentia tecta*, 225. There the house was a mourner, here the abandoned threshold is a corpse over which the ceremonies of mourning have been held. For figures drawn from the same source, cf. Cic. *Cat.*, IV, 6, 11; *Pro Lege Manil.*, 11, 30. Liv., III, 38, 2: *deploratur in perpetuum libertas.* IX, 7, 1: *deploratum paene Romanum nomen.*

absentem . . . *hostem:* Anton, cf. Eurip., *Hipp.*, 44 : κτενεῖ πατὴρ ἀραῖσιν, which is, however, meant seriously, while this is sarcastic, as in Cic., *Cat.*, II, 8, 18 : *magis mihi videntur vota facturi contra rem publicam quam arma laturi:* and Liv., XXII, 14, 14. Cf. Stat., *Theb.*, II, 133 :

> sic excitus ira
> ductor in absentem consumit proelia fratrem.

229. Cf. Lucan, II, 30 f.: hae pectora duro | adflixere solo.

230–231. *grandaevos* . . . *iuventus:* another echo of the *Aeneid*. Cf. Sil. Ital., IV, 27–32 (of the flight from Rome before Hannibal's approach) :

> deseruere larem ; portant cervicibus aegras
> attoniti matres ducentesque ultima fila
> grandaevos rapuere senes ; tum crine soluto
> ante agitur coniunx, dextra laevaque trahuntur
> parvi, non aequo comitantes ordine, nati.
> sic vulgus ; traduntque metus, nec poscitur auctor.

Of course to introduce these details of the heroic age into a picture of Caesar's time was absurd, but it is quite consistent, not only with Petronius's theory, but with Lucan's practice (cf. any of his battle-pieces). The first difficulty arises with *onerisque ignara iuventus*. As this is the subject of what follows, and *patres* the object, the coördinating -*que* is out of place. To remedy this Anton drops it, defending the metrical irregularity by Vergil's example (*e.g. pulvīs*, I, 478). *Humerīs* (Auratus), and *non gnara* have also been proposed. The

first and last of these, although by no means certain, are
by far the best, and have the support, in form and meaning, of Ch. 102, 12: *iuvenes adhuc laboris expertes, i.e.*
unhardened to endurance by toil and suffering. For the
thought cf. also 84.

id . . . trahit: certainly not genuine. It breaks the
thought begun in the preceding line and substitutes a
general statement for it; it is utterly flat, and its style
is suggestive of the equally unworthy : *quantum quisque
timet tantum fugit,* 221 (see note). Moessler is right
in rejecting it as a gloss which displaced the original
words, describing the carrying away of the old men,
although it is rash to venture to replace them as he does
(*in primis aptat cervicibus*).

Some editors have tried to combine 230 with 229
(Anton : *"coniuges uxores secum abducebant, iuvenes
autem patres longaevos quibus ferendis erant impares,
trahebant"*) but, as the language shows, 229 refers to
a farewell embrace, and not to flight together. To
make *patres* the object of *iungant,* as some do, is equally
impossible, as this coördinates it, not with *coniugibus,*
but with *pectora.*

233–237. Cf. Sen., *Agam.,* 138–142, 505–507.

233. *magnus:* Anton, cf. Verg., *Ge.,* II, 334 : *actum
. . . magnis Aquilonibus imbrem.*

inhorruit: refers to the gradual roughening of the
waves as the storm approaches. Cf. Verg., *Aen.,* III,
195 :

tum mihi caeruleus supra caput adstitit imber
noctem hiememque ferens, et inhorruit unda tenebris.

Moessler sees in this a device for telling about those
who fled by sea (cf. 218 f.).   To do this, however, intro-
duces an entirely new idea : a struggle, not with Caesar,
but with the elements, and gives to these fugitives an
importance which quite overshadows the certainly more
numerous party that sticks to dry land.   He forgets,
moreover, that Lucan embodies the same idea in his own
account of the panic (see Introd., p. 16), and that it is
one of the stock similes of Latin poetry.

234. *pulsas . . . aquas.*   Cf. 3.

arma = *armamentum:*   (Caes., *B. G.*, III, 14).   Cf.
Verg., *Aen.*, I, 177 : *cerealiaque arma, i.e.* handmills, etc.
for making bread.

ministris = *nautis:*   cf. Ch. 108, 8 : *navis ministerium.*
Verg., *Aen.*, VI, 302 : *velis ministrare.*

235. *pondera pinus:*   the sails.   Cf. Lucan, I, 500 :
pondera mali.

236. *tuta sinus:*   safe harbors.   Cf. such expressions
as *strata viarum,* Lucr. I, 315 ; IV, 415.   *opaca locorum,*
Verg., *Aen.*, II, 725.

237. *dat vela fugae:*   a poetical variant of *vela ventis
dare.*

238. *quid tam parva queror?*   cf. Ch. 134, 12, 8 : *quid
leviora loquor?*

gemino cum consule: see on 288–289.

For the impression made by the departure of Pompey
and the consuls, cf. Cic., *ad Att.*, VII, 11, 4 : *mira hominum querela est . . . sine magistratibus urbem esse, sine
senatu. fugiens denique Pompeius mirabiliter homines
movet.*   Florus, IV, 2, 20 : *turpe dictu: modo princeps*

patrum, pacis bellique moderator, per triumphatum a se mare . . . fugiebat.   nec Pompeius ab Italia, quam Senatus ab urbe, fugatur prior.

239. *Ponti:* Moessler prints this word with a capital both here and 241, attributing the repetition to the lack of *ultima manus.* Buecheler reads *ponti* here and *Pontus* below. But the opposite seems more natural, as this line would then refer entirely to Pompey's victories in Asia, 241-242 to those at sea. *Fracto gurgite* shows that the kingdom of Pontus cannot be meant in 241.

repertor Hydaspis: Pompey's conquests really did not go beyond the Euphrates, but the mention of the Hydaspes, on whose banks Alexander overthrew Porus, suggests a comparison with the great Macedonian (cf. Plin., quoted on 270). The Romans were not very clear as to the location of the river (Verg., *Ge.*, IV, 211: *Medus Hydaspes*), but its name had power to create a sense of awe and mystery. Cf. Hor., *Carm.*, I, 22, 7 f.: *fabulosus . . . Hydaspes.*

240. *Piratarum scopulus:* an appropriate metaphor with regard to men whose heritage was the sea. It was also common in other connections. Cf. Caes. (in Gell., I, 10): *tanquam scopulum sic fugias inauditum atque insolens verbum.* Cic., *de Or.*, II, 37, 154; III, 41, 163. Florus, IV, 9, 1. Val. Max., III, 7, 9.

Pompey annihilated the pirates in 67.

ter ovantem: cf. Ch. 133, 3; 16 f.:

                         et ter ovantem
circa delubrum gressum feret ebria pubes.

P

Ovare, technically applied to celebrating the lesser triumph on the Alban Mount, here = *triumphare*. Pompey's three triumphs were held for victories in Africa, in Spain, and over Mithridates. Cf. Plut., *Pomp.*, 45. Albin., *Rer. Rom.*, I (Prisc., 305 K. Baehrens, *Fr. Poet. Rom.*, p. 406. App.Verg., *Catalepton*, III):

ille cui ternis Capitolia celsa triumphis
sponte deum patuere : cui freta nulla repostos
abscondere sinus : non tutae moenibus urbes.

241–242. *Iuppiter horruerat:* for the strong expression, cf. *Il.*, V, 362 :

Τυδείδης, ὃς νῦν γε καὶ ἂν Διί πατρὶ μάχοιτο.

fracto gurgite pontus: the conquered sea, with reference, perhaps, not only to the pirates, but also to Pompey's many voyages. Cf. Cic., *pro Lege Manil.*, 12, 34. *submissa Bosporus unda:* cf. Hor., *Carm.*, II, 9, 21 f. :

Medumque flumen gentibus additum
victis minores volvere vertices.

(Wernsdorff.)

Lucan, III, 76 f. : *ut vincula Rheno | Oceanoque daret.*

It was the custom to display figures of "conquered" rivers and seas at triumphs and on temples and arches. Cf. Florus, IV, 2, 88. Verg., *Ge.*, III, 27 f. Ov., *A. A.*, I, 223 f. Pers. VI, 47.

This tendency to personify large bodies of water and to believe in their sympathy with their faithful worshippers and lively resentment of any indignity is a world-wide and natural one. Cf. the story of Xerxes and the Hellespont (Her., VII, 33–35). Verg., *Aen.*, VIII, 711 ff. ; 728 : *pontem indignatus Araxes.* Kipling, "The Bridge-Builders" : "She is Mother Gunga — in irons."

Moessler wishes to cut out everything between *horruerat* and *deserto*, 243, making one line :

Iuppiter horruerat, deserto nomine fugit.

243. *Imperii deserto nomine.* Behaving in a manner unworthy of the *imperium* which had been bestowed on him by the Senate.

244. *Fortuna levis:* cf. 102. Sen., *Med.*, 219: *rapida Fortuna ac levis.* *Tro.*, 2 ; *Octavia*, 454. Stat., *Theb.*, I, 177.

245–246. For the thought, cf. Ch. 89, 53 :

peritura Troia perdidit primum deos.

Octavia, 159–162.

ergo : introducing a natural consequence rather than a logical conclusion. Cf. Verg., *Ge.*, I, 489 f. (following the enumeration of portents. See on 127) :

ergo inter sese paribus concurrere telis
Romanas acies iterum videre Philippi.

The emendation *tergo* substitutes almost impossible Latin for something perfectly plain and simple.

lues: "*débâcle.*" Cf. Sil. Ital., XII, 184 f. :

fertur acerba lues disiectis undique portis
effusaeque ruunt inopino flumine turbae.

vicit: the Mss. reading, *vidit,* while not impossible, lacks force and point. For the combination *lues . . . vicit,* cf. the language of 192 and 201 f.

consensitque: de Salas, cf. Ch. 89, 39 : *consentiunt luminibus.*

fugae: the general panic and flight just described, and already signalized by the presence of Pompey and the Consuls (238).

caeli timor: "*dii caelestes timentes ne in hoc bello et ipsi perturbentur.*" (Anton.)

247. The gods divide into three classes : those who take no part at all in the struggle, those who urge on both sides indiscriminately (254 ff.), and those who become patrons of one leader or the other (264 ff.).

turba: cf. 31. The use of this word becomes a mannerism with the poets of the Empire. Cf., *e.g.,* Stat., *Achill.,* I, 2, 236 : *turba sumus* (Achilles, Deidamea, and the infant Pyrrhus). Propert., IV, 11, 22 : *Eumenidum turba;* 31 (of ancestors); 76 (of Cornelia's children).

furentes: see on 168.

248. *damnatum:* doomed to destroy each other.

avertitur: see Introd., p. 51.

249. *niveos pulsata lacertos:* beating her arms and breasts with her hands in token of mourning, according to the ancient custom.

With the flight of *Pax,* cf. *Octavia,* 424–426.

250. *palla:* cf. Hes., *Works and Days,* 192–200 :

καὶ τότε δὴ πρὸς Ὄλυμπον ἀπὸ χθονὸς εὐρυοδείης,
λευκοῖσιν φαρέεσσι καλυψαμένω χρόα καλόν,

ἀθανάτων μετὰ φῦλον ἴτον προλιπόντ' ἀνθρώπους
Αἰδὼς καὶ Νέμεσις.

Wernsdorff, cf. Stat., *Theb.*, XI, 495 f. :

> deiectam in lumina pallam
> diva trahit, magnoque fugit questura Tonanti.

Covering the head thus was a sign of grief or despair.

Galea, the reading of the Mss., is so inappropriate to the character and attributes of *Pax* as to be inadmissible. The only motive she could have for assuming a helmet would be that of disguise (cf. Juv., VIII, 203 : *nec galea faciem abscondit*), but she is represented here as a mourner (249), and though a fugitive (251), there is no reason why she should attempt to conceal her identity. For the repetition of *palla* (250, 253), see Introd., p. 47.

251. *Ditis petit . . . regnum.* Anton, cf. Aristoph., *Pax*, 223 :

> ὁ Πόλεμος αὐτὴν ἐνέβαλ' εἰς ἄντρον βαθύ.

She takes refuge in Hades as its proper inhabitants desert it and ascend to join in the war (254 ff.).

implacabile: cf. Propert., IV, 11, 1–8.

252. *submissa:* "meek."

crine soluto: in token of mourning. Cf. Ch. III, 2 : *vulgari more funus passis prosequi crinibus.*

253. *Iustitia:* the *Astraea virgo* of the *Octavia*, 424 ff.

lacera Concordia palla: another token of mourning. Cf. the frequent reference to the rending of garments in the Bible. In 276 *Discordia's laceratam vestem* is not for her own mourning, but a symbol of that which she brings upon others.

254. Cf. 67, 101, 124. *Erebus* is used for the Infernal Regions in general. With this and the following lines cf. Verg., *Ge.*, III, 551 f. :

saevit et in lucem Stygiis emissa tenebris
pallida Tisiphone Morbos agit ante Metumque
inque dies avidum surgens caput altius effert.

255. *emergit late:* emerges and spreads far and wide, like a swarm of dangerous insects.

chorus: cf. the "rout" of Comus.

horrida Erinys: bristling with snakes. Tisiphone is probably the one meant. Cf. 97 and 120. Megaera is mentioned in the next line.

256. *Bellona:* she was armed with a scourge, like a Fury. Cf. Verg., *Aen.*, VIII, 703. Lucan, VII, 568. Sil. Ital., IV, 441.

minax: cf. 263.

facibusque armata Megaera: a torch and a scourge of snakes were the peculiar attributes of the Furies. The torch also appears as a symbol of violence and destruction. Cf. 262 f., 277. Sen., *Thy.*, 251 ; *H. O.*, 1003–1007. Florus, III, 12, 13: *atqui haec Caesarem atque Pompeium furialibus in exitium rei publicae facibus armavit.*

257. Cf. Verg., *Aen.*, II, 369 : *plurima mortis imago.* Busch, cf. Ov., *Am.*, II, 9, 41. Verg., *Aen.*, VII, 326 :

iraeque insidiaeque et crimina noxia cordi.

Sil. Ital., XIII, 583 : *Curaeque Insidiaque.*

Letum . . . Mortis imago: " *videtur Letum . . . fatum mortiferum, sicut* κήρ *Graecum; Mors autem moriendi necessitatem significare. Cf.* Stat., *Theb.,* IX, 280 :

mille modis leti miseros mors una fatigat." (Anton.)

lurida: blême. Luror is used of extreme pallor. Cf. Apul., IX, 12 : *lurore deformes* (of the wretched slaves in the mill).

With these personifications cf. Verg., *Aen.,* VI, 273–278 :

vestibulum ante ipsum primisque in faucibus Orci
Luctus et ultrices posuere cubilia Curae ;
pallentesque habitant Morbi, tristisque Senectus,
et metus et malesuada Fames ac turpis Egestas.
terribiles visu formae, Letumque labosque ;
tum consanguineus Leti sopor et mala mentis
Gaudia, mortiferumque adverso in limine Bellum,
ferreique Eumenidum thalami et Discordia demens
vipereum crinem vittis innexa cruentis.

Sen., *H. F.,* 92–103, 690–696. *Oed.,* 588–592, 650 f. Stat., *Theb.,* II, 287 f. Sil. Ital., II, 548–551 ; XIII, 581–587. Stephen Phillips imitates these passages — especially that of Vergil — with modern feeling :

"Right in the threshold Hunger stands, and Hate,
And gliding Murder with his lighted face,
And Madness howling, Fear, and neighing Lust,
And Melancholy with her moony smile,
And Beauty with blood dripping from her lips."

(Ulysses, II, 1).

258. *abruptis . . . habenis:* two lines of Vergilian reminiscence meet here. First, Petronius is, of course, thinking of the closing of the temple of Janus (*Aen.*, I, 294 ff.) :

> Furor impius intus
> saeva sedens super arma et centum vinctus aenis
> post tergum nodis fremet horridus ore cruento.

of which this picture is the reverse. But the language also suggests the simile of the runaway stallion :

> qualis ubi abruptis fugit praesaepia vinclis
> tandem liber ecus, etc.

(*Aen.*, XI, 492 ff., imitated from *Il.*, VI., 506 ff.).

259–260. *sanguineum . . . cruenta:* here synonymous. Ordinarily *sanguineus* means "blood-red"; *cruentus*, "blood-stained," "gory."

261. *Mavortius umbo:* the shield of Mars, borrowed for the occasion, as Pallas borrowed the accoutrements of Zeus (*Il.*, V, 736 ff.).

262. *innumerabilibus telis gravis:* Caes., *B. C.*, III, 53, tells of a shield which showed 120 scars received in one fight. Cf. App., *B. C.*, II, 60. Lucan, VI. 140 ff. (exaggerated according to his custom). Here the missiles are still sticking in the shield and weighing it down. Cf. Stat., *Theb.*, II, 604 f. (of Tydeus) :

> spicula devellens, clipeo quae plurima toto
> fixa tremunt armantque virum.

263. *stipite:* see on 256. Cf. Lucan, I, 572 f. :

> Erinys
> excutitur pronam flagranti vertice pinum.

incendia portat: Anton, cf. Verg., *Aen.*, III, 539: *bellum . . . portas.*

264–270. Cf. Sil. Ital., IX, 287 ff.:

nec vero, fati tam saevo in turbine, solum
terrarum fuit ille labor: Discordia demens
intravit caelo, superosque ad bella coegit.
hinc Mavors, hinc Gradivum comitatus Apollo,
et domitor tumidi pugnat maris: hinc Venus amens,
hinc Vesta, et captae stimulatus caede Sagunti
Amphitryoniades, pariter veneranda Cybelle,
indigetesque dei, Faunusque, satorque Quirinus,
alternusque animae mutato Castore Pollux.
contra, cincta latus ferro, Saturnia Iuno
et Pallas, Libycis Tritonidos edita lymphis,
ac patrius flexis per tempora cornibus Hammon,
multaque praeterea divorum turba minorum.

Moessler considers this paragraph out of place. *Sentit terra deos,* he says, is made to refer, apparently, to *Ditis chorus,* when it properly belongs to the *caelites* who follow. *Discordia,* moreover, is separated by it from the other infernal deities, who should blow the trumpets of 271. He would, therefore, put these seven lines after 294, closing the poem with them, and making *excipit* refer to Pompey's evacuation of Italy (292 ff.), which would not have taken place had the gods been with him. But this transposition involves, first, the rejection of 295 (see note on it); second, the effect of a raw edge at the end of the piece; third, a very abrupt change of subject after *Discordia's* speech. The objec-

tions, moreover, to the present arrangement, are not
so serious as Moessler thinks.   The sequence of thought
is perfectly natural.   The uproar on earth first drives
away the minor divinities who dwell among men during
their periods of good behavior, and who, naturally, are
the first to feel the change (245–253).   Next it attracts
the fiends who delight in strife and bloodshed (254–263).
The great gods, always rather remote and self-absorbed,
are the last to disturb themselves.   (It will be observed
that Jove and his Stygian counterpart (76 ff. and 122
ff.) do not deign to take sides.)   But when, at length,
they have chosen their parties, *Discordia*, as umpire
in the coming contest, steps out and addresses the
combatants.   *Sentit terra deos* does look back as well
as forward, and forms a transition.   The earth feels
the unwonted burden of divinity — and then we learn
that not only Furies and fiends, but the highest gods,
too, are deserting their homès to take part in this Roman
Armageddon.   *Excipit*, of course, refers to Pompey's
flight from Rome (238–244).   As for his faith in the
power of his divine allies (which, by the way, did not
prove of much assistance in the end), it must be remembered that the gods seldom revealed themselves,
even to their favorites.   The retreating Pompey was
probably entertaining them unawares.

264. See Introd., p. 87 f.   Cf. Ov., *Met.*, IX, 273 :
sensit Atlas pondus (*sc. Herculis*).   Sen., *Hipp.*, 972–974 ;
H. F., 73 f. ;   *H. O.*, 11 f., 257 f., 1600, 1909 f.   Juv.,
XIII, 46–9. (Ironical.   The other passages are meant
seriously.)   Sil. Ital., IX, 300 f.

mutataque sidera, etc. : Anton would have this =
sidera terra mutata, citing Hor., *Carm.,* I, 17, 1 f. and
Carm. Saec., 39 f.   But it is better explained as =
mutatum sidera pondus quaesivere.

265. *quaesivere:* "missed." Wernsdorff, cf. *Maece-
nas* (in *App. Verg.*), 129 :

quaesivere chori iuvenum sic Hesperon illum.

regia caeli: i.e. the gods who dwell there.

266. *in partes diducta:* cf. Ch. 108, 7 : *Tryphaena,*
. . . *turbam diducit in partes.*   Lucan, II, 35 : *divisere
deos* means that the women left behind at Rome turned
for help, some to one god, some to another.

Dione: properly the mother of Venus, but often,
as here, Venus herself. (*E.g.* Ov., *Am.,* I, 14, 33 ;
F., II, 461.)

267. *acta:* as this word properly applies to deeds
already done, a number of commentators have rejected
it here, and proposed such emendations as *arma* (Passerat), *astra* (Colladonius), *alma* (Reiske). Moessler,
full of objections, as usual, finds that the gods are not
leading, but merely joining the movement (as shown
by *diducta,* 266), and reads *Dionen . . . acta . . .
ducunt. Acta* then looks back to *Discordia's* exhortations, 290-292 (see on 264-270). Once more, however,
the difficulty has been met by the most difficult means.
Vergil uses the present participle of past time (*Aen.,* I,
492) and the past participle of present time (*Aen.,* I,
481), and it is not too violent a stretch to allow *acta*
here its substantive sense alone without any reference
to time.

sui: cf. Verg., *Aen.*, I, 231 : *meus Aeneas.* Caesar claimed descent from Venus through Iulus and Aeneas. Her head, or the group of Aeneas, Anchises, and Iulus appears on his coins. Cf. Dio, XLIII, 43.

comes additur illi: cf. Verg., *Aen.*, VI, 528, 777 (see on 268) ; IX, 649, 765. Sil. Ital., XIII, 581.

ducit: cf. Verg., *Aen.*, I, 382 (of Aeneas) :

matre dea monstrante viam, data fata secutus.

268. *Pallas:* the goddess of scientific warfare, naturally aids Caesar, the greatest of Roman génerals. Her presence may also, as Anton suggests, be a compliment to his intellect and learning.

Mavortius: Romulus. Cf. Verg., *Aen.*, VI, 777 f. :

quin et avo comitem sese Mavortius addit
Romulus.

and the use of *Saturnia, Titania,* etc. In his own person he represents Rome, showing that Caesar really has the right side of the quarrel. As his father's representative, he stands for the fury of war, so terribly embodied in Caesar's veterans. Caesar has thus an irresistible combination of forces on his side. With the honor that is here paid to Caesar, Moessler, cf. the title of *Pater Patriae*, afterwards bestowed on him (Suet., *Iul.*, 76. App., *B. C.*, II, 106).

Wernsdorff would have *Mavortius* = Mars, because of *Halieut.*, 96 :

nec curru nocturna volat Phoebea nitente.

and Ruf. Fest. Avien., *Aratea*, 127 f. :

> immenso cum iam Titanius orbe
> imbuerit tremulo Tartesia terga rubore.

But to use the adjective when the god is identified with the sun or moon or other natural body (as *Divus* in the phrase *sub divo*, where Jove is again identified with the sky. See on 140) is a very different thing from using it when he appears as an independent personality.

ingentem . . . hastam: cf. 203. Romulus bears one of his father's attributes. Cf. Verg., *Aen.*, VI, 779 f. :

> viden ut geminae stant vertice cristae
> et pater ipse suo superum iam signat honore?

269. It is not clear why Apollo and Diana join Pompey. Apollo especially, the patron of Augustus (see on 115), seems out of place as a Pompeian. Anton attributes his favor to the temple which Pompey built him, and that of Diana to Pompey's great *venationes* (Cic., *ad Fam.*, VII, 1; 3).

Cyllenia proles: cf. Verg., *Aen.*, IV, 258. Hermes (Mercury), the son of Zeus and Maia, was born on Mt. Cyllene in Arcadia.

270. *excipit:* receives him as he withdraws from Rome. See on 264–270.

Tirynthius: Hercules (Heracles), born at Tiryns in the Peloponnesus, loved far wanderers and conquerors of strange peoples (see on 206). From the Roman point of view the overthrow of Gauls, Spaniards, pirates and rebellious slaves (Cic., *pro Lege Manil.*, XI, 30) would rank with purging the earth of monsters. Cf.

Plin., *H. N.*, VII, 27, 1 : *ad decus imperii Romani, non solum ad viri unius, pertinet victorias Pompeii Magni, titulos omnes, triumphosque hoc in loco nuncupari; aequato non modo Alexandri Magni rerum fulgore, sed etiam Herculis prope ac Liberi patris.*

271. With what follows cf. Sen., *Med.*, 13–15, 947–952 ; *H. F.*, 100–103, 982–985. *Octavia*, 261 f., 596, 621, 725 f., 917. *intremuere tubae:* cf. *tremefacta*, 135, and note. Lucan's *insonuere tubae*, I, 578, has tempted some editors to change the verb here.

scisso . . . crine: stronger than *crine soluto*, 252. *Discordia* appears in the guise of a Fury. See below.

Discordia: cf. Enn., *Ann.*, VII (see Hor., *Serm.*, I, 4, 60) : *Discordia taetra;* Verg., *Aen.*, VI, 280 f. (see on 257) ; VIII, 702 :

> et scissa gaudens vadit Discordia palla.

Also Sen., *de Ira*, II, 35, 5.

At the sound of the trumpets *Discordia* appears, and delivers to the embattled nations a speech (283–294) which may be compared to the *hortatio* which a Roman commander addressed to his troops just before joining battle.

272. *extulit . . . caput:* cf. 76 : *extulit ora.* Contrast Verg., *Aen.*, I, 127 : (*Neptunus*) *placidum caput extulit*, and Hor., *Epod.*, II, 17 f. :

> vel cum decorum mitibus pomis caput
> autumnus agris extulit.

Verg., *Ge.*, III (see on 254).

superos Stygium: cf. 170. The collocation in a sentence of the two words most sharply contrasted, or most closely allied in meaning, is characteristic of Greek and Latin. It lends point and emphasis in a manner impossible to imitate in an uninflected language. Cf. Eurip., *Iph. Taur.*, 621 :

αὐτὴ ξίφει θύουσα — θῆλυς ἄρσενας ;

With the following description of *Discordia* cf. Ov., *Met.*, II, 775 ff. (*Invidia*) :

pallor in ore sedet, macies in corpore toto
nusquam recta acies, livent rubigine dentes,
pectora felle virent, lingua est suffusa veneno.

de Salas, cf. Ael. Arist., *Or. de Concord. ad Rhod.*, 44 (838 D), of Στάσις.

273. *contusaque lumina flebant:* cf. Aesch., *Choe.*, 1058:

κἀξ ὀμμάτων στάζουσαν αἷμα δυσφιλές.

and *Eum.*, 54.

Such creatures are often represented as bearing the marks of the violence they wreak upon others. Cf. Sen., *de Ira*, II, 35.

274. *stabant:* for this picturesque use of *stare*, cf. Verg., *Aen.*, VI, 300 : *stant lumina flamma.* Ov., *Met.*, VI, 304 f.: *lumina maestis | stant immota genis.* Lucan, VI, 224 f. : *stetit imbre cruento | informis facies.* Stat., *Silv.*, V, 4, 7 f. :

septima iam rediens Phoebe mihi respicit aegras
stare genas.

aerati . . . *dentes:* Statius, in the *Thebaid*, uses *ferreus* and *ferratus* of the teeth and talons of Furies and kindred monsters.

273. *concretus sanguis:* cf. Verg., *Aen.*, II, 277: *concretos sanguine crines.*

274. *scabra rubigine:* cf. Verg., *Ge.*, I, 495. Ov., *Met.*, VIII, 793 ; *F.*, I, 687 ; *Ex Ponto*, I, 1, 71. Plin., *H. N.*, XVI, 8, 2.

275. *obsessa draconibus ora:* cf. Verg., *Aen.*, VI, 280 f. (see on 271).

276. *atque:* marks the transition from the description of *Discordia's* appearance to the narrative of her acts.

inter . . . *vestem:* a very difficult expression, which many efforts at emendation and explanation have not greatly helped. Moessler reads *intorto inter: "pectore inter vestem laceratam vel anhelitus ducente vel aestuante."* The older editors, Wernsdorff, Hadrianides, Anton, wished to connect *inter* . . . *laceratam* . . . *vestem* with *quatiebat lampada*, which makes the line absurd. *Inter laceratam vestem* depends on *torto pectore*, which, in turn, depends very loosely on *quatiebat.* "And, her breast convulsed beneath its tattered robe, she brandished," etc. For her appearance cf. Apul., *Met.*, IX, 12 : *homunculi* . . . *scissili centunculo magis inumbrati quam obtecti* . . . *sic tunicati ut essent per pannulos manifesti.* For the significance of her rags, see on 253.

277. *sanguineum* . . . *lampada:* see on 256. Cf. Sen., *H. O.*, 672 :

> sequitur dira lampade Erinys.

The adjective might refer to the color of the flame, as

in Verg., *Aen.*, X, 272 f. : *cometae | sanguinei lugubre rubent.* But Ov., *Met.*, IV, 480 f. :

> Tisiphone madefactam sanguine sumit importuna, facem.

and Stat., *Theb.*, X, 854 f. : *facibusque cruentis | Bellona* show that it probably means "sprinkled with blood." See on 259–260.

278. Cocytus, the River of Wailing, was one of the four rivers of Hades (*Od.*, X, 513 f.). Tartarus was properly the place of punishment, guarded by Tisiphone (Verg., *Aen.*, VI, 555 f.), but here the Underworld in general is meant.

279. See Introd., p. 60.

gradiens: the gait of Mars, *Gradivus.*

280. *posset:* purpose.

281. *fluitantes . . . catervas:* cf. 213. But movement on land is meant here, and the word is a strange one to use. The nearest approach to this instance seems to be Tac., *Hist.*, III, 27, and V, 18, where it means "staggering," "wavering."

282. Cf. Verg., *Aen.*, II, 129 : *rumpit vocem;* III, 246 : *rumpitque hanc pectore vocem.* Wernsdorff, cf. Tibull., IV, 1, 86 : *dulces erumpat terra liquores.*

283. *gentes:* cf. Florus, IV, 2, 3 f.: *Caesaris furor et Pompeii urbem, Italiam, gentes, nationes, totum qua patebat imperium, quodam quasi diluvio et inflammatione corripuit, adeo ut non recte tantum civile dicatur, ac ne sociale quidem, sed nec externum, sed potius commune quoddam ex omnibus et plus quam bellum.*

Q

accensis mentibus. Anton, cf. Sil. Ital., IV, 169 f. : *atque in proelia mentes | accendis.* Val. Flacc., IV, 255 : *atque incensa mente feruntur.*

285. *vincetur, quicumque latet:* cf. the saying of the Senatorial party, "He that is not for us is against us," — reversed by Caesar, — and their hostility to neutrals.

non femina cesset: probably a reference to Cornelia, the wife of Pompey, who followed her husband to the war, keeping as close to the "front" as possible, joined him after Pharsalus, and witnessed his murder at Pelusium (see on 63). Cf. also Cic., *ad Att.*, IX, 6, 3 : *de hac re litterae L. Metello tr. pl. Capuam adlatae sunt a Clodia socru quae ipsa transiit (i.e.* crossed to Greece).

286. *desolata:* see Introd., p. 51.

287. The struggle becomes a convulsion of nature. For the hyperbole, cf. Cic., *Cat.*, II, 9, 20 : *tantus enim illorum temporum dolor inustus est civitati, ut iam ista non modo homines, sed ne pecudes quidem mihi passurae esse videantur.*

288–289. In these lines Petronius mentions two of Caesar's bitterest enemies and one of his stanchest and ablest friends. C. Claudius Marcellus and L. Cornelius Lentulus Crus were consuls for the year 49, in which the civil war began, and did much to precipitate it. They persistently opposed the acceptance of Caesar's overtures, and favored measures against him. They also secured the passage of the *ultimum Senatus consultum*, which recognized the existence of a state of war, and gave the consuls almost dictatorial powers. It was this decree which caused the tribunes M. Antonius

and Q. Cassius to flee for protection to Caesar, thus
giving him a legal pretext for crossing the Rubicon.
C. Scribonius Curio, who accompanied the tribunes in
their flight, was a brilliant but unscrupulous man who
had first become active in Caesar's behalf when the
latter paid his enormous debts. For this reason he is
generally represented as a mere unprincipled mercenary,
but his death in Caesar's service raises him to a level
which few of his opponents, who claimed to be fighting
for their country, attained. In Africa, whither he had
been sent by Caesar, he was trapped by Juba and his
lieutenant Saburra, and a large part of his army destroyed. A chance of escape was offered him: *at
Curio numquam se amisso exercitu quem a Caesare fidei
commissum acceperit in eius conspectum reversurum
confirmat atque ita proelians interficitur* (Caes., *B. C.*, II,
42, 4). Lucan, in spite of his ungenerous *fortis virtute
coacta* (IV, 798), pays him a high tribute (IV, 799–
824).

legem: the decree depriving Caesar of his province
and his army. Petronius is identifying the two Claudii
Marcelli: Gaius, mentioned above, and Marcus, consul
51 B.C., the author of this bill. They were, in fact,
much alike in character and identical in politics.

concute plebem: Curio had been Tribune of the
People shortly before and had used all the power of his
eloquence against the Senatorial oligarchy. Cf. Lucan,
I, 269: *venali . . . Curio lingua.*

tu . . . Martem: an unnecessary exhortation. Lentulus was even more eager for war than his colleague.

Cf. Plut., *Caes.*, 30 : Λέντλου τοῦ ὑπάτου βοῶντος ὅπλων δεῖν πρὸς ἄνδρα λῃστήν, οὐ ψήφων.   Caes., *B. C.*, I, 4.

290. *Dive:* Scaliger wished to read *Die*, "god-descended" (cf. Enn., *Ann.*, I, 55 : *Ilia dia*), because Caesar was still alive. But *Discordia* may be supposed to possess knowledge of what was to come, or the title may be purely conventional, merely representing Caesar's greatness. It must be remembered, too, that when once we have placed a halo on the brow of a dead hero, it becomes hard for us to realize that his contemporaries saw him without it.

tuis . . . armis: the arms which you already wear and know so well how to use.

291. With the spirit of this line cf. Lucan, II, 439–446.

> Caesar in arma furens nullas nisi sanguine fuso
> gaudet habere vias, quod non terat hoste vacantis
> Hesperiae fines vacuosque irrumpat in agros,
> atque ipsum non perdat iter consertaque bellis
> bella gerat.   non tam portas intrare patentis
> quam fregisse iuvat : nec tam patiente colono
> arva premi quam si ferro populatur et igne.
> concessa pudet ire via civemque videri.

In reality the Italian towns opened their gates to Caesar willingly, or surrendered after a mere show of resistance. Rome — *Roma capi facilis* (Lucan, II, 656) — was quite untenable.

frangis portas: Hadrianides refers this to Caesar's forcible entrance into the Roman treasury, but as *thesaurosque rapis*, 292, clearly means that, this must contain the same idea as the rest of the line : "will you not be storming towns?"

muris oppida solvis: a strange turn of expression, which represents the walls as bonds to be loosed.

292. *thesaurosque rapis:* Caesar, on his arrival in Rome, demanded the treasure contained in the *Aerarium* (the Temple of Saturn), and when it was refused him, took it by force. Cf. Plut., *Caes.*, 35. Florus, IV, 2, 21. Dio, XLI, 17. App., *B. C.*, II, 41 : τῶν τε ἀψαύστων ἐκίνει χρημάτων ἅ φασιν ἐπὶ Κελτοῖς πάλαι σὺν ἀρᾷ δημοσίᾳ τεθῆναι, μὴ σαλεύειν ἐς μηδὲν, εἰ μὴ Κελτικὸς πόλεμος ἐπίοι. ὁ δὲ ἔφη, Κελτοὺς αὐτὸς ἐς τὸ ἀσφαλέστατον ἑλὼν, λελυκέναι τῇ πόλει τὴν ἀράν.

nescis . . . tueri: Pompey felt compelled to evacuate Italy in order to gain time to organize and drill an army before he encountered Caesar, but the appearance of flight inevitably had a bad moral effect, and called down bitter reproaches from many of his partisans. Cf. Cic., *ad Att.*, VII, 11, 3–4 ; VIII, 2, 2–3.

293. *Romanas arces:* cf. 107. But as Rome was no longer a fortified city, her defense would have meant the successful occupation of central Italy.

Epidamni moenia: Epidamnus was the Greek name of Dyrrhachium, in Epirus, where Pompey now established his base. It was said that the name had been changed because, to Roman ears, it had an ill-omened sound (Plin., *H. N.*, III, 23), and its use here, as Stephanus pointed out, gives a touch of irony to *Discordia's* advice. Cf. Plaut., *Men.*, II, 1, 38 f. :

propterea huic urbei nomen Epidamno inditumst
quia nemo fere huc sine damno devortitur.

The ancients were prone to see special significance in
names, especially after the event :

conveniunt rebus nomina saepe suis.

294. *sinus:* πτυχαί.

Romano sanguine tingue: cf. 160. *Romano* is the
emendation of Cornelissen. *Humono* lacks point:
Thessaly had seen its share of blood from the days of
the mares of Diomed on, and *Romano* brings the line
closer to its model, Lucan, VII, 473 (see p. 84). For the
repetition *Romanas . . . Romano,* see Introd., p. 47.

295. Heinsius and Moessler reject this line. The
latter holds that it is inconsistent with the plan of the
poem because it treats *Discordia's* exhortations as real
when they are only a means of telling what was to
happen, and puts her among the causes of the war.
On these points see Introd., p. 64 ff. The comment
of Anton is more favorable : "*equidem putem hoc
carmen non meliorem exitum posse habere; indicari enim
debebat quid factum esset: idque poeta paucis expressit,
quia historicus nolebat videri.*

TRANSLATION

LORD was the Roman now of all the earth
Where there was sea, or land, or the day-star
At morn or even shone; yet, lord of all,
He was not sated : still the laden keels
Crossed and recrossed the seas with pulsing oars.
If secret port remote or lonely shore
Might yield the ruddy gold, 'twas held a foe.
Thus, while the Fates unholy strife prepared,
Were treasures sought.   Delights well known to
    all,
Pleasures by coarse plebeian touch defiled,
Could charm no more.   The soldier o'er the sea,
Turned connoisseur, old Corinth's bronzes prized ;
Earth's hidden sheen with Tyrian purple vied.
Here the Numidians curse them ; there Cathay
Her fairy fleece surrenders, and the folk
Of Araby despoil their fragrant land.

  Behold another woe, another wound
To outraged peace : gold spreads the hunter's
    snare;
Remotest Afric Hammon is explored
For beasts of murderous fang.   Across the seas,

Measuring with sullen stride his gilded cage,
Stark famine in his wake, the tiger sails,
That for man's sport man's blood may drench
    his jaws.
  Oh, shame to point the signs of coming doom
In hideous deeds foreshadowed ! Persia's crime
Is reënacted : 'neath the mangling knife
The man-child's promise dies (foul sacrifice !)
And flitting youth, arrested, disappoints
The hurrying years, that nature's copy's lost.
Yet everywhere the wretched victims please,
Frail-limbed, with mincing gait and flowing locks
And silken robes of ever-changing name,
Snares for the wanton ! Dragged from Afric
    wastes
Behold the citrus, ringed and streaked, to tempt
The meaner gold. Its burnished face reflects
The herd of slaves, and Tyrian robes : the pride
And ruin of their lords. The unfruitful wood
Ignobly prized, a sodden band surrounds,
While wandering soldiers with dishonored arms
Heap up for them the riches of a world.
  The brain must serve the palate : the great fish,
Pride of Sicilian waters, to their board
Is borne alive, still rocked in its own sea.
Oysters from Lucrine shores commend the feast
And tempt the jaded appetite, with proof

Of squandered gold.   Now storied Phasis' wave
Mourns for her ravished birds : her voiceless shore
Hears but the lone wind whispering to the leaves.

Nor less the madness where the Field of Mars
Records the votes : the purchased freemen throng
By gleam of plunder led and ring of coin
To make their choice.   The People stands for sale,
The Fathers too : advancement knows its price.
Yea, the proud spirit of freedom, once the boast
Of the unbending Senate, was no more ;
But law to scattered largesse was enthralled ;
And the divinity of glorious Rome
By golden venom tainted, lay in dust.
Spurned by the hooting mob, see Cato pass
Rejected : but the victor sadder stands,
Ashamed of power torn by force and fraud
From Cato, for — oh, shame and honor's death !
'Tis not alone a man repulsed ; with him,
With that one Roman, Rome's dominion dies,
Her glory fades.   Then for this wretched Rome—
Herself the price, herself the prize, self-bought
And sold — who shall arise to break her chains ?

The commons too, as caught 'twixt rising tides,
Usury and debt have eaten to the bone :
No house its master's own, no head unpledged.
But as it were a wasting sickness grows

Within the body-politic, deep-hid,
Which through the vitals tears its wolfish way
With maddening pangs and leaves no limb un-
    harmed.
The wretches dream of arms, their fortunes
    breached
By luxury's waste, by wounds must be repaired,
For beggary fears no loss.   Sunk in this slough,
Unconscious Rome! what skill could break thy
    sleep
With healing art ; save by war's trumpet-blast,
And furious blood-lust, roused by touch of steel ?
  Three chiefs did Fortune bear, whose lofty
    heads
In battle-storm the baleful war-fiend whelmed
By divers shocks.   Crassus wild Parthia holds,
Great Pompey sleeps alone on Egypt's sands,
And thankless Rome with Caesar's blood is red.
Thus, as if earth possessed not strength to bear
So many awful tombs, their ashes lie
Sundered.   Behold the guerdon Glory pays!
  There is a place where yawns a chasm deep,
'Twixt Naples and old Cumae, Stygian waves
Eddy below, for the foul vapor's breath
Which rushes thence, with noxious power is
    fraught.
No harvest ripens there, no waving grass

Gladdens the fields, nor does the tuneful spring
Babble through swaying boughs with discord sweet
From feathered throats: black Chaos reigns
    supreme
'Mid scorched volcanic rocks, above whose heaps
The mournful cypress leans. 'Twas in these
    haunts
Black from the funeral flame, his hair and beard
With dead men's ashes white, Lord Pluto reared
His awful head and fickle Fortune called:
  "Power that sway'st the lots of gods and men,
Almighty Chance, sworn foe of stable power,
Thou who dost woo what's strange and spurn
    what's won,
Wilt own thyself by Roman might o'ermatched?
Canst thou not raise the unwieldy bulk to heights
Whence it must fall? Her brood forgets its
    strength,
It scarce can bear what it hath seized. Behold
The orgy of the plunderer! wealth run mad
To its own ruin. Golden palaces
Mount to the stars: their seas are choked with
    stone,
Their fields are turned to sea: they change the face
Of nature, thankless rebels! E'en my realms
Are threatened: earth is pierced with gaping
    wounds;

Her rocky masses melt ; the solid hills
Are empty shells, the mid-world caverns ring ;
And while the useless marble decks their pride,
My slaves, the bloodless shades, grown bold, con-
  fess
They hope once more to greet the light of heaven !
Then rouse thee, Fortune, bend thy brows for war :
Too long thou'st sleeked them : hark these Ro-
  mans on
And give my realm its hecatombs of dead.
No blood hath cooled my cheek, Tisiphone,
My handmaid, hath not laved her parching limbs,
Since Sulla's sword drank deep and shuddering
  earth
Brought forth a harvest rank with blood of men."
  Thus spake the god and strove to clasp her hand
In token of the bond, but as he stirred
Earth yawned afresh. Then fickle Fortune cried :
  "Father, whose rule the realms of woe obey —
If to speak truth unchidden be my right —
Hear ! thou shalt have thy wish : my bosom burns
With anger hot as thine. All, all my gifts
To Rome's embattled hills I hate : my wrath
Consumes my bounty. Let the self-same god
Who gave her power destroy it, for my heart
Craves holocausts ! Their blood shall slake their
  lust.

I see Philippi burdened with the load
Of death redoubled : haunted Thessaly
Burns thick with pyres : Iberia mourns her dead.
Now clang of arms rings thrilling on my ears :
Your woful camps, Egyptian Nile, I see
And Actium's waters, and the faces pale
Of men who blench before Apollo's darts.
Go, Pluto, fling thy greedy portals wide
And thronging souls invite ; thy Ferryman
Shall faint before his bark hath borne across
The warrior shades : the task demands a fleet.
And thou, Tisiphone, pale fiend, thy draught
Be ruin, ghastly wounds thy meat, for down
To Styx and thee the mangled world descends."
    Scarce had she ended when the quivering clouds
Shot forth the bolt that rent them and was gone.
The King of Shadows sank from sight, and drew
Earth's mantle close, fearing his brother's fires.
Straightway the doom of men and woes to come
By signs divine were blazoned : the bright sun,
With bloody orb unsightly, veiled his face
In dark eclipse, as though even then he gazed
On fratricidal strife. O' the other side
His sister quenched her lamp at full and snatched
Its light from deeds of darkness. Mountain crests,
Torn from their roots, rolled thundering down the
    vale.

No more the wandering rivers brimming flowed
Between familiar banks, but dying crept,
Shrunk to the channel's bottom.   In the sky
Was clang of steel, and shrilling from the stars
A trumpet pealed to arms.   Now Aetna burns
With fires beyond her wont, which to the clouds
Dart lightnings.   Lo, mid tombs and bones denied
The rites of pyre and urn strange phantoms flit
With gibbering menace.   Ringed with stars un-
    known
A comet fills with fire the vault of heaven;
And Jove in place of rain sends showers of blood.
Such warnings in brief space the god vouchsafed,
Then ceased.   But Caesar, ending all delay,
And urged by love of vengeance, sheathed the
    sword
That smote the Gaul, but brandished in its place
A keener, dedicate to civil strife.

   Upon the wind-swept Alps where crags which
    once
The Grecian hero trod stoop down and yield
Access to foot of man, there is a place
Which Hercules' great altar sanctifies.
Here winter builds his barrier of snows
Unmelting and a glittering dome to heaven
Uprears, as though the sky had stooped to rest
His burden there.   Not e'en the blazing sun

With all his rays, nor quickening breath of
    Spring
Can tame the icy challenge of the pile,
Buttressed with cold and bound with chains of
    frost
Whose towering shoulders might uphold a world.
  When Caesar with his eager legions trod
This awful spot, his camping-ground assigned,
Down from the height he gazed where, at his
    feet,
Lay Italy unrolled : then eyes and hands
Lifted to heaven and prayed : "Almighty Jove,
And thou, old Saturn's land, glad in my deeds,
And with my laurels crowned : unwillingly —
I swear it — have I summoned Mars to judge
'Twixt thee and me : unwillingly my hands
Are armed, but wrongs compel : My city's gates
Are closed against me, even while the Rhine
Runs red with foemen's blood, and Alpine gates
Are barred against fierce Gauls, who pant once
    more
To scale our sacred Capitol. My crime
Is victory ! For three-score glorious fields
And bleeding Germany exiled. Yet who
Sees treason in my glory ? Hirelings all,
Corruption's journeymen, no true-born sons
Of Rome, my Mother. But not easily,

Methinks, nor unavenged, shall cravens bind
This sword-hand. On, fierce conquerors : com-
    rades, on !
'Tis steel shall plead our, cause. One common
    charge,
One doom awaits us all, but I will pay
To all my debt: I have not fought alone.
Then, since the headsman by the trophy waits,
Since victory hath won the prisoner's weeds,
Let Fortune rule the lots. Take up this war :
Your swords again ! My case is won, I know.
Armèd amid my braves I cannot fail."
  He spoke, and from the sky Apollo's bird
Wheeling, a joyful omen, clove the air.
Then on the left hand from an ancient grove
Of awful sanctity, a wondrous voice
'Mid crackling flames rang out : the sun himself,
Bright with unwonted splendor, round his orb
Dilated, cast a fringe of golden beams.
Emboldened by these portents, Caesar bade
His warlike standards follow, and himself,
Striding ahead, the daring march began.
At first the ice and frost-bound soil, held firm,
Scarce whispered 'neath their tread, but when
    the weight
Of squadrons burst the icy bonds, and steeds,
Plunging in terror, clove the river's mail,

The snows dissolved. Soon torrents from the
    heights,
New gathering, rushed, but these — as by com-
    mand —
Stood still, transformed to ice even as they fell ;
And what a moment since had freely flowed
Now barred their path till hacked away : but
    then —
Treacherous before — it mocked the struggling
    foot
And hold denied : while men and steeds at once
Fell heaped 'mid scattered arms to rise no more.
The clouds as well, by icy blasts convulsed,
Poured down their burden, nor were whirlwinds
    still,
Nor buffeting of hail from shattered skies.
The very heavens seemed heaped upon their arms,
And with the billow's might the sleet rushed down.
The earth was conquered by the drifted snow,
Conquered the stars of heaven, the ice-bound
    streams;
Unconquered still was Caesar : his great spear
His staff, with stride unbroken he traversed
The bristling ice-fields, like huge Hercules
From Caucasus returning, or fierce Jove
When from Olympus' brow in wrath he sprang
And dashed the armèd giants to their doom.

R

While sink the heights 'neath Caesar's angry
    tread,
With rush of startled wings swift Rumor seeks
The topmost ridge of Palatine, and thence
Thunders to Rome her warning: Caesar's fleets
Cover the sea, the Alpine passes belch
Invaders reeking still with German blood.
Then sword and fire and direst shapes of war
Swim red before men's eyes. Their hearts are
    torn
In twain by terror: one by land would flee,
Another o'er the wave; the sea to him
Safer than home. A bolder here and there
Exhorts to arms, since war is Fate's decree.
Fear, flight, and breathless speed! The craven
    throng,
As goading fear may drive — disgraceful sight! —
Desert their city. Rome streams through her
    gates
As flight were pastime, and her citizens
Conquered without a blow, their hearths forsake.
One clasps his children in his trembling arms
Another in his mantle wraps the gods
Of home, then bids that home a last farewell,
And smites the foe — still distant — with a curse.
Men press their wives to bosoms racked with
    grief;

Youths, uninured to toil, their aged sires,
The source of all their cares, bear with them ; one
Unskilled in camps, drags all his treasure forth,
And to the war brings spoil — to glut his foes.

    As when upon the deep the storm-winds rage
And lash the waves ; nor tackle, spar, nor helm
Obeys the seaman's hand : one furls his sails
And runs before the storm, another seeks
The tranquil harbor and the sheltered shore ;
Another crowds his canvas and leaves all
To Fortune —   But why rail at trifles ? Lo !
Where with the Consuls Pompey flees — the Great !
Whom Pontus feared, who trod Hydaspes' strand,
The shoal where pirates shattered, at whose car
Thrice driven in triumph, Jove himself grew pale.
The sea had worshiped him with humbled waves,
The flowing Bosporus cringed, and now, for shame !
Duty and name and fame forgot he flees,
And Fortune looks on Pompey's back at last.

    The avalanche of terror seized in turn
The gods themselves, the trembling heavens con-
    fessed
Its might.   Lo, from the earth the kindly powers,
Loathing its madness, pass with downcast looks
And leave mankind to perish in their sins.
Peace first of all, bruising her snowy arms,
Covers her vanquished head and seeks the realm

Of ruthless Dis, a fugitive.   Meek Faith
Attends her, Justice with dishevelled locks
And Concord robed in woe.   But where the gates
Of Darkness yawn, stream forth the hordes of Dis :
The Fury serpent-wreathed, Bellona fierce,
Megaera armed with firebands, Treachery,
Destruction, and the livid shape of Death.
Among them Frenzy, bursting from her bonds
Raises her gory head : her features scarred
With countless wounds a blood-stained casque o'er-
   shades.
On her left arm she wears the war-god's shield,
Battered and thick with darts : her right hand
   wields
A blazing torch to wrap the world in flames.
   Earth feels the unwonted load and skies the
   lack
Of gods, for all the host of heaven divide
And seek the opposing factions.   First of all
To Caesar bends the Mother of his race,
Venus, bright star of victory : Pallas next,
And Mars' great son shaking his father's spear.
But Phoebus with his sister and the child
Of Maia welcomes Pompey, and his peer
In wanderings and in deeds, great Hercules.
   The trumpets pealed, and Discord to the sky
Lifted her Stygian head and tresses torn.

Upon her face was clotted blood ; her eyes,
Livid with bruises, streamed ; her iron fangs
Stood thick with scales of rust ; her lolling tongue
Distilled corruption, serpents framed her face ;
And as her bosom 'neath its tattered robe
Heaved frantic, with her quivering hand she shook
A torch with blood-fed flame.   When she had left
Cocytus and black Tartarus, she climbed
With eager stride the glorious Apennine,
Whence from the heights she could all lands behold,
All shores and all the armies of the world,
And from her furious heart these words she flung :
      "Nations, to arms ! let wrath your minds in-
         flame :
To arms, and 'mid your cities cast the torch.
Who seeks escape, is doomed ; nor wife nor child
Nor helpless age shall respite find ; the earth
Herself shall shake, the shattered roof-tree smite !
Marcellus, guard thy law : bold Curio,
Stir up rebellion : strive not, Lentulus,
To stem the tide.   Great Caesar, sword in hand,
Dost hesitate?   Wilt thou not break the gates
And loose the cities' girding walls and snatch
Their treasures?   Pompey, canst thou not defend
Embattled Rome?   Retire to conquered Greece,
And dye Thessalian shores with Roman blood."
   Thus Discord, and her orders were obeyed.

CRITICAL NOTES

Note on the Mss.

There are twenty-one Mss. which preserve the fragments of the *Satirae* of Petronius in more or less complete form. Fifteen of these contain the *Bellum Civile*, which, with a few other passages, has been reproduced oftener than any other part of the work. These Mss. are :

Traguriensis. Ms. in the Bibliothèque Nationale, Paris. About fifteenth century.

a. Ms. in the Bibliothèque Nationale, Paris. About eleventh century.

b. Ms. in the Bibliothèque Nationale, Paris. About fourteenth century.

Leidensis.[1] Ms. in the University Library, Leyden.

Vb. Ms. in the University Library, Leyden.

Sc. (Codex Scaligeri). Ms. in the University Library. Leyden.

M.[1] Ms. in the Royal Library, Munich.

V1. Ms. in the Imperial Library, Vienna. Fifteenth century.

V2. Ms. in the Imperial Library, Vienna. First half of sixteenth century.

---

[1] *Bellum Civile* only.

Dr.[1] Ms. in the Royal Library, Dresden. Fifteenth century.

Br. Ms. in the Public Library, Berne. Tenth century.

F1. Ms. in the Laurentian Library, Florence. First half of fifteenth century.

F2. Ms. in the Laurentian Library, Florence. Second half of fifteenth century.

Vat. Ms. in the Vatican Library, Rome. First half of fifteenth century.

Mess. Ms. in the Benedictine Convent, Messina, twelfth century.

These Mss., with the exception of the three which contain the *Bellum Civile* only, and Trag. constitute the class sometimes called *Vulgaria* or *Vulgata Excerpta*. Trag., except in its first part (containing the *Cena Trimalchionis*, Chs. 26–78), coincides with these, and is included with them in the references below. A full account and collation of all the Mss. of Petronius are to be found in Beck, "The Manuscripts of the Satyricon of Petronius Arbiter" Cambridge (Mass.), 1863, on which these notes are mainly based.

The readings here given are a selection of the most important variants. Mere differences of spelling have not been included (*e.g. sydus* 2, *fulfum* 5, *treita* 8). When a reading is found in all the Mss., no reference is given. A reading which appears in a majority of the *Vulgata Excerpta*, and is the only one of importance in that group, is marked O (following the system

---

[1] *Bellum Civile* only.

of Buecheler). After the Mss. readings are given
those of the oldest editors and commentators, and
after these such later emendations as may appear important.

Ch. 118.
1. *decipit* V1.
  quisquis Mess.
  teneriore Br.
  se subito b.
2. *feliciorem* Mess. *faciliorem*, the others.
  vibrantibus a. B.[1] The rest *umbrantibus*.
3. *vanitatem* B. Mess. The rest *sanitatem*.
  concipere B. *conspici* O.
  fulmine Br.
4. *summotae.* Buecheler *semotae.*
5. *curam dum.* Trag. Vb. V1. V2. F1. omit *corpus.*
  orationis Sc. B. Mess. The rest *rationis.*
  vestibus B. Br.
  "fortasse testis est et" Buecheler.
  enim a. b. Sc. B. Br. The rest *autem.*
  versum. visam N. Faber.
6. *sub honore* b.
  misteria Vb.
  animi b. B. Br. Mess. Sc. The rest omit.
  placeret Vb. *placeat* b. V1. F2. Vat.
  accipiat B.

---

[1] Ms. of Jacob Bidermann, Royal Library, Munich. Does
not contain the *Bellum Civile.*

Ch. 119.

3. *pressa* Trag.

   Graiis, Rubenius.

4. *peragrabantur* M. Dr. de Tournes. *perarabantur* Delbenius.

5. *fulvum quae* Sc.

8. *risu* Sc. (in the margin *usu*).

   tracta Sc. (in the margin *trita*).

9. *Spolia Tum Semius* M. *Spolia cum señus* Dr.

   aes pireum cum Trag. *aes epyre cum* Br. *aes Ephyrae regum* Pithoeus. *aes Ephyreiacum* Heinsius. *Assyria concham* de Tournes. *Hesperium coccum* Saumaise. *Assyriae bacam* proposed by Reiske. *in ora* proposed by Stephanus. *in Inda* proposed by Dousa. *in umbra* proposed by Heinsius.

11. *accusant* Sc. (in the margin *crustas*). *accusatius* O. *accurant* Delbenius. *adtulerant* de Guerle. *acculant* Heinsius. *citros* or *Gallos* Reiske. *silices* Stephanus. *lapides* Palmer. b. has lacuna in place of *Numidae . . . Seres.*

13. *elisae* Leid.

14. *an reo* Trag. (in the margin *leo*). *circo* Stephanus. *caveae fera* Colladonius. *fera nunc leo* proposed by Brassicanus. *Euri* Heinsius. *Mauri* Burmann. *Mauris* Hadrianides. *Mauro* Anton.

15. *danti* Moessler.

16. *pretiosa suas* Sc. *pretiosa furens* Reiske. *pretiosa fames. premit*, etc., Burmann.

17. *aerata* Brouckhusius. *ferrata* quoted by Anton.
    rabidus spectatur Cuperus.
19. *paritura* Patisson. *facta* proposed by Burmann.
21. *exactaque* O.
22. *fugere* Leid.
    nobilis O. Sambucus. *mobilis* M. Dr. Leid. V2.
    nubilis suggested by Buecheler.
    aevo O. *tunc Venerem* Brassicanus.
24. *quare se natam non* O.
25. *factique* Trag. M. Mess. Leid.
26. *lassi* Trag. *lapsi* V1. Vat. *pexi* or *flexi* Heinsius.
    fluxi or *lixi* Dousa.
27. *iure quaerit* Trag. *quo iure haec quaerit* Brassi-
    canus. *viri quaerunt* Auratus. *virque* or *quis-
    que virum quaerit* Heinsius.
    eruta tescis or *tesquis* Heinsius.
29. *mutatur* Trag. Vb. V1. Vat. Mess. The rest *imi-
    tatur. heu! maculis mutatur vilibus* Bouhier.
28. *citrea* Leid. V1. Dr. M. *antea* Trag. Vb. V2 (in
    the margin *citrea*). F1. F2. Vat. Mess. (in the
    margin *aurea*). a. b. Sc. (in the margin *citrea*).
30. *sensum turbant hostiale* O. *trahant hosterile* Br.
    turbant sensum hostile M. Dr. Leid. (*sensum
    turbant*). *sensum trahat hoc sterile* Sc. *cen-
    sum turbant* Heinsius. *et sensum turbat tandem*
    proposed by Brassicanus. *o sterile Orelli*. b.
    omits *turbant . . . lignum*.
32. *correptis. conceptis* Heinsius. *corruptis* Buecheler.
    extruit O. *esurit* Sc. Br. b. *adserit* or *adstruit*
    Heinsius.

33. *versus* Erhard.
34. *nimis* a. *unius* Mess.
     deducitur ac inde Sc. in the margin. *ad mensam hinc vivus deducitur* Heinsius.
35. *obruta* Moessler.
     condunt Heinsius. *tendunt* preferred by Cuperus. *reddunt conchylia coeno* Crusius (see 36).
36. *removent* O. *per stagna salem* Crusius (see 35).
37. *cantum* Palmer.
39. *emtusque* Daniel.
40. *sonitum. crepitum* quoted by Anton.
     vincent, vendunt, verrunt quoted by Anton.
44. *iacet nunc* M. Dr. *iacebit* ND. *iam quoque maiestas . . . latebit* quoted by Anton.
45. *vinctus* a. b.
46. *quos* conjectured by Barth.
47. *dedecori* Sc. *dedecus est populo* Auratus. *dedecus est populi* Stephanus. *dedecori est populo* Anton.
48. *invicta* de Salas.
49. Heinsius conjectures *a se prodita*.
51. *praedam. praeda* Colbertinus. *plebem* Crusius. *foeda* Cuperus. *Romam* Moessler. Vb. omits the line.
52. *ingluvies* Sc.
     exciderat Trag. Leid. Vb. M. V1. Dr. Mess.
55. *infra . . . errant* O.
     hiris de Tournes.
     lacerantibus Sc. in the margin. *latitantibus* Colladonius.

57. *tua* Br.
60. *excisa* all but Mess. (*excita ?*).

Ch. 120.
61. *dederat* ND.
62. *Enyo* Sc. b. Br. *emo* a. *eruo* ND. The rest *Erinnys*.
64. *Tertius* Leid. M. Dr. *Tullius* (corrected to *Iulius*) F1. F2.
65. *tellus tot* Br. b. ND.
69. *Cocytia* O. *Cocyta* Leid. *Cocyti* Sc.
70. *iurit* Br.
71. *iurat* a.
72. *aer* Br.
    si verno a.
73. *locantur*.
75. *circumcumulata* conjectured by Colladonius.
76. Sc. in the margin: "*v. c. sepades f. saepes.*"
77. *cava* Ed. Princeps.
78. Cuperus proposed *facessit*.
79. *rex* Trag.
80. Line omitted by all but Br. Sc. a. b. ND. (*tibi nulla*).
81. *tu nova* ND.
    Barth conjectures *vix possessa*.
82. *ecquid* Leid. Sc. *ecquod* Br. The rest *et quod* or *quid*. *fictam* Dr.
83. *permiram* a. *ruituram* conjectured by Colladonius.
89. *rebellat* Dr.
91. *haustis* Sc. a. b. ND. Leid. M. Dr. Br. The rest *austris* (or *haustris*).

92. *astra premunt* Heinsius. *astra tremunt* also proposed by Heinsius. *claustra gemunt* Moessler.
vanius a. Mess. *vanos* ND. *varios* Sc. *varius* M. The rest *vanus*.
usus ND. Vb. The rest *usum*.
varios . . . usus de Tournes. *vanos . . . usus* Delbenius. *Parius . . . usus* Palmer.
93. *iubentur* Sc. in the margin. Mess. (?)
97 *artes* Dr.
98. *sordida* proposed by Burmann. *arida* proposed by Colladonius.

Ch. 121.
102. *tum* Le d. Sc. V2.
fudit de pectore proposed by Wernsdorff.
103. *Cocyti cui* Br. b.
104. *si modo vera mihi fas est impune profari* a. b. Leid. Sc. Br. The rest *si modo fas est mihi vera impune probari* (Dr. *sique*). Brassicanus prefers *haec modo fas impune mihi est, si vera profari*.
105. *tibi* a. b. Sc. Br. The rest *mihi*.
credent Trag.
rebullit proposed by Erhard.
106. *leviorque. leviorve* Colladonius.
107. *omniaque* a. Leid. Dr.
artibus Trag. Vb. V1. V2. F1. F2. Vat. Sc. (in the margin).
108. *destruat* Leid.
109. *est* a. Sambucus.

110. *armare* M. Dr. Gronovius.   *caede creare* Reiske.
     ciere or *gregare* proposed by Moessler.
111. Sc. *gemino* (in the margin) . . . *Marte.*
     stratos a. b. Br.   The rest *strictos.*   *structos* Palmer
113. *auras* M. Dr.
114. *et tua* Mess. (?)   Hadrianides.
     in Libya Cuperus.   *et Libyas* Reiske.   *et Libyam
     cerno et te* de Guerle.   *cum Libye* Moessler.
     claustra a. b. Br. Sc. (in the margin *castra*).   The
     rest *castra.*
115. *trementis* Ed. Lugdunensis.   *frementis* proposed
     by Reichardt.
116. *dirarum* suggested by Wernsdorff.   *scientia* a.
     regna cruorem Crusius.
117. *Porthmeus* b. Br.   The rest *Proteus.*   *proreus*
     conjectured by Scaliger.   *parva, picta, putri* sug-
     gested by Colladonius.
     nauta a.
     arcesse Sc. Mess.   The rest *accerse.*
118. *sufficit ad* Trag.   *sufficit hac* conjectured by
     Heinsius.
     tuba a.
119. *inque* M. Dr.   *tumque* Hadrianides.
120. *funera* or *viscera* proposed by Colladonius.

   Ch. 122.
122. *sulfure* Colbertinus.
123. *infremuit* conjectured by Colladonius.
     abdidit Reiske.
124. *reductus* Leid. M. Dr. de Tournes.   *reductae*
     Heinsius.

125. *palluit* Leid. M. F2. b. The rest *polluit*.
127. *ora cruentus* conjectured by Colladonius.
128. *titubans*. *Titan* Delbenius. *Passerat*.
     vultum a. b. V2. Br. F1. F2. Vat. The rest *vultus*.
129. *sperare* Dr. The rest *spirare* (*spitare* Br. first
     hand). *veritum spectare* proposed by Crusius.
     iam conflictare Moessler.
131. *sceleri* b. Leid. Sc. M. Dr. Br. The rest *celeri*.
     tenebant Delbenius. *trahebant . . . montes* Moessler.
132. *lapsis* V1. V2. F2. Vat. Mess. *lapsi* Vb. The rest
     lassis. *laceris* or *laxis* Heinsius.
133. *torrentia* Reichardt.
134. *crepitu* Brouckhusius. *mortem* Burmann.
134–135. *et tuba trinis | sideribus mortem acta ciet*
     Reiske.
135. *tremefacta* a. b. Sc. Br. *transacta* Mess. (?) *trinis
     acta* Trag. *armis acta* Leid. *sic acta* M. Dr.
     sider: us armis ciet Ed. Princeps. *tumefacta* Col-
     bertinus. *tenus icta* Canter. *ciet acta armis*
     Brassicanus. *trinis acta* Burmann. *trans-
     missa* or *tenus alta* Wernsdorff.
     vocatur Trag. Leid. *notatur* V1. V2. F1. F2.
     micabat M.
136. *flumina* de Tournes.
137. *cumulos* Pithoeus.
     carentia b. Br. The rest *arentia*. Gronovius
     prefers *calentia*.
138. *minatur*.
139. *telis* M. Dr. *crinita* proposed by Delbenius.
140. *rubens* Mess. (?) Cuperus. The rest *recens*.

repens Ed. Princeps. *ruens* Colladonius. *frequens* Moessler. *imbre* a. b. Mess. Sc. Br. Mess. de Tournes. The rest *igne*.

144. *nomine. numine* Reiske.

pulso Trag. Leid. M. V1. Dr. Sambucus. Other Mss. *pulsae. vulsae* Ed. Sec. *celsae* or *pronae* proposed by Barth.

148. *illic* Trag. Dr. The rest *illinc. illuc* Moessler. *illic sedisse* Gronovius.

adulti Mess. (?) Pithoeus. The rest *adusti*.

149. *mansuescit* a. b. M. V2. Dr. Br. The rest *mansuescunt. radii* Leid.

150. *riget* b. Br. *algens* Mess. (?) Colladonius. The rest *rigens. rigent* Lipsius. *glacies concreta riget* Wernsdorff. *glacie crebra assurgens hiemisque* Moessler.

151. *totum terrae* Br.

nutantibus Dr. *mutantibus* Ed. Sec. *immanibus* or *nitentibus* Schrader.

153. *ornavitque* Sc. (in the margin *optavitque*). The rest *oravitque. intravitque* Sambucus. *lustravitque* Colladonius. *purgavitque* Moessler.

154. *latae* Leid.

155. *intendens* Trag.

156. *tu* Trag. Leid. Sc. M. Dr. *Eu* Br. The rest *heu. te* Buecheler.

157. *honorata* Dr.

158. *acres* Palmer. *accersere* Br. A. b. V2. (in the margin). The rest *arcessere*.

159. *vincere* proposed by Crusius.

160. *orbe* Dr. *tingo* b. M. V2. Dr. The rest *vinco*.
162. *vincendo exerceor exul* Reiske.
164. *o quos* M.
165. *vident. iubent* Mess. (?) Gulielmus. *vetant* Gro-
     novius. *timent* Delbenius. Colladonius. *cient*
     Reiske. *volunt* Wernsdorff.
     mercede redemtae Heinsius.
166. *quarum* Trag. in the margin.
167. *ut. ac* Colbertinus. *at* Heinsius. *iudice* a.
168. *furentes* Trag. Mess. (?) The rest *ferentes*.
     frequentes de Tournes. *sequentes* or *nocentes*
     proposed by Colladonius. *recentes* Moessler.
169. *discite* Leid. M. Dr.
170. *namque unum crimen omnes* Trag. V1. V2. F1.
     F2. Vat. Mess. Vb. Line rejected by Schrader.
171. *nobis* Trag. *votis* Palmer.
172. *solum* Vb.
173. *eminet* Dr.
175. *et* omitted by Trag. Vb. F1. F2. Vat. Mess. *inten-
     tate* conjectured by Colladonius.
176. *armatos* M. Dr. *armatos* or *armatis nescia vinci*
     Lipsius.
178. *omnia* Vb. M. V1. V2. Vat. *mentibus* Vb. Mess.
     e mentibus Trag. Leid. *e mentibus iras* pro-
     posed by Stephanus.
180. *insolita* Leid.
     luna conjectured by Colladonius. *frequenti* M.
     Br. Sambucus. *insolita voces flamma sonuere
     sequentes* suggested by Brassicanus.
181. *laetior* a. b. Br.

s

Ch. 123.

184. *insolitos* M. Dr. The rest *insolito*. *gressu* a. b.
Sc. Br. The rest *gressus*. *ausus* Leid. Sc. M.
Dr. *haustus* O. *haustu* Mess. *insolitus gressus*
. . . *ausu* Wernsdorff. *indomito gressus* . . .
ausu proposed by Burmann. *insoliti* preferred
by Stephanus.

185. *glacieque et* proposed by Putsch.
iuncta Leid. Vat. de Tournes. Sambucus.

186. *horrore* a. b. Br. Mess. (?) Sc. in the margin. The
rest *honore*. *vitiique horrore* Colbertinus. *mitique quievit honore* Sambucus.

189. *fulmina* Leid. b.
montis Vat.
alpis Dr.

190. *missa* Leid. Sc. Dr. V2. in the margin. Sambucus.
de Tournes. The rest and Wouwerius *iussa*.
iusta quoted by Dousa. *scissa* Colbertinus.
spissa proposed by Auratus. *stare* proposed by
Dousa.

191. *stabant* Sc. Br. a. b. V1. V2. The rest *stabat*.
et a. b. Sc. Omitted by the rest.
victa Leid. Mess. *vinctaque mox stabant, fluctus*
. . . *ruina* Sambucus.
pruina. *ruina* Reiske.

194. *pariter* a. b. Sc. Br. *passim* Leid. M. Dr. The
rest *partem*.

196. *rigor concusso* Colbertinus. Sambucus.

197. *rupto* M. Dr. Mess. *rapti* Colladonius.

198. *aut* a. b. Br. The rest *ac*.

contractum Schrader. *confarctum* preferred by Palmer. *turbine* Memmius.

199. *iam* omitted by F2. Vat.
200. *correpta* Vb.
     unda b. Leid. Sc. M. Dr. The rest *umbra.*
     lucebat Vb. *ruebant* Erhard.
201. *vincta* &c. conjectured by Colladonius.
202. *ferentia* M.
203. *magnum* suggested by Palmer.
     nisus V1. Vat.
207. *dimisit* M. Dr.
208. *deiecit* Mss. and de Tournes. Sambucus. *disiecit* Gulielmus.
     bella proposed by Gronovius.
209. *timidas* Leid. Sc. (first hand).
210. *volucrum* (in the margin *volucris, volucer*) Sc.
     pinnis Br. The rest *pennis.*
212. *Romana* M. Dr. *Romanos* Bouhier. *"quo probato temptavi: obvia"* Buecheler.
     omina Sc. *omina scaeva* Cuperus. *omnia magna* proposed by Burmann.
     ferri Brassicanus.
     haec Romano attonito fert conjectured by Sambucus. *haec Romano attonito fert nuncia* proposed by Burmann.
214. *germanas perfuso* M. Dr.
215. *notaque belli* Palmer.
217. *per* M. The rest *perque. per dubias* Sambucus.
     finduntur b.
     curas Colladonius. Gronovius.

219. *patriae* Leid. V2. The rest *patria*.
    et Fl. Omitted by Sc. Br. The rest *est*. *etiam* a.
    et iam O.
    timor O. *et patria pontus iam tutior. est magis
    arma* Sc. Br. *et patriae est pontus. sed iam
    timor* Sambucus. *et patria est timor ipsa* Aura-
    tus. *et pontus patria. etiam magis est timor
    arma* Reiske. *et patriae est cunctis etiam timor*
    conjectured by Nodot.
220. *temptare* b. Br. *tentare* Sc. The rest *tentata*.
    uti a. b. Sc. Br. *acti* Leid. M. V2. Dr. The
    rest, Sambucus *icti*.
221. *ipso* Herrmann.
223. *acta* proposed by Erhard. *educitur* preferred by
    Burmann.
224. *suadet Roma fugam* Suringar.
226. *pavida* a. b. Sc. Br. in the margin. The rest
    trepida.
227. *reliquit* Trag.
229. *suntque* Dr.
    lugentia M. Dr.
    iungunt Vb. Vat. Mess.
    pignora Stewech. *brachia* proposed by Anton.
230. *onerisque* Sc. Br. a. b. The rest *oneris*. *humeris*
    Auratus. *umeris fert gnava* Junius and Vahlen.
    parens conjectured by Buecheler.
232. *hic* a. b. Sc. Br. Mess. (?) The rest *hinc*.
234. *magistris* Colladonius.
235. *sinu* Wernsdorff.
238. *magno* M.

239. *repertus* Mess. (?) *saevi quoque terror* Scaliger.
Parthi conjectured by Buecheler.

241. *in gurgite* b. Br.

244. *tuetur* M. Dr. *videres* Nodot.

Ch. 124.

245. *tergo* Gulielmus.
lumina b.
cernit M. Dr. The rest *vidit. vicit* Herrmann.
fudit proposed by Wernsdorff.
Divi Gulielmus.
terga dare ante alios divum quoque numina vidit
Suringar.

246. *caelo* Reiske.

247. *terrasque* preferred by Colbertinus.

249. *pullata* de Guerle.

250. *absconditque* b. Leid. V2. *abscindit* a.
galea. palla Schrader. *absconditque olea* Colladonius. *cavea* Reiske.
vinctum Colladonius.
relictum a. *relicti* b. Br.

252. *sit* Br.
submissa a. b. Br. *sincera* Leid. Sc. M. Dr. de
Tournes. The rest *summa.*
crure Trag.

253. *ac lacera maerens* de Tournes.

254. *ac* Mess.
rapta. V1.

255. *demergit* b.
cohors M.

256. *facibus* Trag.
258. *abrupti* de Tournes. *arreptis* Sc. in the margin.
259. *lateque tulit* Dr.
260. *velant* O.
263. *terrisque* M. Dr.
264. *mutantia* M. *nutancia* Dr. *multata* Reiske.
  mirata conjectured by Colladonius. *nudata* Hadrianides.
  pontus Dr. a. b. Vb. Vat.
266. *deducta* Trag. b. Leid. Dr. Mess.
  primamque Reiske.
267. *astra* Colladonius. *alma* Reiske. *arma* Passerat.
  Dionen . . . ducunt Moessler.
268. *quotiens* F1. F2.
269. *Magnum* Mess. (?) Barth. The rest *Magnaque*.
271. *intonuere* Mess. *insonuere* quoted by Anton.
  iubae Pithoeus. *ac* omitted by a.
273. *flumina* a. b. Br. F1. F2. Mess.
  stabant conjectured by Burmann. *fletu* suggested by Buecheler.
274. *aerati* Sc. The rest *irati*. *serrati* proposed by Heinsius. *erosi* proposed by Crusius. *atrati* conjectured by Burmann.
276. *intertorto* a. b. Sc. Br. The rest *inter toto*. de Tournes. Sambucus. *lacerato* b. *rupta ter intortam* proposed by Barth. *intertorto lacerans* Bouhier. *inter fremitus* Reiske. *atque ferens* or *terens toto* proposed by Burmann. *ter in toto lacerata pectore veste* proposed by Anton. *intorto inter* Moessler.

277. *dextram* Trag. Vb. V1. F1. Vat.
sanguinea tremulam Sambucus.
278. *haec ubi* preferred by Brassicanus.
281. *orbe* omitted by Dr.
282. *efudit* Trag. *arripuit* Dr. *erumpit* a. b. Sc. Br.
The rest *erupit.*
furibunda Dr.
283. *accensi* Dr.
284. *mittite* Vb. *emittite* V2.
lampades urbem a. *lampades urbes* b. Br. *lampada turbas* M. *lampade turbas* Dr.
285. *vincitur* Dr.
cessat Vb. V2. F1. F2. Vat.
286. *pudor* Mess.
287. *rebellant* Dr.
289. *ne* a. b. Sc. Br. *non* Dr. The rest *neu.*
matrem Vat.
291. *miris* a.
293. *Romanasque* Trag. Vb. V1. F1. Vat.
arces Vb. Mess. The rest *acies.*
Epidamni Br. F1. F2. Vat. b. Pithoeus. The rest,
de Tournes, Sambucus *Epidauria,* or *Epidauri.*
nomina Trag. a. b. Vb. Br. F1. F2. Vat.
294. *Thessaliaeque rogos* Gabbema.
Romano Cornelissen.
pingues Heinsius.
295. *Iustitia* Vb. Mess. Trag. (*Discordia* in the margin.)

Note on the order of the lines.

In *a* the lines are given in great confusion, as follows: 1–20, 46, 21–26, 53–60, 27–45, 61–85, 47–52, 88–120, 86–87, 123, 157, 193–194, 121–122, 158–192, 228–229, 195–227, 263–268, 230–262, 280–285, 269–279, 286–295.

Some of the other Mss. present minor variations, as follows: 29. *ponitur* precedes 28 *citrea mensa* in b. only.

ND, which contains only fragments of the poem, gives them in the following order: 33–38, 40–44, 24–26, 87–89, 56–57, 61–66, 79–81, 91–92 (portions of other chapters of the book intervene here), 93.

Attempts have also been made by editors to rearrange the more difficult passages.

19–31 follow 57 in de Tournes.

113 in Hadrianides follows 115. Anton would have it precede 111.

Moessler, in 212, reads: *Romanos tonitru ferit: omnia signa.* This makes a line necessary before 213, and he supplies it with:

> omnes esse aquilas collatas Caesaris ira
>
> (Cf. Lucan, I, 477.)

217 ff. (de Guerle: 217, 224–225, 230–231, 218–223, 229, 226–228, 233 . . .

221 is put before 231 by Vahlen.

221 ff. (Buecheler, Ed. 1862): 221, 231–232, 237, 226–230, 233–236, 222–225, 238 . . .

225 ff. (Reiske): 225, 230–232, 226–229, 233 . . .

264–270 are put after 294 by Moessler.

276 is put after 277 by Reiske.

CPSIA information can be obtained
at www.ICGtesting.com
Printed in the USA
LVHW082358200121
677060LV00032B/922